TEACHING MATHEMATICS TO LOW ATTAINERS, 8–12

Derek Haylock lectures in mathematics education at the University of East Anglia, Norwich, where he is responsible for the Middle Years (7–12) course. He has considerable experience of initial teacher training, INSET and classroom-based research in mathematics education. His research has focused on the two extremes of children with special needs in mathematics: those with creative ability in the subject, and those whose attainment is low. He was co-author (with Anne Cockburn) of *Understanding Early Years Mathematics* (Paul Chapman Publishing, 1989). His publications also include three books of Christian drama for young people (published by Church House/National Society) and frequent contributions to education journals. His work in mathematics education has taken him to Germany, Kenya, Lesotho, Brunei and India.

TEACHING MATHEMATICS TO LOW ATTAINERS, 8–12

DEREK HAYLOCK

P·C·P

Paul Chapman
Publishing Ltd

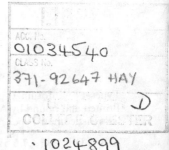

Paul Chapman Publishing Ltd
144 Liverpool Road
London
N1 1LA

British Library Cataloguing in Publication Data
Haylock, Derek
   Teaching mathematics to low attainers 8–12
   Title
   371.9264

ISBN 1–85396–151–5

Typeset by Inforum Typesetting Portsmouth
Printed and bound by Athenaeum Press Limited,
Newcastle upon Tyne.

A B C D E F G   7 6 5 4 3 2 1

CONTENTS

ACKNOWLEDGEMENTS

My thanks are due to the many low-attaining pupils and their teachers, with whom I have been privileged to work over recent years, and who have provided me with the experience on which to base this book. In particular, acknowledgements are due to the staff and pupils of the following local middle schools, who have made me welcome and assisted me in my research:

Angel Road Middle School, Norwich
Bignold Middle School, Norwich
George White Middle School, Norwich
Kinsale Middle School, Hellesdon, Norwich
Larkman Middle School, Norwich
St. Mary's Middle School, Long Stratton, Norfolk
St. Michael's Middle School, Bowthorpe, Norwich
St. Thomas More Middle School, Norwich

My thanks are due especially to the following teachers who have worked with me on curriculum development for low-attaining pupils in mathematics: Gill Blake, Nancy Bridson, Keith Clayson, Peter Cleary, Adrian Day, Sheila Hogan, Frances Hogg, Helen McCabe, John Seaward, Martin Silvester, Debbie Simpson, Angela Skeggs, John Swann, Jane Wilkinson.

Texas Instruments generously provided a supply of calculators for the UCAN project (*Using Calculators to Aid Numeracy*). The Open University have kindly granted permission to include the transcripts from the course EM235 in Chapter 3. The University of East Anglia provided the study leave and the Macintosh-Plus word-processor, without which this book would never have been written.

INTRODUCTION

Teaching Mathematics to Low Attainers, 8–12 is about one of the most difficult jobs in the world. Teachers will not argue with me when I assert that teaching is one of the hardest professions that anyone could enter. The age range 8–12 years is possibly the most challenging phase of schooling: most primary and (8–12) middle-school teachers are required to cover the whole spectrum of National Curriculum subjects for pupils whose range of competences is becoming gradually more diverse. Mathematics is often the subject which is most worrying for many of these teachers. And, judging by my conversations with many primary and middle-school teachers, teaching those who do not do well at the subject is the most demanding aspect of teaching mathematics. Hence my conclusion that teaching mathematics to low attainers in the age range 8–12 years is one of the most difficult jobs in the world.

The age range 8–12 years reflects the middle-school model prevalent in Norfolk, where most of my experience with low attainers has been gained. For a number of years, I have been able regularly to spend time teaching various groups of low attainers in mathematics, or working alongside and consulting with their teachers. For two years, here at the University of East Anglia, I directed a project entitled *Using Calculators to Aid Numeracy*, in which a dozen local teachers worked with me on curriculum development in mathematics for their low-attaining pupils. This book therefore derives directly from my personal experience of low-attaining pupils, their difficulties and achievements, and the problems encountered by their teachers. In this respect, it is very much a personal view. I certainly do not claim to have all the answers. The book does not purport to be either comprehensive or definitive. It describes simply what my personal research and experience lead me to think about the nature of the problems facing low attainers in mathematics and their teachers, the strategies for tackling these, and what might constitute an appropriate curriculum. I have included a large number of suggestions for activities which have been tried with various groups of pupils and which seem to have some potential for helping them. The book, therefore, although deriving from a research perspective, is essentially practical in its tone. I have tried to write something which will be of use to teachers and thus of value to those of their pupils whose progress in mathematics compares unfavourably with their contemporaries.

The major themes of the book are outlined in Chapter 1. To set the scene for the remainder of the book, Chapter 2 provides case studies of six low-attaining pupils. Chapter 3 tackles the question: why do some pupils do so poorly in mathematics? Chapter 4 is the fulcrum of the book, outlining an overall strategy for teaching low attainers in mathematics in the 8–12 age range. This introduces a balanced approach, emphasising both an objectives-and-assessment model and the importance of giving the pupils purposeful activities in meaningful contexts. Chapters 5–8 deal with particular aspects of numeracy for low attainers. In Chapter 9, I provide a number of examples of ways in which low-attaining pupils have achieved surprising success when encouraged to use mathematics to make things happen. Finally, in Chapter 10, I have tried to bring together all the principles outlined earlier in the book to show how they might be put into practice in constructing a scheme of work for a particular topic.

Derek Haylock
University of East Anglia, Norwich
School of Education

1

GROANS, THEMES AND LABELS

GROANS

Some years ago I visited a primary school to do some mathematics with some of the classes. I went into the school assembly at the start of the day, where the headteacher introduced me. 'Boys and girls, today we have a visitor in the school, from the university. He will be coming into some of your classes this morning to do some mathematics with you.' At this, all the children in the hall groaned audibly!

The headteacher's reaction to this was also significant. He exploded in anger and shouted at the children, 'Right, if that's how you behave when we have a visitor, you will all be in here at lunchtime doing extra mathematics!' I must admit to a slight feeling that this threat of extra mathematics as a punishment for bad behaviour would not do much to support my cause of encouraging the children to enjoy the subject.

However the groan has stayed with me as a significant example of a possible response to my specialist area of the curriculum: an indication, perhaps, that mathematics is seen as something boring and unpleasurable. Clearly such an attitude must be reinforced by the unthinking teacher who would use mathematics as a form of punishment.

Then I recall another school, another time and another groan. But this second groan was of a different kind altogether.

I was working with a local teacher and a class of low-attaining 9-year-olds, using calculators to help the children to understand addition and subtraction. They had first collected data from a local supermarket about prices of various items, and had used their calculators to answer questions using all the different models of addition and subtraction. They had learnt, for example, to associate the operation of subtraction not just with take-away situations such as giving change, but also with comparison situations and the language of comparison, such as 'how much more does this cost than that?' or 'how much less?' or 'what is the difference in price?', and similarly with inverse of addition situations, such as 'how much more do you need to buy this?'. Our assumption in this work was that, in an age of inexpensive calculators, it was actually more important for the children to know what calculation to do in a given situation than to be able to do the calculation.

Having built up their understanding of these operations in the familiar context of money and prices, we had, on the day in question, aimed for the children to move these mathematical structures into the less familiar context of measurements of length. Having collected data about the lengths of various items around the room, the children were then given a series of questions to answer such as 'how much longer is this than that?', 'how much shorter?', 'what is the difference in length?', and also invited to make up their own questions to give to each other to answer with their calculators. It was wonderful to see their enthusiasm as they immediately grasped the connections with the previous work on money, bursting to tell the teacher that they knew what operation to enter on their calculators to answer these questions. We must appreciate that these were children who did not usually experience success in mathematics and for whom understanding what was going on was something of a rare experience. Suddenly, in the middle of all this excited activity, the school bell rang to signal the end of the lesson and the beginning of the morning break. At the sound of the bell the whole class spontaneously groaned.

What a contrast with the previous groan! Here the children were so absorbed in their mathematical activities, and so delighted with their experience of understanding, that they groaned because it had to stop. And it was not that we were doing anything particularly sensational with them – all that we had done over the few weeks we had worked together was to try to shift the perception of doing mathematics away from just the mechanical learning of recipes and procedures towards an emphasis on understanding.

THEMES

Developing understanding

This notion of shifting the emphasis in our work with low-attaining pupils in mathematics away from the learning of routines and procedures more towards the development of understanding is one of the major themes of this book. My experience of working with pupils who do not do well at this subject has convinced me that much of the problem is that they are required to spend so much time in mathematics lessons engaged in tasks which have no meaning for them whatsoever. Such tasks provide them with no satisfaction or incentive for learning, particularly if their most frequent experience is of getting the answers wrong. Much of the satisfaction inherent in learning mathematics is that of understanding: making connections, relating the symbols of mathematics to real situations, seeing how things fit together, and articulating the patterns and relationships which are funda-mental to our number system and number operations. It is the experience of learning with understanding which produces the second kind of groan rather than the first, but which is too often, unnecessarily, absent from much of the mathematical experience of low-attaining pupils.

Language

A second recurring theme in this book is the importance of focusing specifi-cally on language development in teaching mathematics to low-attaining pupils. It is so often the case that poor language skills – reading, writing, speaking – are associated with low attainment in mathematics. Mathematics has its own peculiar language patterns and vocabulary, and a major part of the development of understanding of mathematics must focus on building up confidence in handling these and in connecting them with the corresponding mathematical symbols and manipulation of concrete materials.

For example, working with one group of low-attaining 9–10-year-olds, assessing their understanding of place value, I asked them to write down any number between the two numbers I wrote on the board: 37 and 62, for example. This defeated most of them. It became clear that, although they could respond correctly when I asked one child to sit 'between' two other children, they did not yet connect this language with numbers. The asser-tion that, for example, '45 is between 37 and 62' is an example of the kind of mathematical statement with which low-attaining pupils often need spe-cific help. Since this is essentially a spatial idea, it was necessary to help the children to connect the language with the spatial representation of number given by a number line. We did this by playing some simple games involv-ing placing small flags between other flags placed at various points on a number line.

Realistic and relevant objectives

There are basic skills to be mastered in learning mathematics, of course, and routine practice of these will from time to time be essential for all pupils. It is particularly helpful when working with low attainers to specify precise, short-term objectives for the learning of such basic skills, so that those who have experienced repeated failure in this subject can recognise that they are actually making progress. The importance of specifying clear and detailed objectives for numeracy is another theme of this book, but it is stressed throughout that such objectives must be realistic and relevant to the actual needs of the pupils.

For example, is it really worth while having as an objective that low-attaining twelve-year-olds should be able to multiply a two-digit number by another two-digit number, using the method of long multiplication? Is this a realistic objective, given the complexity of the task and the prerequisite skills and knowledge? And is such an objective really relevant to their needs, given that in practice such calculations will be done on a calculator? Much more realistic and relevant would be the objective that the pupils should know which keys to press on their calculators in a situation requiring a multiplication, such as in the purchase of a number of items at a given unit price, and be able to interpret the answer.

Numeracy

Knowing what sum to enter on a calculator in a numerical situation which arises in everyday life is an example of what I would regard as a basic component of *numeracy*. In working with low attainers, if we accept the 'realistic and relevant' criterion, then our most important objectives must be in the area of numeracy.

In my view, a numerate person is basically one who can cope confidently with the numerical situations they encounter in normal life. Confidence with numbers and the relationships between numbers is an important aspect of this. An innumerate person is likely to be so lacking in this confidence that they will unquestioningly accept the opinions and judgements of others when there are numbers around. A numerate person would at least have some idea of the size of answer expected and would thus be less at the mercy of the unscrupulous.

So the major content of this book focuses on those aspects of mathematics which would be essential to numeracy:

- a good understanding of the place-value principle in our number system
- knowing what calculation to enter on a calculator in a range of real-life situations and how to interpret the result
- confidence in handling basic number relationships
- confidence in handling money
- skills and concepts associated with measurement
- the application of mathematical skills in purposeful activities, to solve real problems, to make things happen.

In excluding from this list specific reference to spatial work for low attainers, other than the spatial concepts associated with measurement, I am not suggesting that this should have no part. Some low attainers who struggle with numerical work can have both their confidence and their motivation boosted by their success with spatial tasks, and many of them gain particular satisfaction from exploring spatial patterns. But I am prepared to assert that priority in the systematic development of mathematical knowledge and skills for low attainers in the 8–12 age range should focus on the areas listed above. Many spatial ideas are developed, albeit in a less systematic way, through the kinds of practical projects which are described and encouraged in Chapter 9 of this book.

Calculators

One author (Girling, 1977) goes so far as to define basic numeracy as the ability to use a calculator sensibly. This is perhaps just a little inadequate as a definition, but the use of calculators to *develop* numeracy is an interesting possibility. This is another of the major themes of this book. Examples of calculator activities, evolved through working with low attainers, will demonstrate that calculators are not a threat to the development of pupils' facility with number. Rather, it is argued that calculators, if used skilfully by teachers, especially with those children who do poorly in number work, can help them to develop their understanding of number and number operations, their confidence and competence in manipulating numbers mentally, and their enjoyment and concentration in mathematical work (see, for example: Bell *et al.*, 1978; Moore, 1985). This approach has been demonstrated most convincingly by the achievements of the Calculator-Aware Number Curriculum, promoted by the Primary Initiatives in Mathematics Education Project (PrIME, 1991).

I recall a group of low-attaining eleven-year-olds who spent one lesson working in pairs with tremendous enthusiasm on the following problem using calculators. Each pair was given six cards with the digits 2, 3, 5, 6, 7, 9 written on them, and another card with a multiplication sign. The challenge was to find how to arrange the cards to make a sum with the largest possible answer, recording all their attempts. The calculators freed them to concentrate on the mathematical structure of the problem and the relationships between the numbers involved, without worrying about the difficulties of the calculations. As I went round the groups I insisted that they said to me the largest answer they had found so far. By the end of the lesson, all these pupils were confidently reading and comparing large numbers, such as 'seven hundred and twenty-four thousand, one hundred and seventy-six' (963×752) and 'seven hundred and twenty-six thousand, three hundred and seventy-six' (952×763).

Purposeful activities in meaningful contexts

A major theme which will run through this book is the need to identify activities which have some genuine purpose for low-attaining pupils in mathematics. A key phrase which summarises the approach to be advocated is *purposeful activities in meaningful contexts*. As I go round schools and observe children engaged in mathematics lessons, it constantly strikes me that, from the pupils' perspective, most of the tasks they are engaged in have little or no purpose, other than to satisfy the demands of the teacher.

For some pupils, particularly those who do well at school and experience the rewards of success within the school as an institution, this might well be sufficient purpose. But in the case of many others, I cannot help but sympathise with them if they show little inclination to commit themselves to the tasks which we teachers so often give them to do.

Recently, I observed a low-ability mathematics set of ten-year-olds who spent most of a mathematics lesson, on the topic of time, failing in some exercises in their mathematics scheme which required them to draw hands on pictures of clock faces to show various times of day. They became increasingly frustrated and disillusioned as the lesson proceeded, with some of them eventually becoming quite disruptive. But I could understand their response. The task they were asked to engage in was, as far as I could judge, completely purposeless. Moreover, it was actually more complex than the skill of reading the time from a dial clock, the development of which was being aimed at by the teacher. With a large clock sitting on the wall of the classroom and the usual relationship between times on the clock and events of the school day, it seemed to me that it would not require much imagination for a teacher to find ways of developing the skill in question through activities which had more genuine purpose than this particular task. It is a good discipline and something of a challenge for all of us who teach mathematics to evaluate the tasks we give to our pupils against this criterion of purposefulness.

Small-group games

The use of small-group games and competitions as a way of enabling low-attaining pupils to practise and consolidate their mastery of basic number skills is another recurrent theme in this book. A game or a competition is an effective form of purposeful activity, more interesting and motivating than simply ploughing through pages of abstract sums in a text-book.

For example, here is a very simple small-group game designed to enable children to practise addition of two-digit numbers. The children in the group are in teams of two. One other child acts as dealer, banker and scorer. There are two packs of cards, preferably different colours, with single digits written on them (0, 1, 2, 3, 4, 5, 6, 7, 8, 9), one pack representing tens and one representing ones (in Chapter 5 these are referred to as Packs A and B), and a supply of plastic one-pound, ten-pence and one-penny pieces. Each player is dealt one card from each of the tens-pack and the ones-pack. They then ask the banker in turn to give them the corresponding number of tens and ones. The players in each team of two then combine their winnings, exchanging, through the bank, 10 ones for 1 ten, or 10 tens for 1 hundred (pound), where necessary. The team with the highest total wins a point. For example, in one team, player A is dealt 3 from the tens-pack and 5 from the ones-pack, while player B is dealt 7 from the tens-

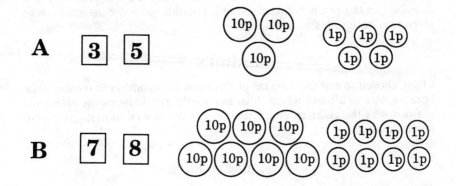

Figure 1.1   A small-group game for practising addition

pack and 8 from the ones-pack, as shown in Figure 1.1. When they combine their winnings they have to exchange 10 ones for 1 ten, and then 10 tens for 1 hundred, and finish up with 1 hundred, 1 ten and 3 ones.

Next time they play the game they may be expected to record their winnings and exchanges in some way, for example, as shown in Figure 1.2.

Through simple games like this children can practise many of the basic skills of mathematics in a more enjoyable, purposeful and meaningful way. When participating in group games, they are often put in a situation where they have to talk about mathematics, using mathematical criteria to justify their moves or to determine who wins or loses.

Another advantage of employing small-group activities of this kind – provided that the children have the social skills to cooperate in a game without constant squabbling and shows of bad temper when they lose – is

	hundreds	tens	ones
A		3	5
B		7	8
TOTAL	1	1	3
Exchanges	1	1	

Figure 1.2   Recording results from Figure 1.1

that this might be an activity which, once under way, makes very few demands on the teacher, thus making it possible for more attention to be given to other groups within the class.

LABELS

I have chosen to call the subjects of this book *low attainers in mathematics*, because this is a label which does not imply any judgements about the reasons why the children concerned do not do as well in mathematics as might be hoped.

Less able children

This is therefore a book which is not just about teaching mathematics to *less able children*. Although this might be an appropriate description of many of those I have worked with over the years, I do not find the term *less able* a helpful one. It implies too strongly that the basis of the problem is the ability of the child. Once the child is labelled in this way the teacher's expectations of what they can achieve are inevitably limited. There are plenty of children in our schools who, compared to their peers, are reaching low levels of attainment in mathematics who nevertheless have abilities which occasionally surface and surprise their teachers when they are given a task which motivates and excites them. The challenge for us as teachers therefore is to find ways of encouraging these abilities to emerge. One teacher, working with what was described as a 'low ability set' of 8–9-year-olds for mathematics, reporting on how the children responded to the responsibility of organising an inter-school football tournament (Haylock, Blake and Platt, 1985), expressed her surprise at discovering some of their hidden abilities:

> They showed themselves capable of work which I would never have undertaken in normal circumstances, e.g. ratio, time-tabling, costing and percentages. There were several occasions when children asked to be taught a mathematical technique because they needed it, and there was no sign of them being backward in learning it.

Slow learners

Nor is this a book which is just about teaching mathematics to *slow learners*. This label seems to imply that all pupils will follow the same learning path, but some will just proceed along it at a slower rate than others. Such a view of learning leads to all pupils being expected to work through exactly the same materials in mathematics lessons, with no allowance made for individual differences, other than the rate of progress from one page of a commercially produced mathematics scheme to the next.

For example, low attainers may need considerably more practical work with coins and blocks, before moving on to recording a particular arithmetic operation with symbols, than might be provided by a scheme designed for average pupils. There will also be sections of the scheme which could justifiably be omitted by some low attainers. For example, I would question the relative usefulness for many low attainers of tackling the section on volumes of cuboids which appears in most schemes, or learning to use index notation for representing squares, cubes, etc. The assumption that because it is there it must be done is clearly misguided. We cannot justify the view that our low-attaining pupils are simply slow learners and so they should just work through the same material as the others, but at their own rate.

Under-achievers

Another term which teachers often apply to some of the subjects of this book is *under-achiever*. This can be a helpful term, if it is interpreted positively. If we talk about some children as under-achievers it might imply that we are optimistic that they have the potential, given the right encouragement and an appropriate curriculum, actually to achieve very much more than they are achieving at present. However the term is often used in a rather negative sense, referring to pupils who achieve very little in school – often right across the curriculum – mainly because of their constant misbehaviour, their antisocial attitudes, their inability to conform to institutional procedures, or their lack of interest in the tasks they are given in school.

Technically, the term *under-achiever* should apply to an individual whose achievement in a specific area is not commensurate with assessments of their general aptitude, such as a score on an intelligence test might purport to be. Although many of the children who struggle with mathematics seem to struggle with most things in school, we do sometimes come across children who appear to have learning difficulties just in this specific area. In such a case teachers understandably feel that there must be some reason why a child who otherwise gets on well at school is 'under-achieving' in mathematics.

Low attainers

Other labels abound: special-needs, remedial, backward, dull, retarded, less gifted, and so on, each with its implied judgements about the nature or cause of the problem. By opting to focus on *low attainers* in mathematics, I am signalling what is essentially a pragmatic approach. There are many children who in fact attain very much less in this subject than most other children of their age. The reasons for this are varied, complex, idiosyncratic and unpredictable, but nevertheless, from my experience of working with such children and their teachers, it is clear to me that there is much we can try to do to help them to make progress and to grow in confidence.

So this book will be concerned about teaching mathematics to all kinds of low-attaining children in the eight to twelve years age range: children who just do not do very well at the subject, whether less able, slow-learning, under-achieving, or whatever else they might be labelled.

It is significant that for mathematics more than for any other subject many schools employ 'setting' as an organisational device for coping with the problems of the range of competences within a year group. This is a system whereby, for particular slots on the timetable, children who are normally grouped into a number of mixed ability classes within a particular year group are regrouped into sets according to their performance in mathematics. In a recent survey of fifty local schools with pupils within the age range 8–12 years, it was found that forty of them used setting for mathematics in one or more of the year groups, whereas only three did this for English language work, and none did this for science, art, music or the humanities.

This fact reflects a recognition by teachers that mathematics spreads pupils out in terms of their competences more than any other subject in the school curriculum. This is nicely illustrated by reference to the 'seven-year-gap', a phenomenon noted in the Cockcroft Report (1982): that there are mathematical tasks which an average eleven-year-old can do successfully, which some seven-year-olds can do, but some fourteen-year-olds cannot.

Furthermore, where setting is used for mathematics, it is often the case that the lowest set consists of a smaller number of pupils than the others. This is itself a recognition of the idiosyncratic nature of low attainment in mathematics, and the consequent need for much individual attention by the teacher for those pupils in these lower sets.

So this book is about those children who find themselves permanently in the bottom set for mathematics in those schools that use this system; or those children who are always one or two books behind the majority of the class in those schools where children work individually through a series of work-books in a mathematics scheme; or those pupils who are in what the teacher identifies as the remedial group within a mixed ability class, the children who need special help and provision in mathematics.

Typically these children would be able to get very few questions correct if they were given a norm-referenced assessment test in mathematics, and would gain standardised scores which put them, say, in the bottom 25% of a notional ability range for their peer group.

The six children described in the next chapter are all identified by their teachers as being low attainers in mathematics. In each case their progress in mathematics is, for one reason or another, a cause of concern. These examples illustrate the kinds of difficulties which many pupils have in handling the concepts and techniques of primary- or middle-school mathematics. They also demonstrate clearly the broad range and great variety of children whose attainment in mathematics compares unfavourably with other children of their age.

QUESTIONS FOR FURTHER DISCUSSION

1. What do you understand by 'numeracy'? Is it justified to focus mainly on the development of numeracy in teaching mathematics to low attainers in the age range 8–12 years?
2. Evaluate a recent mathematics lesson you taught or observed against the criterion of 'purposefulness'. From the perspective of the pupils, how 'purposeful' were the tasks in which they were engaged?
3. What educational judgements or points of view are implied by the use of the following labels: special-needs, remedial, backward, dull, retarded, less gifted, learning-disabled, low-achieving?

2
CASE STUDIES OF LOW ATTAINERS IN MATHEMATICS

In this chapter I will introduce some of the many boys and girls in Norfolk primary and middle schools who have helped me to write this book. All of them are children who have experienced difficulties of various sorts in learning mathematics. The factors associated with their problems in this area of the school curriculum are many and complex, as will become clear as we look at these examples of low attainers in mathematics.

The following case studies are of six pupils, one boy and one girl in each of Year 4 (8–9-year-olds), Year 5 (9–10-year-olds) and Year 6 (10–11-year-olds). They were undertaken in the summer term, when the pupils had been with their particular teachers for about eight months. In each case I have tried to give a pen portrait of the child, highlighting some of the significant features of their personality and their behaviour in mathematics lessons. Then there is an account of some of the performances of the children on a variety of mathematical tasks, showing both some of the things they can do and some of the characteristic problems which they have with mathematical ideas or processes. The main focuses in my interviews with them were: (i) their understanding of number and number notation, particularly the principle of place value; (ii) their grasp of the ideas and language of comparison in a variety of contexts, particularly those of money and time; (iii) their knowledge of number bonds and their facility in simple arithmetic. Many of the points which emerge from these studies will be taken up in later chapters. In these reports the names of the children have been changed.

TWO YEAR-4 PUPILS

Mark and Tracey are members of a class of 8–9-year-olds in their first year at a rather over-crowded 8–12 middle school, situated in a new urban development of mixed private and local authority housing. Mathematics is taught to this mixed ability class in a flexible way, with a variety of organisational styles: some class-teaching, some integrated-day approach and some small-group work. The Scottish Primary Mathematics Group (SPMG) scheme is used as a basis for their mathematics, supplemented by activities and work-sheets designed by the enthusiastic and skilful class teacher.

Mark: aged 9.0

Mark has been fostered since the age of 13 months, his natural mother being mentally disturbed. His foster parents, who have two daughters of their own, aged 16 and 18, are very supportive. They have recently applied to adopt Mark.

He is both physically and emotionally very immature. He is small for his age, looking like a 7-year-old. He has poor mechanical skills, such as in the use of scissors and glue. These contribute to his low attainment in mathematics, since he often performs poorly on the practical tasks which his teacher rightly regards as important for mathematical development at this age.

However the teacher's view is that the main factors associated with his low attainment in mathematics are in the area of social and emotional problems. He behaves in an immature and disruptive fashion in most lessons and has great difficulty in concentrating on most tasks in school. His level of reading and comprehension are actually quite good and he appears reasonably bright in one-to-one conversations, but the fact is that he achieves very little in class. All his written work is very poor and generally untidy, partly related to his poor mechanical skills. It has the appearance of having been done quickly.

In a typical one-hour lesson, Mark is working on one of the tasks which his group of less able pupils has been given to complete during the day. This is to work independently through various pages of the SPMG workbooks, with the instruction to ask for assistance when necessary. Mark is seen immediately to be a very active and animated child, often kneeling on his chair, even sometimes crouching with his feet on it, reaching across the table, frequently preoccupied with what other children are up to. But he is not malicious or deliberately disobedient to authority. In fact, he appears eager to please, and always seems cheerful and lively. He will do what he is told as much as he is able to within the limitations of his personality.

He has a pattern of alternately working on his mathematics for literally a minute or two, then checking up on what is going on around him, looking round the room, listening to conversations going on, and so on. A reasonable estimate would be that he spends about 75% of his time doing this. His first concern, for example, might be which page, compared to him, his neighbour is on. He clearly likes attention and will either call the teacher over or follow her around the room, if no-one else is taking any notice of him.

Early in the lesson the teacher explains to him the point of the questions he is to do, involving adding three single-digit numbers in different orders, for example, '(3 + 4) + 7' and '3 + (4 + 7)'. He appears to catch on fairly quickly, not just to the procedural issue of how to tackle these questions, but even to the idea that you get the same answer regardless of the order. But the impression is given that this insight will not take root in his mind, because he is immediately distracted by another child walking across the room.

All Mark's movements are very rapid and poorly coordinated. He never does anything carefully, including his written work. He does not put something down if he can throw it. For example, an eraser is returned to another child by throwing it, not very accurately, across the table. He adds even small single-digit numbers by counting on his fingers, and this also is done with exaggerated movements. He talks out loud when doing these calculations, and even, on occasions, sings the sums he has to do. (Interestingly, he is, in fact, a very musical child, with a fine singing voice.) He appears to respond rather at random to mathematical symbols, often just adding any two numbers however presented. For example, '11 – ? = 6' produces the response '17', and '6 + ? = 9' the response '15'. For '19 – 7' he gives the answer '26'. Even in cases where he is fairly confident with addition of numbers up to 20, he does not make the connection with subtraction. So, for example, he knows '8 + 2' is '10', but '10 – 2' is done laboriously on his fingers. He knows '10 + 10' is '20', but cannot evaluate '20 – 10'.

Not once does he appear to be absorbed in his work. Other children occasionally find him a nuisance. Borrowing the eraser, for example, is inevitably a cause of disturbance to the rest of the group. Occasionally he will call out unsolicited advice to others, such as, 'Danny, you're not allowed to do that,' this being typical of his preoccupation with what is going on around him. It is noticeable that he interacts with several children in the course of the lesson, but it is always Mark who initiates the interaction. He shouts across the table to impress another child, 'I've done six pages,' but is totally ignored.

Clearly, the biggest challenge facing Mark's teacher is to find some ways of actually getting him absorbed in a mathematical task.

Interviewing Mark reveals that he has a good understanding of concepts of time, probably above average for his age. Talking about his two elder sisters, Sarah, 16, and Katrina, 18, he can tell me that Sarah is 7 years older than him, and that he is 9 years younger than Katrina. Although he solves these problems by counting on his fingers, he nevertheless understands the structure of them. He knows when his birthday is, that we are now in May and tells me that 'we go second year in September'. He correctly works out that this would be in four months' time.

He is able to read the time from a conventional dial clock for quarters to and after the hour, and is fairly secure on days of the week and order of months. A typical conversation about time reveals not just the major role played in his family life by Australian television soap operas, but also the restriction of his knowledge of times of the day to those which are most important to him at school, namely lunch and going-home time:

'What time do you get up in the morning?'
'Usually about a quarter to seven.'
'How do you get to school?'
'I walk. My mum brings me.'
'How long does it take?'
'Don't know.'
'Ten minutes?'
'No, longer than that, about twenty, I reckon.'
'What time does school start in the morning?'
'Not sure. . . . '
'When's dinner time?'
'Twelve o'clock. About half an hour.'
'And do you know when school ends?'
'Half past three.'
'When do you have tea?'
'When *Neighbours* is on.'
'What time do you go to bed?'
'When *Home and Away* finishes.'

He has little idea of the value of money, and apparently gets little experience of shopping and handling coins outside of school. In fact, his only experience of shopping is with 'Mum' in Sainsbury's supermarket. He rarely buys anything himself, and rarely spends any of his pocket money on sweets, drinks, or small toys, as do many children of this age. He has no idea at all of how much a can of drink might cost, for example. He reckons that a pound is more than 10p, knows that it is the same as two fifties, but does not know that it equals 100p. He cannot say how much change from £1 you would get if you bought a can of drink for 30p. He gets £1 pocket money a week and appears to be expected to save this most weeks, but he has no idea how much his savings are. This is clearly an area where he suffers from being over-protected and from having very limited experience outside of school compared to many children of his age. This is a case where a teacher may need to develop ways of bringing into the classroom some examples or simulations of the range of experiences on which Mark is missing out in his everyday life. For instance, he would benefit from playing various kinds of shopkeeping games, or even serving in the school tuck-shop alongside a more capable friend.

His grasp of place value is patchy and this might be a useful focus for initial remedial work. For example, although he can write numerals up to 99 correctly, when asked to write down 'one hundred and sixty-four' he writes '100064'. However he can correctly say in words the number that is represented by '124', and even knew the names of '6000' and '22000'. He can confidently order a set of numbers up to 99, but is shaky on the idea of 'between' applied to numbers. He can correctly associate numbers up to 99 with positions on a number line, for example, placing 45 midway between

40 and 50, and placing 29 just to the left of 30. He can only answer a question about how much older I am than him (49 against 9) by counting in ones on his fingers – and, not surprisingly, getting lost in the process.

When asked to give me 64p, with a pile of plastic coins – tens and ones – on the table, he apparently does not have immediately available the relationship between the symbols and the materials. Instead of giving 6 tens and 4 ones, he counts up all the ones on the table until he has exhausted the supply (this happens to be 29), then adds a ten, counting on his fingers to 39, then another ten counting on to 49, another to 59, and then counts on his fingers to 64 and announces that he needs a five! We do this again, with me giving him the tens first, and he correctly assembles six tens and four ones. When I point out the connection between the coins and the symbols (i.e. the 6 tens and the 6 in 64, the 4 ones and the 4 in 64), he smiles, and appears to find genuine pleasure in making the connection. He says excitedly, 'I get it!' and then demonstrates that he understands this with 23p.

He has done plenty of work in bundling in tens and ones in his SPMG work-books, and recognises 2 longs and 4 units as representing 24. But, even though he is clearly capable of grasping the place-value principle, he has not made the necessary firm connection between the symbols and the materials. This is probably typical of the effect of his lack of concentration on his activities in mathematics lessons.

As for number operations, he often appears to have very little idea of the connection between the operation and the practical situation to which it might be applied, for example in shopping contexts. When asked how much more does he have (with 64p) than me (with 23p), he has no idea how to manipulate the coins or what to enter on a calculator to answer this question.

Tracey: aged 8.10

Tracey is from a stable family background, with very supportive parents. Her mother is especially anxious about Tracey's slow progress in school. She is a very quiet child in class, relying heavily on her friends. She is generally poor in all aspects of the school curriculum, and her teacher sometimes wonders if she takes in anything at all. Tracey is very lacking in confidence and is completely thrown if a question is reworded or posed in an unfamiliar way. She does not easily see connections between experiences. She finds reading very difficult. Her 'reading age' was assessed at the start of the school year in September as 6.10 and five months later, in February, assessed as 6.9. Her written work is however fairly tidy and has the appearance of having been done with care.

In a typical one-hour mathematics lesson she spends a good deal of time sitting doing nothing in particular, not being naughty or disruptive, just gazing into space and looking around the room. For the first half of the lesson she has a number of interactions with two other girls in the class, whispered conversations about an incident with some jewellery. She has a work-sheet to do on symmetry. After a while she gets a mirror, but does not seem to know what to do with it, so she spends a few minutes looking at herself. Occasionally she turns hopefully to a neighbour, but this girl has a different work-sheet and ignores Tracey's gentle interruption. Tracey looks frustrated for a second or two and then returns to gazing around the room. When the teacher talks to her she appears to understand the task, but is very hesitant to do anything.

There are many demands from other children for the teacher's attention and Tracey seems quite content to do very little and to be ignored. There is a marked contrast with the other children, all of whom seem to be on-task most of the time. She discovers that wiggling the mirror on the sheet of shapes produces an amusing diversion. She shows no sign of distress or concern about her lack of progress with the work-sheet. She takes to looking in the mirror again and smiling at herself.

After twenty-five minutes she eventually joins a queue of three children and seeks reassurance from the teacher about what she should do. After twenty-nine minutes she actually draws a line on the sheet and immediately seeks out the teacher to see if it is right and to ask what to do next. Eventually, having completed the sheet she moves on to the SPMG work-book, doing examples like '$12 - 9 = ?$' and '$3 + ? =$'. She counts on her fingers for both addition and subtraction, getting in a muddle with most questions. She produces several wrong answers, such as '8' for '$12 - 9 = ?$' and '14' for '$3 + ? = 11$'. When these errors are pointed out to her she appears to be not the slightest bit worried about having got the questions wrong. If anything, she finds it quite amusing, as though failure somehow fits her image of herself. She proceeds very slowly, seeking help and reassurance about the procedure to be followed for almost every question. She seems particularly lacking in confidence with questions which do not indicate an established procedure. For example, she is completely thrown by a question about adding darts scores, even though this actually requires simply the addition of three small numbers. So she sits and does nothing until eventually the teacher arrives and tells her what to do.

This attitude of dependency is demonstrated nicely by a conversation about times (the classroom dial clock is showing 11.30):

'What time is it now, Tracey?'
'Don't know.'
'Do you know what time school starts in the morning?'
'No.'
'What time is lunch?'
'I don't know. Miss knows.'

The teacher sees her major challenge as how to get Tracey motivated to make quicker progress in mathematics, so that she actually gets more done in the space of a normal lesson. She might consider, for example, trying to set her specific goals to achieve each fifteen minutes, making use of the class clock as a reference.

But a bigger challenge must surely be to wean Tracey off her dependency on the teacher and to get her to be more independent, less anxious and more of a risk-taker. She looks currently to be heading for a classic case of female dependency, a behaviour syndrome reinforced by the way in which we adults tend to be more supportive of girls experiencing difficulties than we are of boys. It might be argued that it would actually be more helpful to Tracey to be less kind and gentle with her, and to force her to get on and work things out for herself.

She has made a start in getting to grips with the place-value principle in our number system, but a number of gaps and misunderstandings emerge in conversation. She can, for example, write numbers up to 99 correctly, with no confusions between 14 and 41, or 17 and 70. She can then confidently put a set of such numbers into order from smallest to largest. She is very good at locating numbers such as 29 and 72 on a number line marked in tens. She can also put out and recognise any number in tens and ones, using either coins or base-ten blocks.

She can put out correctly sums of money, such as £2.34, with pounds, tens and ones, but is likely to get in a muddle in writing the number that goes with a collection of blocks or coins if there is a zero involved, such as 307, or £3.07. When asked to write down the number 164 she writes '100', hesitates, crosses it out and, typically, remarks: 'We haven't done them.'

Questions to do with comparison baffle her, even in the context of ages. For example, she cannot say how much older I am than her, given that she is 8 and I am 48. (The reader may note a tendency to vary my age according to the circumstances.) Given two sums of money, such as two prices, she knows which is the greater, but cannot work out how much more one costs than the other, either practically with coins or with a calculator.

However, she clearly has some useful experience of handling money outside of school. For example, she understands the principle of giving change, although she consistently works this out on her fingers. For example, she can find correctly the change from £20 when buying something for £12, by counting 12 on her fingers and then noting that there were eight further fingers to be counted. However this process leads her to state incorrectly that you get 38p change from 50p when spending 22p.

She does, in fact, tend to rely very heavily on the security of counting on her fingers, even with very small numbers: her actual recall of number bonds with numbers up to 20 is weak for her age. Questions such as '3 + 5' and '9 + 2' are done on her fingers, by counting on. Subtractions, such as '10 − 2' and '12 − 4', are done by a counting-back process, again using her fingers. She has instant recall of those results which she will have met frequently through experiences of handling coins, such as '10 + 10', '20 − 10', '10 − 5' and '20 + 10'. Others, such as '20 + 30', '30 + 40' and '60 − 20', she hesitates over, but solves quickly when some coins are made available.

The counting-on process is used also for '23 add 14' and '39 add 14', successfully but laboriously working her way along fourteen fingers. She gets in a muddle, not surprisingly, when she tries this method with '37 add 32', losing track of how many she has counted on. However it is significant that she completes this addition successfully in no time at all when given coins to use. She can also find '37 + 32' correctly when it is set out in vertical form, by dealing with the '7 + 2' and then the '3 + 3' separately on her fingers.

However, when then asked to work out '26 + 48' in vertical form, she resorts to trying to count on 48, using her fingers, and, of course, gets lost in the process.

This behaviour seems to typify a tendency in Tracey, when faced with the slightest of difficulties, to revert to a routine with which she is confident, in this case counting on her fingers.

A strategy for helping Tracey should probably therefore focus on developing her confidence with numbers and number relationships. At present, she has so little confidence in her knowledge of number bonds that she automatically resorts to the security of her fingers. Her familiarity with money might be used to establish the number bonds up to 20p securely, for both addition and subtraction. She should probably tackle addition and subtraction with two-digit numbers only using the support of 10p and 1p coins, and not with numerals in isolation. This experience would be designed to enable her to internalise the process of dealing with tens and ones, and exchanging, rather than the naive one of counting on in ones using her fingers. It would help her confidence with number enormously to make the connections between the addition and subtraction processes and the corresponding situations in shopping with which she seems familiar. For example, to relate addition to finding the total cost of a number of items, and to relate subtraction to 'how much more for this?', 'how much less for that?', or 'how much change?'. Asking her to make up her own problems like this might prove to be an effective way of reducing her dependency on the teacher. So would the opportunity to participate with other children in some small-group games focusing on some of the weaknesses identified above.

TWO YEAR-5 PUPILS

Sarah and Ben are in the second year of an 8–12 middle school in a small market town. It is a school with a good reputation locally, with good modern buildings and facilities, and plenty of parental support. Mathematics is taught in ability sets for four lessons a week, during which time the pupils work through the school's mathematics scheme, the Scottish Primary Mathematics Group series. They also have one lesson per week of mathematics within their mixed ability class, where there is more of an emphasis on investigative mathematics and problem-solving. Sarah and Ben are in the bottom set (set 3) for their year, a group of fifteen children. This small number makes it possible for most lessons to be organised to allow the children to work individually through the SPMG work-books, with the teacher moving around the room dealing with their problems as they arise. The objective of each lesson is for each pupil to make progress through the scheme.

Sarah: aged 10.3

Sarah lives with her mother, her step-father, and a younger brother who is the baby of the second marriage. The home background is fairly stable now, the parents supportive, always attending for parental consultations. They are anxious about Sarah's progress at school and often seek reassurance about this.

Her teacher's judgement is that her low attainment in mathematics is associated mainly with her personality and attitude. She tends to panic and give up quickly if she thinks she cannot tackle something. She had lagged behind in the first school and found it difficult to keep up in her first year in middle school. In fact, her level of attainment in most subjects is lower than average, although her reading skills are about average for her age. However, she has difficulty in following written instructions. Often this seems a matter of lack of confidence, so the teacher has to interpret instructions for her and explain precisely what she has to do in a mathematics question. She is noisy, demanding, insisting on help when she needs it, and requiring considerable reassurance. She does not mind exposing her weaknesses.

In mathematics lessons, it is clear that Sarah is more concerned with what is going on around her and what other children are up to, than she is with the exercises in her mathematics book. She will, for example, volunteer her advice and opinions to the teacher about seating arrangements, while the teacher is organising this at the start of the lesson. She will get up, uninvited, and write the date on the board, and she will engage in idle chatter with anyone within earshot.

In a typical one-hour mathematics lesson, the longest period of time which passes without her interacting with someone else is fifty seconds. It is noticeable that she is always the one to initiate the interaction – usually about school and class social aspects, such as who likes whom – and often the other children in the class do not even respond to her.

It is ten minutes before she starts to work at all. In this time she flicks through her mathematics book, announcing in a loud voice, as though assuming that everyone would be interested, 'Done that . . . done that . . .' When she does start working she makes constant loud comments on what other children in the room are doing, wearing, where they are sitting and so on. The teacher reprimands her for this, but it makes little impression.

When she has to go to the waste-bin to sharpen a pencil, she passes a boy called Paul. 'All right, Paul?' she says, again in a loud voice, quite unconcerned by the fact that Paul ignores her. Returning to her seat, she informs a near neighbour: 'Rebecca, this time last year I was still on the red book. Were you?' Typically she makes this remark in a loud voice, without actually looking at Rebecca, or even apparently expecting a reply. When a child from another class comes to the door of the classroom, it is, of course, Sarah who calls out: 'Come in!'

It is clear that Sarah is a very social person. She is concerned mainly about her relationships and standing with others. It might be suggested therefore that she would benefit from some experience of mathematics as more of a social subject, and less as a matter of individual, personal progress through a series of work-books on tasks which mainly have very little purpose or value from her perspective.

Sarah immediately impresses one as being a very fluent talker. She clearly enjoys talking about her home, school, and so on.

> 'At first school I found maths hard, but here it's easier. They explain things better. I whizzed through the red books and I'm starting on the green books today.'

She can tell the time with confidence and has a good grasp of time intervals, and time concepts generally. She knows when she goes to bed ('about 8'), when she gets up ('twenty-five to 7'), how long it takes to walk to the bus stop ('about 25 minutes'). She can work out how much older or younger than her are various individuals, knows the order of months and in which months various things happen, such as the start of the new term and Christmas. She is probably better than average for her age at this aspect of mathematics, no doubt because she is so involved with people and events around her. She knows that there are seven days in a week, but surprisingly does not know how many hours in a day, or minutes in an hour.

She also has good day-to-day experience of handling money. She goes to the village shop and spends money herself. She has a good idea of the cost of things, and how she spends her pocket money, but struggles a bit with working out how much change to expect.

> 'I usually buy pop magazines. They cost about 50 or 55p. Sometimes I get a can of drink for 30p.'
> 'If you bought a can of drink with this 50p, how much change would you get?'
> '20p.'
> 'And how much change if you had a pound?'
> 'It's 7 something . . . I keep thinking it's seventy or something.'

She writes numbers less than 100 correctly and does not confuse 14 and 41, or 17 and 70, for example. However, she does not yet write numbers over 100 with confidence. For example, she makes the common errors of writing 'one hundred and sixty-four' as '1064', and 'three hundred and twenty' as 3020. Generally her application of the place-value principle, especially to numbers over 100, is weak, and she would clearly benefit from having experience designed to clarify the connections between the symbols, the concrete embodiments (e.g. 100p, 10p and 1p coins, or base-ten blocks), and the associated language. For example, when given a small collection of base-ten blocks (hundreds, tens and ones) representing the number 673, she does not know which block is associated with which symbol or what language. She is quite happy to count the hundreds as ones.

It is not surprising therefore that she has little idea of the principle of exchange ('ten of these for one of those') applied to calculations. A typical error in subtraction calculations is to subtract the smaller digit from the larger regardless of position, as follows:

$$\begin{array}{r} 60 \\ - 27 \\ \hline 47 \end{array}$$

When given coins (tens and ones) to help her with this question she does not appear to have the procedure of exchanging a ten for ten ones available.

Surprisingly, she cannot work out the total cost of two articles costing 30p and 24p, getting in a muddle with her fingers and coming up with the answer '31p'. She can cope with both 'how much less' and 'how much more' in comparing prices, if she can count on her fingers from one price to the other, but does not associate this with subtraction. So, for example, given two TV sets costing £257 and £349, she cannot work out on a calculator how much more one costs than the other. First of all she enters '257 + 349', then realises the answer (606) must be wrong; so she then tries '349 + 257', and is surprised – and amused – to find that she gets the same answer!

She has a fairly good grasp of addition bonds with single-digit numbers, but is inclined to use counting back (with fingers) when given the corresponding subtraction questions. For example she knows instantly that '5 add 5' is 10, but counts back when asked '10 take away 5'.

She does not seem very sure about how many pennies there are in a pound, and when asked how many centimetres in a metre replies: 'I think it's a hundred and something, or three hundred.'

In fact, her concepts of length measurement are generally very weak. For instance, she has no idea how tall she is, responding that she thinks she is 'less than 20 cm,' and sticking with this assertion even when shown a ruler marked up to 30 cm.

It is interesting, however, that in spite of her weaknesses with some aspects of number, she shows a particular fascination with pattern in numbers – as instanced by her amusement at discovering that 257 + 349 = 349 + 257 – and she is surprisingly quick at seeing similarities. For example, she puts out '205p' with coins correctly, two hundreds (pound coins) and five ones. Some time later, when we have done some work with base-ten blocks which clarifies which blocks are hundreds, which tens and which ones, she can immediately put out '205' in blocks correctly, with the comment: 'I remembered there were no tens when I used the money.' Significantly she makes the connection with no prompting. This ability to see pattern might therefore be something which could be built on to encourage Sarah's motivation and commitment in mathematics lessons.

Ben: aged 9.8

Ben is a cause of some worry for his teacher because his attainment in mathematics appears to be not commensurate with his general ability. He is judged therefore to under-achieve in this subject.

He is the middle of a family of three children, with a stable and supportive background. His parents are anxious about his slow progress in mathematics and have made arrangements for him to take extra work home. He has a cheerful personality and a generally low level of anxiety about school work, including mathematics. He does fairly well in school, is lively in discussion and ready to make suggestions, often very interesting ones. He is quite mature intellectually and can, for example, appreciate alternative viewpoints on an issue being discussed. He seems to grasp scientific ideas quickly, and is accomplished in practical tasks. He is less good in written work, where he is hampered by rather untidy hand-writing. His assessed reading age is roughly the same as his chronological age. The concern of his parents and teachers is that his attainment in mathematics is disappointing. In particular his teacher is concerned that he is inclined to forget procedures which he had apparently learnt and mastered.

He has a tendency in mathematics to give quick answers to questions without thinking. He is an independent character and does not seek assistance when he really needs it. It seems at times as though he has unjustified confidence in his ability in mathematics. In fact, he is quite prepared to get a whole page of questions wrong rather than seek help.

In a typical mathematics lesson Ben is seated at a table on his own, because, as the teacher explains to him, he will work better that way. He does not appear to have a very easy relationship with the teacher, clearly resenting being separated from other boys in the group. Five minutes into the lesson the teacher helps him to identify which page he should be working on, but when she moves on he just sits fiddling with a piece of paper, still looking resentful. It is ten minutes into the lesson before he starts doing any of the questions from his mathematics text-book. He works quietly, without interacting with anyone or calling for assistance throughout the entire lesson. He never once initiates a contact with the teacher. He appears to be absorbed in what he is doing, and quite unconcerned about other children in the room. He actually has quite impressive oral language skills, and is well able to talk about what he is doing and to explain his working. It seems a pity therefore that he should spend the majority of time in mathematics lessons working independently and hardly ever talking about what he is doing. When he is given the opportunity to talk about mathematics, he actually shows an impressive level of confidence in manipulating important concepts in the context of time and shopping:

'How old are the other children in your family?'
'My brother's eleven and my sister's eight.'
'How much younger is your sister than your brother?'
'Three years younger.'

'What's the time now?'
'Nearly half past eleven.'
'When does school end?'
'Half past three.'
'How long till the end of school then?'
(Counting on fingers) 'Four hours.'

'How much pocket money do you get?'
'50p.'
'What do you spend it on?'
'Airfix planes.'
'How much do they cost?'
'It varies really – about one pound fifty.'
'How long would it take you to save up to buy one with your pocket money?'
'Three weeks.'

Ben handles the mathematics in this discussion so well that it seems surprising that he is perceived as having difficulty in this area of the curriculum. Clearly he does not translate his grasp of mathematical concepts and relationships into success in the tasks he is required to undertake in mathematics lessons in school.

In one lesson he is observed working on his own as usual, without interacting with either the teacher or other pupils, doing some simple division questions, such as '20 ÷ 3'. He uses a standard layout and procedure which he seems to know well, looking up the results he needs (such as $3 \times 6 = 18$) in his multiplication tables. The way he does this suggests that he has recently memorised this rather complex procedure, and it will not be surprising if in a few weeks' time he has forgotten it. When he gets to questions such as '65 ÷ 3', where the result is outside the range of his multiplication tables, he makes repeated and random errors, and typically does not ask for assistance.

In spite of this, the impression is given that Ben does have a desire and the ability to understand what he is doing, rather than just to carry out routines. For example, when I explain to him the idea of sharing the tens first, using a drawing of 6 tens and 5 ones, he picks this up quickly and is able to apply it to other questions. Later, when the teacher checks up on his progress, he is able to explain to her what he is doing. Then, when he gets to the next level of difficulty with these division questions, with problems like '97 ÷ 2' where the principle of exchange is involved, he succeeds with these by drawing pictures of tens and units in a note-pad and manipulating the drawings. This drawing procedure shows a good level of understanding of place value and the principle of exchange.

It is significant that the mathematics text-book he is using suggests the use of base-ten materials for these division questions, but these are not available for use by the children in this year group. This would seem to be a pity, since it is likely that Ben's understanding would be enhanced by further experience of connecting the base-ten materials with the arithmetic procedures. He is a boy who wants to understand and who can grasp principles. He will respond positively to explanation and discussion of mathematical ideas, but his present experience of learning mathematics, in which he works independently most of the time without assistance, means that he actually gets very little of this.

He certainly seems to be quick at making connections and grasping mathematical principles. For example, he correctly evaluates '4 fives', '5 tens', and '7 fives', but, typically for children of his age, does not know '5 sevens'. When I ask him to find '3 fours', he evaluates this correctly by counting-on: 4, 8, 12; and likewise '4 threes' is also obtained by counting on: 3, 6, 9, 12. At this point, without prompting, he says: 'So that other one [i.e. '5 sevens'] is 35, isn't it? It doesn't matter which way round it is, it's the same.'

The ability to formulate immediately and to apply generalisations like this is an intellectual behaviour which one would associate with a mathematically more able pupil. The challenge for the teacher is clearly to find a way in which Ben's ability to grasp mathematical structures and principles can emerge, be recognised and be encouraged in the context of a class of children learning mathematics.

His knowledge of addition bonds for single-digit numbers and multiples of 10 is good. Significantly, he makes intelligent use of reconstruction in mental arithmetic. For example, for '5 + 8' he clearly uses some form of mental reasoning rather than just straight recall in obtaining the result '13'. When asked to explain how he worked out the answer he says: 'I know in 8 there are 5 and 3; 5 and 5 is 10, so the answer is 13.' Likewise for '17 – 9' he explains his reasoning like this: '7 . . . . you have to add 2 to make 9, so take 2 from 10 to get 8.'

This shows really good understanding of mathematical structure and relationships. Again it appears unfortunate that he does not get opportunity in class to discuss these informal procedures and for them to be validated by the teacher's approval and recognition.

He tries to memorise the routine procedures of arithmetic, but it is clear from talking to him that this is the aspect of mathematics that gives him the least satisfaction. He can correctly carry out subtractions, such as '436 – 152', using the decomposition method as a routine, when given a question set out in the conventional way with one number above the other. But when asked to work out '23 – 17' written horizontally, he gives the (not uncommon) answer '14'.

This error leads to a conversation which illustrates Ben's potential for understanding in mathematics, provided he can be given the time and the space to resolve conflicts himself and to make connections between experiences. He is asked to compare the prices of two pens costing 23p and 17p. He asserts that the first costs 14p more. He then draws two lines for me, one 23 cm long and the other 17 cm long. (He does this well and remarks that he likes measurement best in maths.) However when asked how much longer is the one line than the other, he insists it is 14 cm longer.

Later in the interview I ask him how much more would he need to buy a £23 kit if he had only £17. The answer is predictable: £14. We then simulate this problem with coins, with Ben holding £17 and me playing the part of a rich uncle. He correctly works out that I have to give him £6 so that he can buy the kit. As he takes the coins from me he can see immediately that there is some conflict in his answer.

> 'I don't understand this!'
> 'What's the problem?'
> 'Well, I needed £6 more, but it should be 14.'
> 'Why is that?'
> '23 take 17 is 14, isn't it? But you only had to give me six. I don't get it.'
> 'So, what do you think?'
> (Looking at the coins in his hand)
> 'It's six, isn't it?'

Then, without prompting, Ben turns back to the drawings of the two lines, and to the problem of '23 – 17', immediately recognising the implications of his deduction: 'So that's 6 cm longer . . . . and that's 6 as well.'

TWO YEAR-6 PUPILS

Sharon and Michael are members of a mixed ability class of 10–11-year-olds in a city 8–12 middle school serving a local authority housing estate. This an area with more than its fair share of social problems, so that the hard-working and dedicated teachers at the school expend much of their energy on dealing with the effects of these on the children's social behaviour in school and on providing them with the security which many of them lack at home. Overall the level of educational attainment in the school is understandably depressed compared to schools with less educationally disadvantaged intakes. Certainly Sharon and Michael have the greatest problems in mathematics of the six pupils studied in this chapter.

All mathematics teaching takes place in mixed ability classes, with the Nuffield Mathematics scheme forming the basis throughout the school. There are thirty-three pupils in Sharon and Michael's class. For mathematics they are organised into four groups, so that the pupils in each group work on roughly the same material at the same time. The school is able to arrange its staff resources so that an additional teacher joins the class for mathematics and works with Sharon and Michael's group of eight particularly low-attaining pupils.

In a typical lesson, most of the class might be doing work from their Nuffield work-books on, say, ordering decimal numbers and adding/subtracting decimal numbers, while Sharon and Michael's group might be tackling a work-sheet on addition of tens and units.

Sharon: aged 10.10

Sharon is the third of four children. In common with the other children in the family, she has a slight hearing problem. Her father left home following the birth of the fourth child, but her family life has been fairly stable since. As the only girl in the family, she fulfils a stereotype female role at home, cooking, cleaning and undertaking other housekeeping duties. She appears to have a very narrow outlook and limited experience of life. Her immediate family life is the sum total of her experience and knowledge.

She is a podgy, slow-moving child, with a rather dull personality. She speaks in a monotonic voice and has poor mechanical skills. She is as good as gold in class and very cooperative. She hardly ever talks, looks generally listless and totally lacking in animation. She rarely interacts with other children and seems in a world of her own most of the time. Although she occasionally looks up from her work to watch other children fooling around, she does not participate and even appears a little shocked – or envious – that anyone should misbehave like this.

Sharon is limited in every aspect of school work. She always achieves very little on written tests. Both her written work and her reading skills are very poor. She needs one-to-one help constantly in class, being able to do very little on her own without constant reassurance and specific direction from the teacher. She shows no imagination or initiative in her work at school.

When she is doing mathematics she forms her figures very laboriously, with her mouth open and her tongue stuck out. She is left-handed and holds her pencil very awkwardly. In fact, she has her exercise book rotated anti-clockwise through an angle of about 85 degrees from the normal alignment, so consequently she actually writes more or less vertically, rather than horizontally.

The following is a typical example of Sharon's work in a mathematics lesson. First, she is seen counting on her fingers as she tackles addition of two-digit numbers, set out in vertical form:

$$
\begin{array}{r} 25 \\ 17 \\ + \ 19 \\ \hline \end{array} \qquad
\begin{array}{r} 36 \\ 18 \\ + \ 27 \\ \hline \end{array}
$$

She initially gives the answer 21 to both these questions, achieved by counting up the units on her fingers and ignoring the tens altogether. Since she had in recent lessons been practising the addition of strings of single-digit numbers (e.g., '5 + 6 + 3') this behaviour is perhaps understandable. The teacher, moving around the group, spots Sharon's errors and helps her to correct her additions. Wisely, the teacher decides to simplify the task by putting Sharon on to adding two numbers rather than three. With guidance she gets the idea of adding the tens as well as the units, and ten minutes later she has completed successfully three questions like this:

$$
\begin{array}{r}
26 \\
+\ 36 \\
\hline
62 \\
\hline
1
\end{array}
$$

Other children in the group have done about eight questions in this time. After more success with a few more examples of this sort, the teacher tries her again on the addition of three numbers. Immediately Sharon reverts to ignoring the tens again and just adding the units.

She looks thoroughly bored and quite uninterested in the tasks she is given to do. She is clearly used to getting things wrong in mathematics, and whether her work is right or wrong appears to be a matter of total indifference to her.

Some of Sharon's misunderstandings about mathematical concepts seem quite surprising for a child of her age. For example, most primary-school children have a very clear concept of age and handle relationships of 'older' and 'younger' with confidence. A discussion with Sharon about her family reveals that she has three brothers: Simon, aged 11, 'but little', Kevin, aged 6 and Jamie aged 2. When asked whether she is older or younger than Simon, Sharon insists that she is older than him, 'because my birthday is before his.' Sharon knows that her birthday is in July, when she would be eleven, and that Simon's birthday is in August, when he would be twelve. But she is quite convinced that she is older than Simon, because her birthday comes first.

However, she is fairly confident with other concepts related to time. She wears a digital watch and refers to it with apparent understanding. For example, at 10.57 she is able to tell me that next it will be 10.58, then 10.59 and then 11 o'clock. She has a fairly good idea of times of events in her life – she knows that she leaves for school at half past eight, that 12 o'clock is dinner-time, that school finishes at 3 o'clock, and that she goes to bed at half past eight or nine o'clock. On Saturdays, she explains, she goes to bed at half past twelve, because her brother goes to the club, and she stays home and gets a pound. This is presumably payment for baby-sitting with the two younger brothers.

Discussion with Sharon about money again indicates surprisingly patchy knowledge of an aspect of mathematics related to life outside of school, at which most of the children in the class are fairly adept. She is getting a new bike for her birthday, but has no idea at all whether this will cost one pound, ten pounds or a hundred pounds. With her £1 pocket money she buys sweets. These, she says, are 1p each and she buys about 40 at a time, but she cannot tell me how much this would cost. She can tell me that a can of drink costs 30p.

'How many cans could you buy with £1?'
'Eighty.'

Given a pile of £1, 20p, 10p, 5p, 1p coins, she is able correctly to work out that there is eight pounds, six pence, in total, although she makes the not-unusual error of writing this down as £8.6. However, she cannot even begin to handle questions about change:

> 'If you bought a can of drink for 30p with your one-pound coin, how much change would you get?'

Sharon is unable to offer a response, even when I try role play with her as a shopkeeper and me buying a drink with a £1 coin – she just has no idea how to deal with this.

I try again with smaller amounts of money. This time, as I ask the question, I draw a sweet and a coin, writing 5p on the sweet and 20p on the coin:

> 'If you buy a sweet costing 5p with a 20p coin, how much change would you get?'
> '25p.'

Sharon's response is simply to add up the two numbers written on the paper, counting on her fingers. Presumably this is what she normally has to do with any numbers she sees written down. She is apparently unable to interpret this as a real situation and sees it just as some numbers to be manipulated in the only way she knows.

When asked to write down various numerals she makes two classic errors: first 'one hundred and sixty-four' is written '10064' and 'one hundred and fifty' is written '10050'. Secondly, 'seventy' is written '17'. Given her suggested hearing problem, I repeat this one very clearly and carefully, and she says 'seventy' quite clearly back to me. But she still writes '17', and, in fact, seems to interpret it as 'seventeen', since when she (correctly) arranges the set of numbers in order she puts the 17 between 14 and 29.

She does not have much understanding of the word 'between' applied to numbers. For example, she cannot give me a number between 12 and 92. When asked to show me where various numbers are on a number line marked in tens, she places 59 between 40 and 50, and 43 between 30 and 40.

Any notion of comparison of two quantities floors her completely. For example, she is unable to give any answer to the following two questions:

> 'I am 40 and you are 10. How much older am I than you?'
> 'Here are two cans of drink, one costing 40p and the other 10p. How much more for this one?'

She is able to use her ruler to draw two lines, one 14 cm and the other 12 cm long, and when asked which one is longer, answers correctly, even though the 12 cm line is projecting further to the right. But her response to the question, 'how much longer?' is simply a puzzled expression.

Sharon's understanding of place value is extremely sketchy. When I put out 2 hundreds, 4 tens and 5 ones in base-ten materials and ask her what number this is, she just counts the pieces and gives the answer 'eleven'. Not surprisingly, she cannot put out a number like 143 with these materials. She is not unfamiliar with the blocks, since they are used extensively in the school, but clearly she has so far totally failed to make the connections between the number symbols and the blocks and does not know the 'one of these is ten of those' principle.

Sharon's confidence in operating mentally with numbers is limited to simple addition, and subtraction expressed in terms of 'take away'. She can cope with the addition of two single-digit numbers, such as '3 + 4', '6 + 8', sometimes knowing the result immediately (e.g. '8 + 8'), other times counting, surreptitiously using her fingers and moving her lips silently. She makes no use of the relationships between numbers which she does know to deal with those that she does not. She copes with subtraction slowly, with questions like '7 – 3' and '9 – 4' again being done on her fingers. For '10 – 9' she gives the answer '2'.

For questions like '17 – 3' she uses an idiosyncratic procedure with a 30-cm ruler: this involves counting back three from 17, covering over the 14 with her thumb, then counting all the other marks on the ruler from 13 to 0, to get the answer '14'. She does this repeatedly and never seems to notice that the number under her thumb is always the answer to the question.

Sharon's teacher justifiably recognises her as an example of a less able child who is generally unsuccessful in the kinds of tasks which schools conventionally give to children.

Michael: aged 10.11

Michael is seen as an enigma. His attainment in mathematics is just as low as Sharon's, but he is a very different person, demonstrating vividly just how idiosyncratic the pattern of mathematical competences and misunderstandings in any individual learner can be.

Michael is the youngest of four children in a stable family. He is excessively mollycoddled by his mother who, for example, walks him to school and meets him each day. He is always well turned out, looks healthy and active. He is a lively boy, with a vivid imagination and a tendency to exaggerate.

He does not take much care with his work and is very slapdash, although quite capable at practical tasks. He has plenty of ideas for written work, but needs a lot of help getting them down on paper. He forms his numerals unconventionally and awkwardly, for example, starting '7' at the bottom.

He is lively and interested in class, and contributes orally. His reading skills are average for this group. His teacher remarks that he has occasional flashes of inspiration in mathematics when he shows surprising insights and knowledge. But these contrast markedly with equally surprising misunderstandings and errors.

He is quite well-behaved, but is inclined to be moody and sulky with other children, probably because he is used to getting his own way at home. He finds it fairly easy to pass the time away without doing the tasks set for him, without being especially naughty. He is very involved in everything going on around him in his group. He calls out immediately whenever he wants advice or help from the teacher – and normally makes sure that he gets it.

Michael is most unpredictable in his responses to mathematical questions. There are things which he can do successfully, which you would not expect him to be able to do given the things he cannot do, and vice versa. Very typical of Michael is a tendency to give what might be termed 'intuitive' responses to mathematical situations. In this respect he is characteristically intellectually immature.

For example, he knows the ages of his older brothers and sister: Sean 18, Mark 14, Haley 13 – and he is 10. The following is a conversation with Michael about ages, normally an aspect of number which children handle with confidence:

'Is Sean older or younger than you?'
'Older, of course.'
'How much older than you is Sean?'
'Eighteen.'
'Yes, Sean is eighteen, and you are ten, so how many years older than you is he?'
'About nine.'
'So, how much younger are you than Sean?'
'Ten . . . hang on . . . no . . . two.'
'I'm 40 and you're 10 – how much older than you am I?'
'Four . . . . and you'll be one year older than me.'
'How many years will it be till you're 40, Michael?'
'About fifty.'

Michael often seems unable to deal with simple relationships between numbers in practical situations like this, even though in his mathematics lessons he is currently carrying out the procedure for the additions of three two-digit numbers with considerable success. Sometimes it seems as though there is no connection whatsoever between the numbers he writes down and operates on in his mathematics book and the numbers he encounters in everyday situations. He cannot accurately recall the order of the months of the year and he has a surprisingly limited knowledge of annual events and time scales for a child who is nearly eleven.

'When is your birthday, Michael?'
'July 4th.'
'When is Christmas?'
'September.'
'How long is it till then?'
'Ages.'

He has a digital watch and seems confident about times in his day – he tells me that school starts at 8.45 and finishes at three o'clock, that he has tea at about six o'clock, and that he goes to bed about ten or eleven, but at nine o'clock when he has to go to school the next day. However, when I ask him at half past one what the time is he looks at the dial clock and says: 'nearly 2 o'clock.' This is typical of his rather carefree and approximate approach to measurements and quantities. The word 'about' appears frequently in his responses.

> 'What time do you leave home for school in the morning?'
> '8.20.'
> 'And what time do you get to school?'
> '8.30.'
> 'So, how long does it take?'
> 'About three or four minutes.'

He gets £1 a week pocket money, spends 50p on sweets and saves 50p for Saturday. He likes Kinder eggs, which he says cost 32p. He tells me that you could get a can of Coke for 29p at the Spar shop. I draw a can of Coke, labelled '29p', and a Kinder egg, labelled '32p'.

> 'How much more does the Kinder egg cost?'
> 'About 2p.'

I ask Michael to put out coins for these amounts, using ten-pence and one-penny pieces. He does this correctly, but when I ask which pile of coins he would rather have he opts for the 29p, 'because it's the most.' Here he again responds intuitively to the number of coins rather than to their value, in a way more typical of an average six-year-old.

This response seems at odds with the fact that he seems confident in a number of procedures indicating a well-developed sense of place value. He is, for example, very quick at putting out 3-digit numbers (such as 125, 240, 303) with both coins and base-ten blocks, and seems to have a clear grasp of the coins–symbols and blocks–symbols connections. He is able correctly to write two- and three-digit numbers in symbols, as I call them out. He then very confidently puts them in order: 12, 14, 29, 70, 71, 92, 164. He also handles the concept of 'between' very well, more or less correctly locating 31, 45, 54 and 69 on a number line marked out in tens.

In particular, he is likely to respond apparently at random to any questions requiring the comparison of two numbers or quantities in a practical context. He cannot handle relationships of comparison, such as 'older', 'younger', 'longer', 'shorter', 'costs more than', 'less than', and simply makes an intuitive guess. For example, he can draw lines of 14 cm and 12 cm, and knows which one is longer. But when asked, 'how much longer?' he answers immediately, 'about four.'

Although he is quite confident at carrying out some written arithmetic procedures, he is clearly very weak in mental manipulation of numbers and has very limited knowledge of simple number bonds. So, when carrying out, for example, additions of two-digit numbers, he can be seen counting on his fingers at each stage. When I ask him for the answers to '6 + 3', '4 + 2', '2 + 5' he counts on his fingers every time, slowly and laboriously. When he gets the answer '7' for '2 + 5' he expresses some surprise, 'because two fives are ten.'

Similarly, when he is asked to work out 'six take away three', 'seven take away two', and so on, he is very slow and hesitant, uses his fingers, and makes the comment, 'I'm not very good at these'.

Because of his limited recall of simple number bonds, he cannot answer '15p, spend 5p – how much left?' other than by laboriously counting back, using his fingers again. He knows that two £5 notes make £10, but has to work out the value of three by counting on, once more with his fingers. His inability to recall basic number bonds and his lack of confidence in simple number relationships clearly contribute to his unpredictable behaviour in real-life situations: one can understand his preference for making a wild, intuitive guess, rather than engaging in a slow, laborious procedure.

When I ask him to do some of the questions on a calculator he does not know how to operate it. He tells me that he would not use a calculator at school, because that would be cheating.

QUESTIONS FOR FURTHER DISCUSSION

1. Mark, Tracey, Sarah and Sharon all make the common error of inserting extra noughts when writing down numbers involving hundreds, such as 10064 for 'one hundred and sixty-four'. How would you help them to eradicate this error?
2. Mark, Tracey and Sarah especially show little commitment to the tasks they are doing in their mathematics lessons. By what means might such pupils' commitment be increased?
3. Discuss the suggestion that Sarah might benefit from some experience of mathematics as more of a social subject. How might this come about?
4. What would be your advice to Ben's teacher to help his obvious potential in mathematics to be realised?
5. Where would you start in sorting out the mathematical problems of Sharon and Michael?

3
FACTORS IN LOW ATTAINMENT IN MATHEMATICS

In this chapter I will address the question: why do some children do so poorly in mathematics? The case studies in the previous chapter have already suggested that there will be no straightforward or universal answer to this question. For any given child the factors associated with their low attainment in mathematics may be numerous and related to each other in a complex manner. A *deficit model* of low attainment would consider the problem merely in terms of the intellectual deficiencies or immaturity of the child. Such a model would emphasise mainly the diagnosis of the child's difficulties in understanding and mastering mathematics (see, for example, Underhill, Uprichard and Heddens, 1980). It is generally recognised that such a model is an inadequate way of analysing the problem and that an *ecological model*, which attempts to describe the relationships between the child and the whole learning environment, is likely to give more useful insights (see, for example, P. Mittler in Womack, 1988).

There are at least three strands to the question raised in this chapter. We can consider: (a) some of the significant characteristics of school mathematics which make it a particularly difficult subject for many pupils; (b) some of the specific intellectual or behavioural characteristics which are frequently noted in mathematical low attainers; (c) some of the shortcomings in the way the subject is often taught. It is likely that low attainment in mathematics is the result of a complex interplay between components of these three strands. When, for example, some of the characteristic difficulties inherent in mathematics are identified, then it becomes clear why children with some specific intellectual deficiencies or behaviour patterns might have problems with this subject, and there are inevitable implications concerning the way the subject might be taught. Consequently, although the points made in the following discussion are organised under these three headings, there is inevitably the need to hold all three strands in mind at the same time, and there is, therefore, much overlap between the headings.

SOME SIGNIFICANT CHARACTERISTICS OF SCHOOL MATHEMATICS

Mathematics is a distinctive subject, with its own particular ways of proceeding, its own characteristic concepts and ways of manipulating and relating together these concepts. It may be helpful for those who teach children with particular difficulties in mathematics to be explicitly aware of some of the characteristics of the subject which may contribute to these difficulties.

Right or wrong

First, it has always seemed to me to be particularly significant that in mathematics, more than in any other aspect of the school curriculum, pupils are given tasks to do for which their responses will be judged to be absolutely right or absolutely wrong. Nearly always in a mathematical situation there exist criteria by which the response may be evaluated in this hard and fast, objective manner. For children whose attainment in the subject is low, the effect of this might be that they have frequent experiences of their work in mathematics being returned to them marked 'wrong'. This does not happen to anything like the same extent in their other activities in school. Their creative writing might be judged to be 'rather dull', their descriptive writing might provoke the comment 'you have missed out some important points', they might be told that their drawings are 'scruffy', their singing 'out of tune', their efforts on the games field 'lazy' or 'uncoordinated', their attempts at scientific observation and recording 'careless', their writing on a humanities topic 'very disappointing', and so on, but rarely will they hear in subjects other than mathematics the word 'wrong' used in judgement of their work. In mathematics more than any other subject there is the possibility that they will experience absolute failure at the tasks they are given. Of course, for many pupils this is precisely the characteristic of mathematics which gives them so much motivation – they get things absolutely right, ten out of ten, red ticks abound, they experience frequent success, and this is a very satisfying experience. But for those pupils at the other end of the spectrum, the constant failure, the repeated judgement that their responses are wrong, and the red crosses proliferating in their exercise books, all add up to a depressing and frustrating experience.

Cumulative effect of failure

Perhaps one other aspect of children's work in schools which shares this feature of being subject to absolute judgements of right or wrong is spelling.

But there is a significant difference here. If I cannot spell a particular word, this does not usually stop me from going on to try to learn to spell other words; nor does it prevent me from using the word I cannot spell correctly, in my talking, in my reading or even in my writing right across the curriculum. But if I cannot succeed with a particular mathematical skill, the hierarchical nature of much of mathematics will mean that I am likely to find it nearly impossible to succeed with a whole host of other mathematical skills, and I will experience failure in a whole range of mathematical tasks which call upon the skill in question. For example, if a child cannot master the addition bonds for numbers up to 10, it would appear to be impossible for them to go on to succeed in subtractions with these numbers, with additions of two-digit numbers, and so on; and they may also fail at many of the practical, problem-solving tasks they might be given, in, say, shopping and handling coins, because of their lack of knowledge of the addition bonds which are likely to be required. This cumulative effect of failure is again more of a distinctive characteristic of learning mathematics than of most other aspects of school learning.

Accuracy and concentration

Another significant characteristic of school mathematics is that success in this subject often requires a considerable degree of care and accuracy. Pupils need to concentrate on their tasks and be self-disciplined in their approach to their work in mathematics, in a way which is alien to many pupils in our contemporary western society. Growing up in a world dominated by fast-moving television, videos, instant entertainment and popular culture, many young people are conditioned to lose interest in anything which requires concentration for more than two minutes. Some aspects of learning mathematics successfully may require therefore some personal and social development in the areas of patience, care, accuracy, concentration and self-discipline, which for some pupils will be a considerable undertaking.

Lack of concentration on the task in hand is a pervading characteristic of children whose progress in school is limited. They appear to be unable to refrain from reacting to any external stimulus, such as movement of other children around the room, conversations, activity through the windows, and so on. Since mathematical tasks in school especially, by their very nature, require concentration, it is therefore not surprising that children such as Mark, Tracey and Sarah, described in Chapter 2, make little progress with this subject.

Successful teaching of mathematics to pupils who find it difficult to concentrate on one kind of activity for very long may therefore require some concessions on the part of the teacher in the way mathematics lessons and activities are organised.

Abstractions

A major difficulty inherent in mathematics for many pupils learning the subject is that it deals so much with abstract concepts and relationships between these abstractions. From the earliest years of schooling, the symbols and language of mathematics are used to represent abstractions and relationships between abstractions. The symbol '5', for example, might represent the attribute shared by all concrete examples of sets of five things. When it is used on its own, unattached to a specific set, it is therefore an abstraction. A simple mathematical statement such as '3 + 5 = 8' is then a relationship between the abstractions 3, 5 and 8, and itself represents an abstraction derived from all the examples experienced of putting together sets of 3 things and 5 things and finding you have a set of 8 things. Of course, the abstractions represented by mathematical symbols can always be traced back to concrete experiences with real things, but this gets more and more difficult as new mathematical concepts are developed by a process of abstracting from abstractions. For example, 'multiple of 3' is a concept formed by an abstraction of the attribute shared by the abstractions 3, 6, 9, 12, and so on, and is therefore two steps removed from the concrete experiences of manipulating sets of counters or fingers.

An important aspect of school mathematics is the application of numerical and spatial concepts and skills to various kinds of measurement. This gives pupils much opportunity for direct, practical application of mathematical ideas. However, many of the concepts of measurement, such as volume, mass and time, are themselves very abstract and require a highly sophisticated degree of organisation of one's perceptions in order to focus on the particular attribute being measured. It is characteristic of many pupils who find mathematics difficult that they show a range of immature misunderstandings and confusions about such fundamental, but abstract, concepts of measurement. The confusion of the Year 6 girl called Sharon about whether she was older or younger than her brother described in Chapter 2 is a typical example of this kind of failure to focus on the attribute being measured. On another occasion, I recall a ten-year-old boy comparing the capacity of two containers by filling one with water and pouring it into the other: he then insisted that the smaller one was the bigger because the larger one was only half-full, whereas the smaller one had been full right to the top.

Symbols

Mathematics is therefore a difficult subject for many pupils because of its characteristic way of using symbols to represent and to manipulate abstract concepts. This is at one and the same time the reason for the power of mathematics and the reason for its complexity for many of those trying to learn it. As these manipulations get further and further away from the real contexts which give them meaning and purpose, the subject becomes for many pupils more and more of a bewildering mystery. A major challenge for the teacher therefore is to enable the pupil to make the connections between the manipulations of the symbols and the corresponding concrete experiences.

But there is a further peculiar difficulty in the way symbols are used in mathematics, particularly in the area of number and number operations. This is the potentially confusing practice of using one symbol to represent more than one category of experience. For example, the division symbol in '18 ÷ 6' could mean in concrete terms 'share a set of 18 counters equally between 6 people and see how many they each get'. But it could also mean: 'put a set of 18 counters into groups of 6 and see how many groups there are'. The same symbol '÷' is used here in two completely different ways, both valid models for the mathematical concept of 'division'. This is not an isolated example, since similar things occur with the symbols and concepts of addition, subtraction, multiplication, fractions, and even the symbols for numbers themselves. Figure 3.1 shows, for example, just some of the great

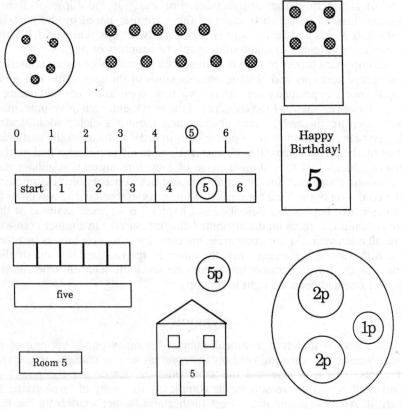

Figure 3.1   Some experiences of 'five'

variety of concrete experiences which a young child may have to learn to connect with the symbol '5' and the word 'five': a set of five counters; a line of five counters and then a longer line with the same number; a familiar pattern for five shown in the dots on a domino; a point labelled '5' on a number line; a square labelled '5' on a board game; five years of age; five cubes joined together in such material as Stern or Unifix; a five-rod in, say, the Colour Factor or Cuisenaire set; a room or a house labelled number five; a 5p coin; and a set of three coins worth 5p. Surely this characteristic habit of using the same symbol to represent such a vast range of differing experiences must be one of the reasons why mathematics is so difficult for many pupils.

Unstable truths and models

A surprising feature of mathematical experience is that there are many instances where children may learn 'truths' and develop models in their early experiences of number which later on have to be unlearnt or modified in some way, as their experience of number widens. For example, they may learn early on to think of a number as a set of things, a model constantly reinforced by the majority of concrete examples used by their teachers; then later, because the idea of a number as a label for ordering is not a major part of their understanding, they cannot make any sense of negative numbers which cannot be interpreted as sets of things. They may learn to say things like 'three take away five, can't do . . .', only to be told later that you can do it and the answer is '–2'. They pick up the ideas that subtraction makes things smaller and that multiplication makes things bigger, and are confounded when they meet '6 – (–2) = 8' and '75 × 0.2 = 15'. This phenomenon is not peculiar to learning mathematics, of course. The concept we develop through our early experiences of what constitutes a 'foreigner', for example, has to be modified radically later on when we travel abroad and discover that we are now the foreigners. But when this happens in mathematics, where we are conditioned to think that what is right and what is wrong is always clear-cut, it can undermine the confidence of the poor student struggling to make sense of what they are being taught. (For a fuller discussion of this and the issues raised in the previous two sections the reader is referred to Haylock and Cockburn, 1989.)

Complex language patterns

A mathematical statement which we might expect a young child to formulate would be: 'seven is two more than five'; or its equivalent, 'five is two less than seven'. These are typical of the complex language patterns which are peculiar to mathematics and which do not come easily to many children. So specific help in getting some of these language patterns established in their talking and writing repertoire will be required. To make statements of this kind, or to understand many of the instructions which appear in mathematics text-books or work-cards, the child must hold and relate together in his or her mind a number of abstract concepts.

Here is an example of a question for 10–11-year-olds taken from a primary mathematics scheme: 'Which number between 25 and 30 cannot be divided exactly by either 2 or 3?' (SPMG Stage 4 Progress Tests).

A child might very well be able to read and understand each of the individual words in this question, but put them all together and a complex intellectual task emerges: the child must hold in his or her mind that the task requires the identification of one number; that to find this number each number greater than 25 but less than 30 must be tested; that the test must determine firstly whether the number is divisible by 2, secondly whether it is divisible by 3, and then each number rejected if either of these is the case; they must be able to call to mind in turn the procedures for testing for divisibility by 2 and by 3, while remembering which numbers have been tested and which have passed or failed which tests, and all the time retaining the aim of the task. This is typical of the level of intellectual demand in many apparently simple mathematical statements, questions or instructions.

Many children with experience of only a limited range of language structures and vocabulary in their everyday lives, will need help with some of the key words which are required to communicate mathematical ideas: words such as 'either', 'each', 'altogether', 'between', which feature surprisingly infrequently in their normal conversation. They will need help in clarifying the subtle differences in meaning implied by different prepositions, such as 'sharing with' and 'sharing between'. The formation of sentences such as '18 shared between 6 is 3 each' and '6 sets of 3 makes 18 altogether' is a major difficulty for many pupils, but is also an essential component in their learning of mathematics.

Sequencing

One further characteristic of mathematics is that many of its processes and routines involve the learning of a sequence of steps, which, for successful mastery, must be carried out in the prescribed order. The formal processes of arithmetic, such as addition of three-digit numbers set out in vertical form and subtraction by decomposition are examples of such ordered sequences of steps. This then is another factor which makes mathematics a difficult subject to learn for many children. The inability to sequence successfully is typical of many children with learning disabilities, and this deficiency will be felt most acutely in mathematics. Many teachers find it necessary to provide some pupils with tasks specifically designed to develop their ability to sequence, as a prerequisite for the development of their mathematical skills.

SOME CHARACTERISTICS OF MATHEMATICAL LOW ATTAINERS

In a survey of some 215 Year 6 schoolchildren, in their third year in 8–12 middle schools, teachers were asked to consider a list of statements which referred to various factors often associated with low attainment in mathematics (Haylock, 1986). For each child with a score on a standardised mathematics test which put them in the bottom 20% for mathematical attainment, the teachers were asked to indicate whether, in their judgement, the statements described the child. The statements concerned were based on reports of possible factors associated with low attainment in mathematics in previous studies, such as those undertaken by Ross (1964), Lumb (1978), Denvir, Stolz and Brown (1982). Twenty-two of the statements used are listed below, together with the percentage of mathematical low-attaining pupils for whom their teachers thought the statement definitely or probably described them.

- has been considered low-attaining in mathematics from the first year in this school (82%)
- is low-attaining in most areas of the curriculum (79%)
- has poorly developed reading skills (77%)
- is equally poor in all aspects of mathematics (74%)
- has poorly developed language skills (70%)
- shows perceptual difficulties such as reversal of figures or poor spatial discrimination (45%)
- has immature motor skills (44%)
- is immature in relationships with other pupils (39%)
- shows little commitment or interest in mathematics lessons (39%)
- shows little commitment and interest in school in general (33%)
- has difficulty in relating to adults (33%)
- is nearly always preoccupied, appearing to find school and learning irrelevant (30%)
- has emotional problems related to an exceptional home background (30%)
- experiences social difficulties with the peer group (29%)
- displays behaviour problems, such as hyperactivity, in most lessons (26%)
- shows an abnormal level of anxiety towards most tasks in school (26%)
- shows an abnormal level of anxiety towards mathematics (26%)
- responds sensibly in a one-to-one conversation with a teacher but behaves badly in front of other children (24%)
- some physical factor such as deafness, poor eye sight, colour blindness, contributes to their low attainment in mathematics (18%)
- has been absent frequently in the last year (17%)
- seems excessively tired much of the time (14%)
- has suffered frequent changes of mathematics teachers or schools (5%)

A number of points emerge from this survey and some of the more significant of these are discussed below.

First of all, the item at the top of the list suggests that pupils can be identified as low attainers in mathematics by the age of 8 (Year 4), if not earlier, and often remain in this category throughout the upper primary years. This lends some support to my view that these are the crucial years for tackling the problems of these pupils. There is evidence to suggest that many of the mathematical tasks at which low-attaining pupils fail around the age of 12 will still be beyond them when they leave secondary school at the age of 16 (Hart, 1981). So, if by Year 4 we can confidently identify pupils who have particular problems in mathematics, then we should surely set about devising an appropriate curriculum for these pupils from that age onwards and not just subject them to exactly the same mathematical diet as that provided for average and above-average pupils.

Reading and language problems

It is striking to note how frequently it is the case that poor reading and language skills are associated with low attainment in mathematics. In the survey quoted above this was true for about three-quarters of the children sampled. It was also significantly more often the case for low-attaining boys to have poorly developed reading skills than for low-attaining girls.

This reinforces the points made above about the particular difficulties associated with the complex language structures of mathematics. But it also underlines how inappropriate for these pupils must be any teaching method which relies heavily on the written word as the medium for instruction in mathematics. One study of children's errors in written mathematical tasks (Clement, 1980) found that 24% of the errors made by low-achieving 12-year-olds were simply reading or comprehension errors. If children are struggling with their comprehension of written English, then it is self-evident that they will fail in learning mathematics when almost all the tasks they are given to do in mathematics lessons are communicated to them by written instructions in text-books or work-cards. The sheer cognitive strain of reading the instructions for the task makes it most unlikely that they will comprehend the mathematics. I recall a typical conversation with one pupil who was struggling with a work-card and called for assistance.

'What's the problem?'
'I don't understand what I have to do.'
'What does the card say then?'
(Hesitatingly) 'Draw a square . . . with side ten centimetres . . . and divide it into five equal parts.'
'So, what's the problem?'
'What do I have to do?'
'You have to draw a square with side ten centimetres and divide it into five equal parts.'
'Oh, I see!' (Proceeds to do it)

The extraordinary thing about this conversation is that all I did was to repeat back to him exactly what he had said to me, and yet because he was hearing it, rather than reading it, he was able to understand what was required.

Perceptual problems

It is interesting to note the frequency with which perceptual problems and poor spatial discrimination are associated with low attainment in mathematics. Success in many mathematical tasks will require confident handling of basic spatial concepts such as left, right, above, below, over and under. Intellectual deficiencies of this kind will show up in reversals of figures, and confusions between, for example, 14 and 41. Some mathematical processes become particularly difficult for some children, since they involve a right to left movement, such as starting with the units when doing addition and subtraction set out in vertical form, contrary to the standard left to right movement which is reinforced in reading.

Social problems

Quite a number of the statements in the list used for the survey refer to difficulties in social behaviour. Roughly speaking, it seems as though about one-third of the pupils sampled were judged by their teachers to be badly behaved in class, to be immature in their relationships, to show off in front of other children, to find school irrelevant, to show little commitment or interest, and to experience social difficulties with their peers. It is interesting to note that the survey also showed that these kinds of problems were significantly more frequently associated with low-attaining boys than with low-attaining girls.

Whether these kinds of factors associated with low attainment in mathematics are the cause of low attainment or the result of it is, of course, impossible to say. It seems likely that the frustration of constant failure in school would contribute to antisocial behaviour within the institution, just as much as a lack of social skills and unwillingness to cooperate with teachers and other pupils would contribute to the failure.

It would seem that an obvious implication of the frequent association of bad social behaviour with low attainment in mathematics is that teachers must aim to provide pupils with tasks to which they will commit themselves. It will not be enough simply to demand that pupils undertake a task just because the teacher says so. The more we can provide such low-attaining pupils with purposeful tasks which they themselves recognise as being worthwhile the more likely we are to see some progress.

Mathematics anxiety

About a quarter of the pupils sampled were judged by their teachers to show high levels of anxiety towards most tasks in school, and a similar proportion towards mathematics in particular. This is consistent with the previous comments about social behaviour. Those pupils who are more accepting of the rules and conventions of the institution are likely to be more anxious about failing at the tasks set for them by the authorities within the institution. Since mathematics is the subject in which failure is experienced most overtly, a high level of anxiety towards the subject can be expected. Anxiety towards mathematics was a factor significantly more frequently associated with low-attaining girls than with low-attaining boys.

Again it is not possible to determine whether this high degree of anxiety is a cause or an effect of low attainment in mathematics. It seems likely that this is another case of one characteristic reinforcing the other. Repeated failure in mathematics increases the level of anxiety, because of the fear of further failure; then the anxiety inhibits the child's performance and leads to further failure.

The challenge for the teacher is to find ways of breaking into this vicious circle, to reduce anxiety, and to foster the pupil's self-concept and confidence in mathematics. For pupils with high levels of anxiety towards mathematics, teaching strategies must ensure that they have considerable experience of success. This will probably require very detailed analysis by the teacher of what existing competences in mathematics the pupil has, and then a teaching programme designed to build on these in very small steps.

SHORTCOMINGS IN THE TEACHING OF MATHEMATICS

The tyranny of the scheme

Most primary and middle schools invest a considerable amount of their budget in a mathematics scheme. This might consist of boxes of work-cards or a series of work-books, often with the expectation that one box of cards or one set of books will determine the mathematics syllabus for one year of schooling. It is interesting to note that there is more reliance on the use of commercially produced schemes for teaching mathematics than for any other subject in the primary and middle school curriculum. In a subject where many teachers are traditionally lacking in confidence themselves, the scheme provides them with security, ready-made decisions about the order and quantity of various mathematical exercises and experiences, some confidence about what the children will have done already, and enough activities to keep children occupied in mathematics for the four or five hours a week allotted on the timetable. But, nevertheless, it is always a surprise to me that a teacher can apparently believe that an author of a mathematics scheme, who has never met the children concerned, can determine exactly what mathematical activities, in what order, and in what quantity, should be given to each and every individual in the class. One teacher complained to me about the particular mathematics scheme he was using with his mixed ability class of 11–12-year-olds:

> 'One of the things I don't like about this scheme is that there are too many of these division questions for some of these children, page after page of them.'

'So, why don't you just let some of the children miss some of them out?'
'I couldn't do that – we've been told that it's essential that every child works through every exercise.'
'Who told you that?'
'We had this representative come round from the publishers – he told us.'

It is almost inevitable that a scheme of this sort, usually produced with average and above-average pupils in mind, will provide an inappropriate curriculum for our low attainers in mathematics (see Low Attainers in Mathematics Project, 1987). Teachers concerned to do the best for these pupils must be prepared to break away from the tyranny of the scheme; to view the scheme as a resource to be used and not as a master to be obeyed; to make their own judgements about the appropriateness of the learning tasks provided in the scheme and to supplement them with activities of their own devising, based on their own knowledge of the particular difficulties and characteristics of the individual children they have to teach. Learning mathematics, particularly for the low-attaining pupils, must not be perceived as simply getting through the scheme. I am convinced that this is a serious shortcoming in the teaching of mathematics, contributing to the lack of progress of many pupils.

Individualised learning

Associated with the tyranny of the mathematics scheme is what I regard as the misguided reliance on individualised learning as a teaching style for mathematics, which has become very common in primary schools in recent years. In this approach, each child in the class spends most mathematics lessons working individually at their own pace through a series of work-cards or pages of a work-book. When a card or page is completed they get it marked and then either do their corrections or go on to the next card or page. Sometimes they do the marking themselves using the answer sheet provided, but more often they will join a queue of children at the teacher's desk. If they have problems with a task they must either signal for the teacher's attention or join the queue.

Again, it is quite understandable why some teachers have opted for such an approach. In a mixed ability class the range of competence and rate of progress in mathematics will be so enormous that there seem to be many advantages in allowing pupils to progress at their own pace. Even in schools where setting across year groups is employed for mathematics, the range of ability in the bottom (and, incidentally, the top) sets will be considerable and probably greater than those in the middle sets. This is simply a statistical consequence of the way in which human attributes (height, weight, life-span, IQ, mathematics attainment, etc.) tend to be distributed, with most people clustered around the average and fewer people coming in the extremes: for example, more men would be described as 'about average height' than would be called 'giants' or 'dwarfs'. So, if the mathematical attainment of the population in a school year group of 100 pupils were to be measured in some way, by, say, using scores on a standardised mathematics test, it is likely that a distribution would emerge with a large proportion of children scoring around the average, and with a gradually decreasing density of scores moving outwards from the average towards the lowest and highest scores. Then, when the population is divided into four equal groups of twenty-five pupils, on the basis of their scores on the test, the range of attainment in the top and bottom groups will be much wider than that in the middle two groups. To cope with this range of attainment many teachers have turned to individualised learning schemes. However, there are many potential difficulties with this approach. My observations of mathematics lessons in many schools lead me to a strong conviction that often an unquestioning reliance on this method of organising pupils' learning experiences in mathematics is disastrous for many children and particularly for low attainers.

First of all, as I have already argued above, there is the basic mistake that this approach relies on the written word as the medium of instruction. For most low attainers the best way for them to come to understand many mathematical ideas and processes is for someone to explain these to them, and the worst way is for them to have to rely on their poor reading skills. In many classes where the individualised learning approach is used pupils get hardly any direct teaching from the teacher. With twenty-five pupils working on twenty-five different tasks, the teacher becomes little more than a marking machine, frantically trying to keep the queue at the desk to a manageable size. In an hour's lesson any given child cannot expect more than two minutes of the teacher's time on average. Instruction from the teacher is only ever in response to a difficulty with a card and is inevitably almost entirely procedural, that is, telling the child what they have to do in order to comply with the demands of the card or page in question. In one lesson of sixty minutes which I observed using this approach, a typical pupil spent only twelve minutes working on mathematics, and the rest of the time doing nothing because they were stuck on a problem, queuing, chatting to friends, wandering round the room, organising their desk, looking for materials, and so on.

Sometimes I have even come across children who, when they come to a card requiring some materials for practical work, such as jugs of water or weighing scales, tell me that their teacher has told them to miss these cards out. This unforgivable policy is adopted presumably because, with each child working individually like this, the teacher is unable to predict, and therefore unable to make available, the practical materials which might be required in any given lesson. Given the fundamental importance of practical experience in mathematics, particularly in the primary years, such a policy is clearly misguided.

It is also generally agreed by mathematics educators that discussion – both between pupils and between teachers and pupils – is an important component of good mathematics teaching. By trying to articulate their mathematical ideas children clarify their concepts and gain mastery of the language patterns of mathematics. Another potential weakness of the individualised learning approach is that there can be little opportunity for such discussion. A report on the special needs of girls in relation to learning mathematics (Royal Society and IMA, 1986) emphasises the importance for girls, in particular, of encouraging pupils to talk about mathematics and to attempt to listen to each other, so as to bring a 'social' (perceived as 'female') element to the teaching. In Chapter 2, the Year 5 pupil, Sarah, was identified as an example of a girl who would probably benefit from a more social experience of learning mathematics, rather than spending all her time on individual tasks.

Now, to some extent, the picture I paint of the individualised learning approach may be something of a caricature. I know many teachers who use variations of this approach skilfully and effectively, organising the children in ways which allow opportunities for instruction, for explanation, for discussion and for practical work. Some teachers employ this method for half the mathematics lessons in a week and adopt different organisational styles, such as whole-class or small-group activities, for the others. And, of course, there are problems and compromises involved in any method of organisation of pupils' learning activities in a large class of individuals. But, nevertheless, I know that the kind of mathematics lesson I have described above is all too common, and my conviction, based on the observation of many such lessons, is that such an approach, for the reasons stated, is a major contributory factor in the lack of progress in mathematics of many children.

More haste, less speed

Another potential shortcoming in the way mathematics is taught is the temptation to move a child on to the next process to be learnt before the previous one is thoroughly mastered and understood. The result of this can be a total muddle in the child's mind, particularly when the processes are taught by rote. It is quite distressing at times to see children struggling with a routine such as subtraction of three-digit numbers by decomposition, crossing out zeros, writing little ones and nines apparently at random, and muddling up the addition process with the subtraction. An illuminating example of this is given in a video which accompanies the Open University course, *Developing Mathematical Thinking*, (EM235, 1982). A 12-year-old girl, Nicola, from what is described as a remedial class, attempts to deal with the subtraction '109 – 70', set out in vertical form (see also Easen, 1985). Her working is shown in Figure 3.2.

As she does this she 'explains' what she is doing:

> You can't do nine from nought, so you . . . cross out the nought . . . and put a . . . nine . . . put a one up the top (*pause, counting from 9 to 19*) . . . ten . . . then put

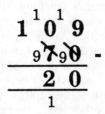

Figure 3.2   Nicola's working for '109 – 70'

a nought there and . . . put . . . under there (*'carrying' the one*) . . . nought from seven you can't do, so cross out the seven and put a . . . nine . . . put a one up the top . . . ten from nine leaves one . . . (*adding in the one carried*) . . . two.

It seems most likely that this pupil's total muddle of addition and subtraction routines derives from the experience of trying to master new processes before previous ones have been thoroughly mastered and understood.

Meaningless routines

Nicola's 'explanation' is a typical example of a child desperately trying to remember which meaningless routine she is supposed to apply to the collection of mathematical symbols arranged in a particular way on a piece of paper. She has been 'taught' several recipes for cooking these symbols. Sometimes you have to cross out numbers and write little ones in various places, sometimes when you cross out a nought you have to write a little nine somewhere, sometimes you get a two-digit answer in one column and have to carry the first digit into the next column, and so on. Quite what you do in any given routine appears to be completely arbitrary, so poor Nicola just plucks various steps from various routines at random.

A shortcoming of much mathematics teaching must surely be an overemphasis on the teaching of routines and recipes for manipulating symbols, without any basis in understanding. For many pupils this can be a meaningless and totally mystifying experience. In aiming for understanding, rather than mere rote learning of abstract routines and recipes, teachers must help the pupils to form secure connections between their manipulations of real things, such as coins and blocks, the language they use to describe these manipulations, and the symbols they use to record them.

Algorithms and adhocorithms

The formal routines for dealing with calculations (such as subtraction by decomposition and long multiplication) are examples of what are called *algorithms*. An algorithm is a step-by-step process, which, if followed correctly, will lead inevitably to a correct solution to a problem. Many pupils find security in these algorithms and they have an important part to play in the development of numeracy. But it is also the case that many pupils are capable of developing and using their own informal, *ad hoc* ways of dealing with calculations. I call these *adhocorithms*.

Another pupil shown on the Open University video referred to above, a 12-year-old boy called Dean, fails repeatedly when he tries to apply the decomposition algorithm to some subtraction questions. But then, when given '716 – 598', he writes down the answer (118), without any apparent working, and explains his reasoning:

> I'm trying to figure out . . . . five from seven leaves two hundred . . . but as it's ninety-eight, it's a hundred and eighteen.

Then, when given '311 – 214', he again demonstrates an impressive ability to devise an *ad hoc* way of manipulating the numbers involved that makes sense to him, writing the correct answer (97), and explaining his thinking:

> Well, I worked out, if that was eleven (*pointing to the 14 in 214*) that would be one hundred dead. But as that's fourteen instead of eleven, you take three away from a hundred, that's ninety-seven.

One shortcoming of much teaching of mathematics, particularly when dealing with the many low-attaining children who find it difficult to remember and make sense of all the steps of the algorithms, is the failure of teachers to give validity to the use of these adhocorithms. The Year 5 pupil, Ben, described in Chapter 2, is another example of a low-attaining boy who would probably benefit from a greater acceptance by the teacher of the use of informal ways of dealing with calculations rather than just being required to try to remember algorithms. The value of encouraging pupils to use and share their own informal, *ad hoc* ways of dealing with calculations is that these are necessarily based on the pupil's understanding of the mathematical structure of the problem and the relationships between the numbers involved. Adhocorithms, by definition, cannot be learned by rote.

Disembedded tasks and purposeless activities

It seems most unlikely that Dean learnt his skill in informal manipulations of numbers from doing exercises in mathematical text-books in school. Much more probable is that he has developed this confidence with three-digit numbers through practical experience out of school, handling money, maybe doing a Saturday job. There is considerable evidence that pupils are much more capable of learning and demonstrating mathematical skills when these are embedded in a context that makes sense to them (Donaldson, 1978, Hughes, 1986). An intriguing study of Brazilian children (Saxe, 1988), for example, found that many 10–12-year-olds with minimal schooling, working as street candy-sellers, developed a level of performance in complex, but informal, mathematical skills for handling money and ratios, far superior to that of children who attended school regularly.

Too much school mathematics can consist of disembedded tasks, without any meaningful context for the child. Activities have neither meaning nor purpose. The difference in the ways in which pupils might respond to embedded tasks and disembedded tasks is demonstrated by another pupil on the Open University video, a boy called Charlie. His first attempt to deal with '109 – 70' produces the following:

$$\begin{array}{r} 1\,0\,9 \\ -\,7\,0 \\ \hline 1\,0\,0 \end{array}$$

Charlie's explanation for this is another example of a desperate attempt to recall the correct steps:

> Nought from nine you can't do that, so you put nought down. Then it's seven take nought, you can't do it, so you put nought down again. Then there's nothing to take from one, so you put one down.

Charlie's teacher then simply asks, 'What if you had £109 and you took £70 pounds away?' Now the task is suddenly embedded in a meaningful context and Charlie immediately gives the correct response, '39', with an explanation showing a level of understanding which contrasts remarkably with his pathetic attempt at recalling the steps of the algorithm:

> It's seventy, eighty, ninety, a hundred . . . that's thirty, and there's nine, so it's thirty-nine.

On one occasion I went to work with a teacher and a group of low-attaining 10–11-year-olds, and found the pupils making very little headway with some exercises in their mathematics work-books. These presented them with some drawings of coins (10p, 5p, 2p, 1p), and the instructions were to shade the coins required to make up various amounts: a typical example of the purposeless activities that pupils are often asked to undertake in mathematics lessons. Given the pupils' sense of frustration, we abandoned these exercises (in fact, we abandoned the scheme). Instead, the children were put into groups of four, given a supply of plastic token coins, and given the challenge to find as many different ways of making up 19p as they could, recording their answers in the form of a table. The actual mathematical skills being developed were exactly the same as those in the exercises we had abandoned, but the difference in the pupils' performance was quite dramatic. They were now engaged in a task with some purpose, even if only trying to be the winning group. Most of the groups found about thirty solutions to the problem, with one group coming up with all the 34 possibilities. This was quite an achievement for pupils who were supposed to be no good at mathematics, and who had, in the previous lesson, failed at a corresponding (but purposeless) task in their mathematics scheme.

QUESTIONS FOR FURTHER DISCUSSION

1. Consider two or three mathematical low-attaining pupils that you know well. What are the aspects or characteristics of school mathematics which make it such a difficult subject for them? Which of the statements given in the list of 'characteristics of mathematical low attainers' in this chapter would you say are true for each of these pupils? Which seem to you to be most significant in their lack of progress in the subject?

2. In your experience, are my comments about the tyranny of the scheme and my criticisms of individualised learning justified?

3. Can you match my low attainers and find all the 34 ways of making up 19p in coins? (See the final paragraph above.)

4
STRATEGIES FOR TEACHING LOW ATTAINERS IN MATHEMATICS

TWO DIMENSIONS: ATTAINMENT AND EXPERIENCE

In the previous chapter I have, on the one hand, stressed the need for careful sequencing of small steps in learning mathematics for those who have special problems with the subject, and, on the other hand, I have described some of the shortcomings of much mathematics teaching which provides such pupils with too many tasks which are low in purpose and disembedded from meaningful contexts. These two points of view indicate the two dimensions of the overall strategy which I would advocate for teaching low attainers in mathematics in the age range 8–12 years. First of all there is what can be called the objectives-and-assessment approach: specify a sequence of objectives to be attained by the pupils, assess the pupils' current attainment against these objectives, and then design a learning programme to move them forward. (See, for example, Duncan, 1978; Ainscow and Tweddle, 1979.) I shall argue that this can be effective and justified provided that the target objectives are realistic and appropriate for the particular pupils being considered, that they are relevant to their real needs, and that the emphasis in these objectives is shifted from the learning of recipes and routines to the development of understanding. Then there is the approach which seeks to identify meaningful situations and genuinely purposeful activities in which low attaining pupils can develop their mathematical skills and confidence. These two approaches should be seen not as alternatives, but as complementary. Some of the time our emphasis is on providing pupils with success through the attainment of objectives. At other times, it will be on increasing their commitment and motivation to engage with mathematics by providing them with activities in meaningful contexts which have purpose from the perspective of the pupil.

Two curriculum models

These two approaches represent two traditional curriculum models, often viewed as opposing ways of approaching teaching. Some educators argue that the curriculum should be defined in terms of learning outcomes: objectives, goals, attainment targets, and so on; others that it should be defined in terms of the kinds of experiences we wish pupils to enter into.

Personally, I am quite happy to take what appears to be useful for guiding my thinking about the problems of teaching from either camp. In working with low attainers in mathematics I have found it useful at times to specify precise, short-term objectives, to assess the pupil against these objectives and then to undertake a teaching programme to enable the pupil to attain them. At other times I have found the only way to get some youngsters switched on and committed to mathematical tasks is to give them the opportunity to engage in activities with real purpose, in which the actual learning outcomes might be somewhat diffuse or unspecific. It is possible in our teaching to maintain a balance between being concerned about the pupil's *attainment in mathematics* and the quality of the pupil's *experience of mathematics*.

The National Curriculum approach

The Mathematics National Curriculum document for pupils aged 5–16 in England and Wales (DES, 1989) demonstrates nicely the tension between these two approaches to the curriculum. The structure of the curriculum is based on what appears to be essentially an objectives-and-assessment model, in which a pupil's progress is assessed by reference to specific criteria.

Mathematics is broken down into fourteen *attainment targets*, towards which pupils must work through the *programmes of study* provided by their teachers. (The details given here refer to the original 1989 version of the Mathematics National Curriculum. This is under review at the time of writing, with the intention being to reorganise the content into a smaller number of attainment targets.) The pupil's progress on each attainment target is determined by regular assessment against *statements of attainment*. If a pupil demonstrates that they have achieved certain statements of attainment then they are deemed to have attained a particular *level* on the attainment target in question. For most targets, ten levels of attainment are defined.

For example, Attainment Target 11, in the area of 'Shape and Space', states that 'pupils should recognise location and use transformations in the study of space'. Some examples of the statements of attainment used to assess the pupil's level of attainment on this target are:

- state a position using prepositions such as: on, inside, above, under, behind, next to, etc. (level 1)
- understand the notion of angle (level 2)
- understand eight points of the compass (level 3)

This is clearly an objectives-and-assessment approach to the curriculum. The teacher must determine the pupil's current level of attainment by reference to the specific criteria in the statements of attainment for each level. This assessment is expected to have a diagnostic function, assisting the teacher in planning the teaching required to enable the student to progress from their current level of attainment to the next.

However, accompanying this highly structured delineation of the mathematics curriculum is the *Non-Statutory Guidance* (National Curriculum Council, 1989), which is advice to teachers on its implementation. In fact, very little of the guidance actually focuses on how to enable pupils to achieve the objectives specified in the statements of attainment. Instead, it appears that the authors of this non-statutory guidance are concerned mainly with considerations of the kinds of experiences which they would judge to be components of a good mathematics education, and with the need to motivate pupils and to develop a positive attitude to the subject. So, for example, advice on the range of activities in which pupils should engage in mathematics, includes the following:

- activities should be balanced between those which are short in duration and those which have scope for development over an extended period
- activities should, where appropriate, involve both independent and cooperative work
- tasks should be both of the kind which have an exact result or answer and those which have many possible outcomes
- activities should be balanced between different modes of learning: doing, observing, talking and listening, discussing with other pupils, reflecting, drafting, reading and writing, etc.
- activities should enable pupils to develop their personal qualities
- activities should enable pupils to develop a positive attitude to mathematics

Clearly, the authors of this mathematics document found that the structure of attainment targets and levels of attainment was not a satisfactory or sufficient description of a good mathematics curriculum, and it was necessary to complement this with (admirable) advice of the kind quoted above, focusing on mathematical experience rather than simply on mathematical attainment. Any attempt to define a curriculum solely in terms of learning outcomes, whether these be called objectives, assessment criteria, or statements of attainment, is bound to be inadequate, because we are dealing with human beings, and not with Pavlov's dogs, Thorndike's cats or Skinner's pigeons. Experience of teaching low attainers in mathematics suggests that, although there is some value in an approach based on assessment of their progress through a careful sequence of learning objectives, this must be balanced by a concern to provide them with activities which they perceive as purposeful, activities which will motivate them, activities to which they will commit themselves.

OBJECTIVES AND ASSESSMENT
The objectives-and-assessment approach is dependent on the determination of objectives the attainment of which can be achieved over a fairly short period of teaching and is observable by the teacher. I shall therefore explain, first of all, in considering this model, the notion of a *behavioural* objective. Because of the hierarchical nature of some mathematical material it may be possible sometimes to determine a logical *sequence* of the behavioural objectives for a particular topic, but I suggest below that this is not always as easy to do as it may appear at first sight. In selecting objectives for teaching low attainers in mathematics the criteria of *realism* and *relevance* must be prominent. Various *categories* of such objectives can be identified, but I suggest below that only four categories are actually useful in this objectives-and-assessment model when applied to teaching mathematics to low attainers, namely, knowledge, skills, understanding and, to some extent, application. An emphasis on objectives related to *understanding* is especially important when working with low attainers, rather than merely drilling them in routines and recipes. These would include objectives specifically related to the development of key patterns of *mathematical language*. Finally, a central and major objective for numeracy in today's world is that the pupil should know what calculation to enter on a calculator for the whole range of numerical situations which might be encountered in everyday life.

Behavioural objectives
The traditional approach to tackling the problems of low attainers in mathematics, particularly with reference to arithmetic skills, has been the specification of precise target objectives, followed by diagnosis of the pupil's performance against these objectives, and then a programme of remediation or instruction. There is clearly some value in an approach which, by making specific objectives explicit, makes success and progress more obvious both for teachers and pupils. The teacher can specify a target skill which is currently not attained by the pupil, encourage the pupil to commit themselves to its achievement and then, subsequent to an effective learning programme, demonstrate that progress has been made.

However, in order to undertake assessment of the pupil's learning with any degree of confidence, it is argued by those who advocate this approach, the objectives must be *specific* and *behavioural*. They must be statements of specific, observable behaviours. The difficulty with many of the statements of attainment in the Mathematics National Curriculum is that they are either unspecific or use words which do not refer to observable behaviours. Consequently teachers find it very difficult to assert with any confidence that a particular level has actually been attained by a pupil.

The examples of statements of attainment from Attainment Target 11 quoted above illustrate this problem. How will a teacher be able to determine that a pupil is able to 'state a position using prepositions such as: on, inside, above, under, behind, next to, etc.'? Just the inclusion of the 'such as' and the 'etc.' is sufficient to introduce an element of vagueness. How many of these and what other prepositions must the pupil use correctly in order to achieve this statement of attainment?

And how will a teacher decide that the pupil 'understands' the notion of angle or the eight points of the compass? 'Understand' is a good example of a non-behavioural verb, which must be translated into statements of the specific behaviours which can be demonstrated by the pupil and observed by the teacher, if this approach is to be employed. An emphasis on objectives which indicate understanding is important and laudable, but the challenge is to state clearly what is meant by understanding of the ideas in question, to specify performances by the pupil which would count as understanding.

For example, the statement 'understand the notion of angle' might be translated into the following collection of specific, observable, behavioural objectives. The pupil should be able:

- standing, with one arm pointing forward, to turn through the following angles when instructed: a quarter-turn, a half-turn, three-quarters of a turn, and a whole turn
- when asked to turn from pointing at one object to another, to state whether the angle rotated through is less than or greater than each of a quarter-turn, a half-turn, three-quarters of a turn, and a whole turn
- to state that a quarter-turn is also called a right angle
- to recall the equivalence in right angles of a half-turn, three-quarters of a turn, and a whole turn
- to indicate an example of a right angle in the classroom environment
- given two lines meeting at a point, drawn on a piece of paper, or two edges of a solid object, to state whether the angle between them is a right angle, less than a right angle, or more than a right angle
- using just a ruler and pencil, to draw 'by eye' a line at right angles to a given line (to within 5 degrees either way), where the given line is parallel to one of the edges of the paper
- using just a ruler and pencil, to draw 'by eye' a line at right angles to a given line (to within 5 degrees either way), where the given line is not parallel to one of the edges of the paper
- given two pairs of lines of varying lengths, meeting at different angles, to state which is the greater angle and which the smaller
- given three pairs of lines of varying lengths, meeting at different angles, to state which is the greatest angle and which the smallest.

The reader may very well wish to argue with me as to whether this collection of objectives constitutes what is meant by 'understanding the notion of angle'. We can, after all, only guess at what the National Curriculum authors had in mind by the phrase, precisely because it is unspecific and non-behavioural. But, having decided on a set of objectives along the lines of those given above, I would now be in a position to determine with some degree of confidence the extent of the pupil's understanding of the notion of angle. This is because each objective is fairly specific and uses a verb which refers to an observable behaviour: to state, to draw, to turn, to indicate, to recall, and so on. Each objective is a statement which indicates quite clearly how it could be assessed. I should be able to answer confidently 'yes' or 'no' to the question, 'can the pupil do this?' Then, if the pupil shows me, on, say, two occasions separated by some weeks, that they can do a particular item, I may feel justified in asserting that the objective has been achieved.

Furthermore, because the objectives are specific, when I have determined that a pupil has not yet achieved one of them, it would not be difficult to devise an appropriate teaching programme to enable the pupil to make progress. And, because each represents a fairly small step in the development of understanding of the notion of angle, some actual progress may be achieved in a fairly short space of time and can be made explicit to the pupil.

Hierarchies of objectives

Because we can analyse much mathematical learning in a hierarchical way, showing how one step in the learning process leads to another, it seems particularly appropriate to apply the objectives-and-assessment model to this subject. However, experience and research into mathematical learning suggests that pupils do not by any means follow what appears to be the logical route in their learning of mathematical material. The authors of the Mathematics National Curriculum *Non-Statutory Guidance* (NCC, 1989) recognise this:

> Although mathematics does contain a hierarchical element, learning mathematics does not necessarily take place in completely predetermined sequences. Mathematics is a structure composed of a whole network of concepts and relationships . . . .

So we need to be aware that, when we are determining what seems to us to be a logical, hierarchical sequence of objectives as the basis for an assessment and instructional programme for some pupils, many pupils will achieve these in an order different from what we would expect. Children are individuals, they have vastly differing kinds of experiences in their backgrounds and everyday lives out of school, and they learn in idiosyncratic ways. The case study of Michael in Chapter 2 is a vivid demonstration of this.

Working with one group of low-attaining 10–11-year-olds, on the topic of capacity and liquid volume, I specified a number of objectives in what seemed to me to be an appropriate sequence. First of all, they should be able to order a set of two or three containers for capacity by pouring from one to the other. Logically this seemed to be the starting point for this topic: direct comparison and ordering, using the attribute to be measured, but with no units involved. Much further down on my list I had the objective that the pupils should be able to estimate the capacity of a container in millilitres, up to 1,000 ml, to within 40% either way. (For example, given a container holding 100 ml, any estimate between 60 ml and 140 ml would be acceptable.) When I assessed the group at various times in the teaching programme, I found, as I would have expected, that most pupils who could do the estimating could cope successfully with what I judged to be the lower-level task of direct comparison and ordering. However, there were one or two individuals who could do the higher-level task quite impressively, but got in a terrible muddle trying to order a set of containers, sometimes making what appeared to be quite naive errors. Incidentally, it seemed that the crucial factor in the children's experience which enabled them to do better at the estimation objective than would have been expected from their failure on lower-level objectives, was their familiarity with the capacities of Coke cans (330 ml) and wine bottles (750 ml).

Realistic and relevant

The objectives-and-assessment approach for mathematical low attainers in the primary or middle school can only be endorsed if the target objectives are realistic and relevant. They must be reasonable targets for the pupils concerned to aim for, given our judgements about their abilities and intellectual deficiencies; and they must be relevant to the real needs of the pupils in the world in which they live and in which they are growing up. We may have to accept that, when we are working with some low attainers, we cannot try to teach them everything in the mathematics curriculum. We may have to make a selection. If this is the case, the principles of realism and relevance must be high on our list of criteria for making such a selection.

This is particularly important in the area of methods of doing calculations. Many pupils' sense of failure at mathematics has been produced by failure to remember and master the different routines which have to be followed in order to carry out abstract calculations by standard, formal, written methods. Yet what the teachers are aiming for in this respect may well be neither realistic nor relevant for the pupils in question.

For example, the Mathematics National Curriculum (NCC, 1989) specifies at level 5 that pupils should be able to divide a three-digit number by a two-digit number, without using a calculator. We may very well decide that this is a quite unrealistic target objective for most low-attaining pupils in the age range up to 12 years, given the complex sequence of steps and prerequisite knowledge and skills required for such a calculation. We may also judge that, since the need for such a calculation, without the use of a calculator, would probably never arise in reality, then it is not only an unrealistic objective but also an irrelevant one.

In specifying our objectives for low-attaining pupils, we must consider carefully the appropriate balance between their mastery of formal algorithms, their use of their own informal adhocorithms, and the use of calculators, given that in the real world outside of school most of the exact calculations they will be required to undertake will be done by electronic machines.

The principle of relevance would also lead us to put a greater emphasis on encouraging the pupils to develop skills of numerical estimation. This is because in the real world, as opposed to exercises in mathematics books, we are rarely called upon to do exact calculations. Most of the time we require just an estimate: about how much will it cost me in petrol to travel the 120 miles from Norwich to London?; roughly how much longer will it take me to drive than to go by train?; about how much will half a pound of this cheese cost?; eight rolls of wallpaper at £4.80 a roll, that will cost us something less than £40. When exact calculations are required, such as when adding up the bill in the supermarket, working out the price of the petrol you put in your tank, or calculating the Value Added Tax on a purchase, almost invariably this job is handed over to a machine. So, if we are concerned to meet the genuine needs of the pupils for coping with the demands of the world outside of school, we should send out the message that good estimates are legitimate and authentic mathematics. Many of the skills required for being a good estimator may be too demanding for low attainers in the 8–12 age range, but we should at least include in our objectives the thorough grasp of the place-value principle, sufficient number knowledge and confidence in mental arithmetic, which are pre-requisites for their development (Poulter and Haylock, 1988).

Categories of objectives

There are a number of different ways of categorising objectives. Perhaps the most well-known and influential of these is the 'taxonomy of educational objectives' produced by Bloom (Bloom,1956; Krathwohl, Bloom and Masia, 1964). This makes a distinction between objectives in the *cognitive domain*, dealing with memory, understanding, reasoning, problem-solving and concept development, and those in the *affective domain*, dealing with emotions, feelings, interests, attitudes and values.

Although we will have very definite intentions in terms of pupils' positive attitudes towards and interests in mathematics, objectives in this affective domain are long term rather than short term, are developed gradually over a period of time rather than attained through a specific programme of teaching, and are therefore not amenable to the particular objectives-and-assessment model which is being discussed here.

In the cognitive domain, Bloom proposed a number of categories of objectives, arranged in a hierarchy from what is judged to be the lowest order of learning outcomes to the highest: knowledge, comprehension, application, analysis, synthesis and evaluation. This idea of categories of objectives may be useful for guiding our thinking about what we are aiming for in our teaching, but the categorisation proposed by Bloom requires some modification when applied to school mathematics. In particular, there is the need to include some reference to mathematical techniques and skills. I would propose that there are essentially four categories of objectives for mathematics teaching which should guide our planning within the objectives-and-assessment approach when working with low attainers. These are four categories within which we will be able to specify objectives which can be readily assessed, which are realistic, in terms of what might be achieved by our low attainers, and relevant to their needs.

- knowledge of terms, facts, definitions, principles
- mastery of techniques and manipulative skills
- understanding of concepts, procedures, principles
- application of knowledge, skills and understanding

Of course, there are other purposes in teaching mathematics, higher objectives, such as the development of analytical thinking, inductive and deductive reasoning, problem-solving strategies, the ability to formulate hypotheses, creativity, and the ability to make evaluative judgements. But such purposes as these, to be realistic, are unlikely to be a major focus in our work with low attainers. They also are not amenable to the objectives-and-assessment model. It is not possible, in my experience, to specify precisely, in behavioural terms, targets for these categories of learning, in such a way that the teacher can ever determine with confidence that the objective has been achieved. This is clearly demonstrated in the first Attainment Target in the Mathematics National Curriculum (NCC, 1989), which attempts (and fails) to break down some of these aspects of learning mathematics to specific statements of attainment at various levels. A teacher will never be able with confidence to assert that a student has *attained* such statements as these: 'to make predictions based on experience' (level 1); 'to ask and respond to the question: what would happen if . . . ?' (level 2); 'to explain work being done and record findings systematically' (level 3). These are, of course, important aspects of learning mathematics, but they are abilities to be developed rather than objectives to be attained. They are the kinds of purposes which a teacher may have in their mind when determining the range of experiences of mathematics which pupils should have, and therefore might figure in the second dimension of the balanced approach to mathematics teaching which I am advocating in this chapter.

It is, however, possible, and in my experience useful, to try to specify precise objectives for low attainers in mathematics in the four categories listed above: knowledge, skills, understanding and application. I should stress that these categories are useful only for directing our thinking about the range of objectives we should be setting for our pupils. The categorisation of any given objective is in itself a pointless exercise. There could well be disagreements or uncertainty about the category in which a particular objective, such as the examples quoted below, should be placed: such discussions serve no useful purpose whatsoever.

First of all, for any given mathematical topic we can state precisely what things we want the pupils to know and to be able to recall. For example, in the topic of time, realistic and relevant objectives in this category might be that pupils should be able:

- to state the number of seconds in a minute, the number of minutes in an hour, the number of hours in a day, and the number of days in a week
- to recite the names of the days of the week, the months of the year and the seasons, in order, starting from any day, any month or any season

These are simply knowledge of basic facts and terms, but they are important and necessary for coping confidently with the demands of everyday life both within and outside of school. Even our low attainers must learn facts like these and be able to recall them when necessary. It is a useful exercise for the teacher of low attainers to determine what knowledge the pupils need to be able to recall.

Then we can spell out fairly precisely the techniques and manipulative skills which we judge to be realistic and relevant for our low-attaining pupils, within any given mathematical topic. These will probably be techniques or skills in which the children are instructed, then drilled through repeated practice. So, for example, again within the topic of time, some of the objectives in this second category might be that the pupils should be able:

- to time activities or events in seconds using the second counter of a digital watch, starting from zero, or a simple stop clock or stopwatch
- to tell the time to the nearest five minutes from a dial clock or watch, giving the answer in the form '3.40 am'
- to calculate, by an informal adding-on process, the time-interval from one digital time to another

Such techniques and skills as these are, of course, useful, even essential, components of numeracy. But sometimes there is a temptation for those who work with mathematical low attainers to go no further than this in their thinking. They restrict the intended learning outcomes for the pupils merely to knowledge, techniques and skills. One of the major thrusts of this book is that we should also specify objectives in the category of understanding. As in the example quoted earlier in this chapter, 'to understand the notion of angle', we should determine what behaviours would count as demonstrating understanding. Examples of such behaviours might be: organising, comparing, estimating, classifying, ordering, relating, conserving (in measurement), translating, explaining, making connections.

For example, again within the topic of time, the ideas of ordering, translating and making connections as aspects of understanding might prompt the teacher to specify as objectives that the pupils should be able:

- to order a set of times of the day given in a variety of forms (e.g. 3.40 pm, 12 noon, twenty to four in the morning, 18:00) from earliest to latest
- to make sensible statements about what could be done in one minute, two minutes, five minutes, ten minutes

By including objectives of this kind the teacher will be aiming for the child's mathematical skills to be built on a foundation of understanding, and will thus put the child in a better position to go on to apply their mathematical learning.

This brings us then to the fourth category, application. We will not be able to specify all the applications of the pupil's knowledge, skills and understanding which we might hope to develop, but there may be, within any given mathematical topic, some particularly important or significant instances of application which we would want to state as specific objectives. For example, within the topic of time, useful and relevant objectives in today's technological, electronic age are that pupils should be able:

- to set automatic timing-devices (for example, time-switches and electric cookers)
- to program a video-recorder to record a sequence of television programmes

I have categorised these objectives as 'application' because they require the coordination of the pupil's knowledge about time and a number of skills, such as the calculation of time intervals, and they are based on the pupil's understanding of the relationships between time intervals and times of the day.

Objectives for understanding number

Because of the importance of the development of understanding, rather than simply focusing on knowledge and skills in our work with low attainers in mathematics, it is helpful to clarify further how understanding in mathematics might be recognised.

A simple model which I have found useful for talking about understanding in mathematics, particularly in the area of number and number operations (i.e. number, place value, addition, subtraction, multiplication, division, equals, and so on) is to view the growth of understanding as the building up of cognitive connections (Haylock and Cockburn, 1989).

When a child encounters some new experience I reckon that they understand it if they can connect it to previous experiences or, better, to a network of previously connected experiences. The more strongly connected the experience the more they understand it. Learning without making connections is what I would regard as learning by rote. Such learning is easily confused or forgotten, particularly by many low attainers with poor memories, and is of little value in application to real-life situations.

In order to specify objectives for understanding number and number operations, rather than just techniques for doing calculations, we need therefore to identify behaviours which indicate that the child is making connections. There are four kinds of experience which children have when they are engaged in mathematics, namely, the manipulation of concrete materials, symbols, language and pictures.

They manipulate concrete materials, such as blocks, rods, counters, fingers and coins. They manipulate symbols, such as numerals and signs written on paper or on the keys of their calculator. They manipulate language, both the formal, technical language of mathematics and the everyday language which describes their actions with concrete materials. And finally, they manipulate pictures, such as number lines and set diagrams. I have found it helpful, therefore, in specifying objectives for understanding the concepts of number and number operations, to include behaviours which indicate that the pupil is making cognitive connections between these four types of experience: concrete situations, symbols, language and pictures. These connections are illustrated in the diagram shown in Figure 4.1. For example, what observable behaviours might indicate that a child has some understanding of the concept of subtraction? The connections model of understanding outlined above leads me to specify the following important behavioural objectives. The child should be able:

- to interpret a subtraction-fact written in symbols by putting out two sets of objects and comparing them (connecting symbols with manipulation of concrete materials)
- to interpret a subtraction-fact stated in words, as a movement on the number line (connecting language with a picture)
- to enter the appropriate calculation on a calculator for a problem using the language 'how many more' or 'how many less' (connecting language with symbols)
- to make up a story to fit a given subtraction-fact in the context of shopping, using the language of comparison, e.g. 'dearer' or 'cheaper' (connecting symbols with language and a concrete situation)

This is just a small selection of objectives which might indicate some aspect of understanding of the concept of subtraction. Targets such as these,

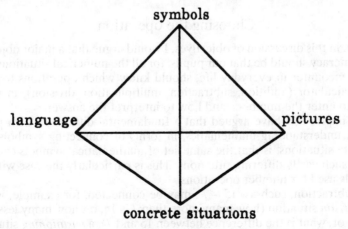

Figure 4.1   Important connections in understanding number and number operations

which emphasise understanding rather than the mastery of abstract routines and recipes, will be prominent in the discussion of various aspects of number work for low attainers in Chapters 5, 7 and 8. That discussion will also indicate some of the kinds of activities which might be used with low-attaining pupils to enable these important connections to be established.

Language objectives

We have already noted in Chapter 3 that it is frequently the case that pupils whose attainment in mathematics is low have poorly developed language and reading skills. As part of our emphasis on developing understanding, those of us who work with low-attaining pupils in mathematics might find it helpful to include some objectives specifically related to the development of particular language patterns in mathematics. This is simply to underline the special importance of language in the connections model of under-standing outlined above. For example, we might set as an objective that the pupils should be able:

- to find the difference between two numbers using a calculator and to formulate sentences of the form 'X is Y more than Z' and 'Z is Y less than X' (e.g. '245 is 58 more than 187' and '187 is 58 less than 245')

Other objectives might target similar patterns with other aspects of the language of comparison, such as 'longer than', 'shorter than', 'heavier than', 'lighter than', 'cheaper than', 'dearer than', or such key mathematical words as 'each', 'between' and 'altogether'. My point is that if we make the use of these language patterns into specific targets then we will have to ensure that we devise activities to enable the pupils to attain these objec-tives. Examples of such activities are given in later chapters in this book.

Choosing the operation

Finally, in this discussion of objectives, I would argue that a major objective for numeracy should be that our pupils, for all the numerical situations they might encounter in everyday life, should know which operations to enter on a calculator (addition, subtraction, multiplication, division), in which order to enter the numbers, and how to interpret the answer.

In Chapter 3, I have argued that a fundamental difficulty which pupils face in understanding mathematics, in terms of connecting symbols with concrete situations, is that the same set of mathematical symbols can rep-resent such vastly differing situations. This is particularly the case with the symbols used for number operations.

A subtraction, such as '15 – 7', may be connected, for example, with a *comparison* situation (how many more than 7 is 15, or, how many less than 15 is 7, or, what is the difference between 15 and 7), a *partitioning* situation (15 take away 7), a *complement of a set* (in a set of 15, 7 have some attribute, how many do not), a *counting back* or *reduction* situation (start at 15 and count back 7), or an *inverse of addition* situation (what must be added to 7 to make 15). Each number operation can be analysed like this in terms of a number of different models, that is, categories of concrete situations to which the number-facts must be connected. The pupil has to learn to connect each operation correctly with the various models.

Since each of these models may be encountered in a variety of contexts, such as manipulating sets of objects, money, measuring length, weight, time, capacity, and so on, I come to the conclusion that the most basic and important objective for numeracy is that the pupil should be able:

- to state what calculation should be entered on a calculator in order to solve a practical problem, for each of the operations, addition, subtraction, multiplication, division, using any of the models of the operation, and in any appropriate context, and to be able to interpret the answer.

So, for example, for *subtraction*, using the comparison model in the context of money, the pupil should know what to enter on a calculator in order to work out how much more expensive one item is than another (a task which defeated the Year 5 pupil, Sarah, described in Chapter 2, for example, when she was asked to work out on a calculator how much more one television set cost than another).

This key objective for numeracy is the focus of Chapter 7, where a complete analysis of the operations, models and contexts is undertaken. It represents a considerable task for the teacher of the low-attaining pupil. But it is surely much more relevant to their needs than drilling them in the algorithms of arithmetic. In the age of the calculator, knowing what calculation to do is far more useful and significant than being able to do the calculation yourself.

PURPOSEFUL ACTIVITIES IN MEANINGFUL CONTEXTS

A major shortcoming in the objectives-and-assessment approach to teaching mathematics to low attainers is that it tends to focus too much on what the pupil *cannot* do. The starting point for the design of a teaching programme is likely to be the pupil's failure on a particular objective. One benefit of the second dimension in the balanced approach being advocated in this chapter is that pupils are given opportunities to show what they *can* do, when they engage in purposeful activities in meaningful contexts. Often low attainers can surprise us with what they can do in mathematics, when they are committed to a task which makes sense to them.

For example, we may find that some low-attaining 9-year-olds fail at a task assessing their understanding of the principle of conservation of weight. When they are asked to comment on the weight of some joined-up cubes compared with that of the same cubes separated, they appear not to realise that the weights are the same. But when these pupils are participating enthusiastically in a cookery lesson we may observe them measuring out 100 grams of flour, transferring it from one container to another, mixing it with other ingredients into their cake mixture, and so on. They certainly do not appear to think that the 100 grams of flour they started with might no longer be 100 grams after all the transformations they have applied to it. In the context of this purposeful activity the pupils seem to use the concept of conservation of weight with no difficulty. The task with the cubes, like many of the tasks pupils are given to do in school mathematics, is purposeless and disembedded from any meaningful context. In contrast, my experience suggests that when we find purposeful, meaningful tasks, then even, or, especially, low-attaining pupils can show unexpected competence and determination to succeed.

Unexpected competence and commitment

An impressive illustration of this assertion is provided by the following problem, which does not look like an appropriate task for a group of low-attaining 8–9-year-olds:

> How much will it cost to purchase enough orange squash to provide three drinks each for ninety participants in a football tournament? The capacity of an orange squash bottle is the same as 26 cupfuls, the squash has to be diluted in the ratio 2 parts of water to 1 part of squash, and a bottle of orange squash costs 90p.

In fact, a group of 8–9-year-olds, in what was called a low-ability set for mathematics, found themselves in the position of having to solve this problem, when they were given responsibility for providing refreshments for an inter-school football tournament (Haylock, Blake and Platt, 1985). Of course, it was not presented to them in this form. The task they had been given was to organise the drinks, so they had to find out how many bottles to buy and what budget would be required. Gradually they determined what information would be required to solve the problem. They found out from other groups planning other aspects of the event that 3 drinks would be needed during the day and that there were 90 participants. They found out the price of squash from the local supermarket. They then did some direct measurement to determine how many cups could be poured from one bottle, recording their progress like this:

> Refreshments – how many containers of drink needed?
> We had to work out how many cups of orange we needed.
> There were 90 players so we needed 3 × 90 drinks.
>
> $$\begin{array}{r} 90 \\ 90 \\ \underline{90} \\ 270 \text{ drinks} \end{array}$$
>
> We could get 26 drinks from 1 container.

So we needed to find out how many containers.

1 container	26
2 containers	52
3 containers	78
4 containers	104
5 containers	130
6 containers	156
7 containers	182
8 containers	208
9 containers	235
10 containers	260
11 containers	287

so we needed 11 containers.

The occasional arithmetical error in this work can surely be forgiven, in view of the genuine mathematical thinking – based on their own understanding of the relationships involved in this real problem – which they demonstrate. One boy gained a significant insight from this activity, shown by the remark he made to his teacher before suggesting the above method to the group:

'You can use adding for this, Miss. I reckon this is why we learn it, so we can use it for things.'

They then realised that the squash had to be diluted and decided to do some market research, using children in their class, to determine the ratio of water to squash:

Refreshments – how strong should it be?
We borrowed a measure from Mr Brown and we put 1 orange and 1 water and we got somebody to taste it and they said yuk. We tried 1 orange and 2 water and they still said yuk, and then we tried 3 water and 1 orange and they all said yuk, and then we tried 4 water and 1 orange and they all said yuk. And the best one was 2 water and 1 orange.

And so, somehow or other, step by step and with great determination, they solved their problem. Using their own informal methods which made sense to them in that context, and, incidentally, without using a calculator, they decided they needed to buy four bottles of squash and put in their bid for a budget of £3.60. In the process they amazed their teacher by both their commitment to the task and their success with the mathematics involved. Time and time again low-attaining pupils surprise their teachers with what they can do when they are given purposeful tasks, real problems, and the opportunity to use mathematics to make things happen.

Categories of purposeful activities

There is a wide range of activities which pupils will find purposeful, and a number of categories might be suggested. These are not hard and fast categories, and they are not suggested as a method of analysing or categorising activities. Rather they are put forward as a framework for generating ideas for useful learning experiences for low-attaining pupils in mathematics.

The activity described above, for example, might come in the category of *planning an event*.

Other mathematical tasks with real purpose, such as deciding where the staff should park their cars in the school playground, might come within the category of *solving a real problem*.

Some pupils will show real commitment to tasks which involve the *design and construction* of something useful, such as making a box to store some teaching materials.

Within the constraints of our school organisation we may not be able, as often as we might wish, to allow pupils to develop their mathematical skills through planning actual events, through solving real problems, or by undertaking the design and construction of something useful. However, sometimes we may find that pupils will show real commitment to realistic *simulations* of real-life problems or activities. There is available nowadays a range of very effective computer software of this kind, such as simulations of running small businesses or sporting events, giving the pupil the opportunity to make decisions about the values of the variables which determine the degree of success or failure in the simulated real-life situation.

A related category of activity, which can work with some pupils, is that of *role play*. Pupils can act out a real situation, such as a family dispute over pocket money, and then seek to solve the problems which emerge.

Finally most children enjoy participating in *games* and *competitions*. These are two further categories of activities which, from the pupil's perspective, have some purpose, namely, to be the winner. We can harness pupils' willingness to commit themselves to playing a game, or to participation in a competition, in order to develop their mathematical skills. Games and competitions are purposeful activities which can often be used much more specifically to target particular objectives than the other categories suggested above.

Meaningful contexts

Alongside the categories of purposeful activities a number of categories of meaningful contexts might be suggested. By 'meaningful context' I mean some aspect of the pupil's everyday experience in which mathematics is or can be embedded. The first two obvious examples of such meaningful contexts would be *school organisation* and *the classroom*. These are clearly contexts in which pupils encounter problems which they can make sense of, and in which events occur in which they are actively involved. Solving the problem of where the staff should park their cars in the playground, or deciding on the best arrangement of the furniture in the classroom, or planning the school disco, or dealing with the class monthly book club order, for example, are tasks which have real purpose and which arise in contexts which pupils understand. They know what the task is about, they can recognise a solution when it is achieved, they appreciate the criteria which are significant in the context concerned. These are meaningful contexts for the development and application of their mathematical knowledge, skills and understanding.

Other aspects of the pupils' lives which may serve as meaningful contexts include: *television and video, life at home, shopping, fund-raising, earning money, cookery, travel, sport.*

A framework for devising purposeful activities in meaningful contexts

Figure 4.2 provides a framework which can be used to suggest tasks we might identify that have purpose and meaning for our pupils. Along one axis are listed some potentially meaningful contexts. The reader will, of course, be able to suggest additions to this list. Along the other axis are some of the categories of purposeful activities: solving a real problem, planning an event, design and construction, simulation, role play. (The category of 'games and competitions' has been omitted from this framework, because a game or

PURPOSEFUL ACTIVITIES

MEANINGFUL CONTEXTS	solving a real problem	planning an event	design and construction	simulation	role-play
SCHOOL ORGANISATION					
CLASSROOM					
TV AND VIDEO					
LIFE AT HOME					
SHOPPING					
FUND-RAISING					
COOKING					
TRAVEL					
SPORT					

Figure 4.2   Purposeful activities and meaningful contexts

competition effectively provides its own context of meaning and its own criteria for success.)

Each cell in this grid might suggest to us various purposeful activities in meaningful contexts which would give opportunity for the development and application of the pupils' mathematics.

For example, the intersection of *travel* and *planning an event* might suggest that a group of low attainers could be given responsibility for planning the travel arrangements for a class trip. This is something which teachers might normally do themselves, thus missing the opportunity to give their pupils a purposeful task in a meaningful context, with considerable potential for developing and using mathematical skills. The intersection of *cooking* and *design and construction* might remind teachers of the mathematics involved in baking a cake. Consideration of the intersection of *solving a real problem* and *fund-raising* might lead us to give our low-attaining pupils responsibility for handling a charity appeal.

Some of the computer programs available which simulate the running of small businesses include those for a tea-shop, a stall at a school fete, and a car-wash. These would come in the category of *simulation* set in the meaningful context of *earning money*. Pupils make decisions about the purchase of materials, the prices they will charge, and how much they will spend on advertising, all of which affect their earnings in an imaginary business. Simple simulations such as these, as substitutes for the real thing, calling upon and developing a wide range of relevant mathematical skills, are often very effective as purposeful activities for many low-attaining pupils.

The current educational climate in the United Kingdom is one which very much emphasises attainment targets and assessment of the pupil's progress through various levels towards these. With the special needs of low attainers in mind, it is more essential than ever therefore that those who work with such pupils maintain the balance advocated in this chapter. We must ensure that we complement the current emphasis on an objectives-and-assessment model of teaching and learning with an equal emphasis on providing those who find progress in mathematics difficult with some purposeful tasks in meaningful contexts.

A more detailed consideration of this second strand is given in Chapter 9, and Chapter 10 provides an example of how the dual approach might be put into practice in the teaching of one particular topic. Before that, in Chapters 5–8, I deal with the teaching of some important aspects of numeracy, particularly with the needs of low attainers in mind. In considering the teaching of place value (Chapter 5), choosing the operation (Chapter 7), and other aspects of number (Chapter 8), the main emphasis is on the specification and attainment of realistic and relevant objectives; purposeful activities related to these topics will be mainly small group games, targeting specific objectives. The context of measurement (Chapter 6) provides rather more opportunity for pupils to engage in some of the other categories of purposeful activities suggested in the framework of Figure 4.2.

QUESTIONS FOR FURTHER DISCUSSION

1. How would you determine that the following statements of attainment from the Mathematics National Curriculum (NCC, 1989) had been achieved by a pupil? Try to rewrite them as sets of specific, behavioural objectives:

   - understand eight points of the compass (Attainment Target 11, level 3)
   - understand the meaning of 'a half' and 'a quarter' (Attainment Target 2, level 2)
   - recognise and understand simple percentages (Attainment Target 2, level 4)

2. Are the objectives you have devised in answer to question 1 realistic and relevant for low-attaining pupils up to the age of 12 years?

3. For which cells in the diagram in Figure 4.2 can you identify an example of a purposeful activity in a meaningful context? How useful is this framework for generating ideas for learning experiences for low-attaining pupils in mathematics?

5

PLACE VALUE

When the Year 6 pupil, Sharon, described in Chapter 2, writes '10064' for 'one hundred and sixty-four' she reveals that she has not yet mastered the essential principle on which our number system is based, that of *place value*. She has not yet, apparently, realised that we do not just have symbols acting like abbreviations for words – she writes '100' as an abbreviation for 'one hundred' and then '64' for 'sixty-four' – but that, in our number system, the meaning of each symbol is also determined by the place in which it is written in relation to other symbols. Place value is a highly sophisticated and powerful system, enabling us to express large numbers in a concise form without the need to invent further symbols. We have only to compare the numeral '888' with its Roman numeral equivalent, 'DCCCLXXXVIII', to appreciate the superiority of a place-value system over one which depends essentially on the value of the digits and not on their positions relative to each other. Both numerals represent the same number, but the first version is so much more compact than the second, more readily interpreted, easier to compare with other numbers, and more amenable to arithmetic manipulations. The whole modern world is indebted to the Indian and Arabic cultures which contributed to a number system without which it would be difficult to imagine most of the mathematical, scientific and technological developments of the last thousand years taking place.

In order to cope confidently with handling numbers it is essential therefore that our pupils develop a good basis of understanding of the principle of place value on which our number system is based. In working with low attainers I have found that this requires a considerable amount of work and attention. But you really cannot make sense of the numbers you encounter in the world and the procedures of arithmetic without some degree of confidence with this fundamental principle, and I am convinced that this should be a major target area for our work with low attainers. So, in this chapter, I will first outline some of the important features of the system which have to be understood by children. The connections model of understanding suggests that we should aim to help pupils to connect the symbols we use for numbers (i.e. the numerals) with the language (i.e. the number names), with the picture of number in a number line, and with concrete materials. Two particular concrete embodiments of the place-value principle which are especially helpful are base-ten blocks and coins. From this discussion of what is involved in understanding place value I go on to specify a set of objectives for low attainers, with some indication of how these might be assessed. The remainder of the chapter is given over to some suggestions for activities to achieve these objectives. Many of these make use of calculators and, I hope, demonstrate that the calculator, far from being a threat to numeracy, can, in fact, be a positive aid to its development.

UNDERSTANDING THE PLACE-VALUE SYSTEM

The components of the system

In thinking about helping our pupils to understand the principle of place value it is helpful to analyse the basic components of this number system. These are:

- a set of *digits* : 0, 1, 2, 3, 4, 5, 6, 7, 8, 9
- the *base* of the number system: i.e. 'ten'
- *powers* of the base: ones, tens, hundreds, thousands, ten thousands, and so on
- the *places* in which the digits are written
- certain *conventions* about the way the numbers are read

We can see how these components contribute to the meaning of, for example, the numeral '453'. The digits '3', '5' and '4' mean that we have 'three of something', 'five of something' and 'four of something'. But what are these 'somethings'? As we work from right to left (not the conventional direction for reading, of course) the places of the digits indicate that they represent respectively the powers of the base: in this case, ones, tens, hundreds. These powers are connected by the simple, recurring principle that 'one of these is ten of those': one ten is ten ones, one hundred is ten tens, one thousand is ten hundreds, and so on. So the '4', by virtue of being in the third place from the right, represents 'four hundreds'; likewise, the '5' represents 'five tens', and the '3' represents 'three ones'. Our number is 'four hundreds, five tens and three ones'. The convention is that, although we work from right to left in determining the place values, we actually read the number from left to right, giving the largest place-value digits first. There are then further conventions: we abbreviate the 'four hundreds' to 'four hundred', the 'five tens' to 'fifty', and the 'three ones' to 'three', we insert the word 'and' between the hundreds and the tens, but we omit it between the tens and the ones. So finally we read the number as 'four hundred and fifty-three'. (Numbers which have 11, 12, 13, 14, 15, 16, 17, 18 or 19 as the last two digits are exceptions to these rules.)

I have deliberately laboured this explanation in order to make overt the complexity of the system. Helping our pupils to make the correct connections between the words and the symbols for numbers is a major part of the task of developing their understanding of place value.

Zero

Children have many difficulties with 'zero'. Sometimes they find it hard to accept that zero is actually a number, since it is often referred to as 'nothing'. We should note that the number 'zero', represented by the symbol '0', does not always mean 'nothing'. For example, a temperature of zero degrees does not mean there is no temperature, a place does not cease to exist if it is found to be at zero feet above sea level, and, as I write this sentence, I am actually sitting in an office situated on Level 0.

However, the function of zero in the place-value system, often referred to as that of a 'place-holder', is, in fact, to indicate 'nothing'. If there are no tens in a number, we put a zero in the tens place, and so on. This means that, when we come to interpret a numeral, we actually have to ignore a zero, apart from recognising the existence of the place it occupies. So, for example, in the numeral '400', strictly speaking, it is the *position* of the '4' which leads us to say 'four hundred', not the '00' which follows it. The two zeros simply serve to indicate that the '4' is actually in the hundreds place, and that there are no tens and no ones. We can see how this is the basis of the confusion which leads a child to write '10064' when they mean '164': they interpret the '00' as signalling the word 'hundred' rather than two empty places.

Learning to handle zeros correctly in their function as place holders must also be part of the pupil's development of understanding of the place-value system.

The principle of exchange

The principle that 'one of these is ten of those', as we move right to left from one place to the next in a numeral (and its equivalent, 'ten of these is one of those', as we move from left to right), is at the heart of our number system. In helping pupils to understand the procedures of arithmetic this is a phrase I find myself using frequently. The digits represent different things, depending on their position: ones, tens, hundreds and so on. Whenever we get ten of one sort (when, for example, we are adding two numbers) we can exchange these for one of the next sort (i.e. 'carry one'), going from right to left. Similarly, when we need to, we can always exchange one of one sort for ten of the next (for example, when using the decomposition algorithm for subtraction), going from left to right.

Practical experience of this principle of exchanging one for ten (or ten for one) should form a major component in the development of under-standing of place value.

Connections

I have found the connections model of understanding to be particularly helpful in guiding my thinking about helping pupils to understand place value. First of all, some of our objectives, as has been suggested above, will be to help pupils to connect the words we use for numbers with the corres-ponding symbols. So, given a number in words they should be able to write it down in symbols, and vice versa.

Other objectives are suggested by the connections between pictures and words or symbols. The most significant picture of number in this respect is a *number line*, where numbers are used to label points. The spatial imagery involved here is particularly helpful in developing such concepts of order-ing as 'greater than', 'less than', and 'between', applied to numbers.

The ability to order a set of numbers at sight is an important component of mastery of the place-value system. This involves recognising that the number of digits in a (whole) number is more significant in indicating its magnitude than the actual digits themselves. So, for example, any four-digit number must automatically be greater than any three-digit number. Then, when comparing two numbers with the same number of digits, we have to learn that the most significant digit is the one on the left, and that the digits become less significant as we move from left to right.

Learning to position numbers on a number line labelled in hundreds, for example, is therefore a helpful contribution to a pupil's development in understanding place value, since it reinforces these procedures for ordering and gives them a spatial interpretation. The connections made in this way between the words or symbols for numbers and the picture of number in the number line all contribute to a deeper level of understanding.

Most important in developing this understanding of place value is the building up of connections between concrete materials and the language and symbols of number. The *multi-embodiment principle* (also called the *perceptual variability principle*) enunciated by the influential mathematics educator, Zoltan Dienes (see, for example, Dienes, 1960) is helpful in guiding our thinking about these connections.

THE MULTI-EMBODIMENT PRINCIPLE

Dienes suggests that our understanding of some abstract mathematical con-cept or principle is more secure if we experience it in a variety of concrete *embodiments*. In fact, his view was 'the more the merrier'. So, for example, if we were aiming to establish the mathematical notion of 'the intersection of two sets', pupils could encounter this idea by considering the overlap between the set of pupils in the class who walk to school and the set of boys; or between the set of story-books in the class library and the set of books with more than 50 pages; or between the set of triangles in the 'logic-block' set and the set of red shapes; or between the set of whole numbers less than ten and the set of even numbers; and so on. Each of these is an embodiment of the same mathematical idea, and the more embodiments the pupil encounters, it is suggested, the more secure is their understanding. In fact, there is some evidence to suggest that mathematically more-able pupils are characterised by their ability to formulate a general principle from a single embodiment, so that subsequent experiences are merely applications of the general principle which they have already abstracted (Krutetskii, 1977). Less able pupils, however, may benefit from more than one embodiment of the principle and specific help in making the connections.

Embodiments of the place-value principle

When it comes to teaching place value, the problem is to determine what useful embodiments of the principle are available. We need sets of concrete materials which embody the 'one of these is ten of those' idea. Some materials which Dienes himself developed are the base-ten blocks shown in Figure 5.1. The principle incorporated in these blocks is simply that one of the 'longs' can be made from ten 'units' and one 'flat' from ten 'longs'. Also available in the set are 'blocks', equivalent to ten 'flats'. The same principle can be experienced in practical work with money, length and weight, and is

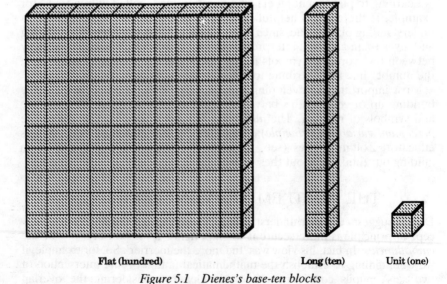

Flat (hundred)   **Long (ten)**   **Unit (one)**

Figure 5.1   Dienes's base-ten blocks

also the basis of the abacus. So these are five possible embodiments we might consider using in teaching place value (up to three-digit numbers only):

- base-ten blocks: units, longs, flats
- coins: using just pennies, ten-pences and pounds
- rods: using just centimetres, decimetres, metres
- weights: using just one-gram masses, ten-gram masses, hundred-gram masses
- an abacus: using different coloured counters on pegs to represent ones, tens and hundreds

Each of these provides a concrete situation in which the principle of exchanging ten of one sort for one of another operates. In my experience, when working with low attainers in mathematics, the first two of these are the most effective. With the blocks, the pupils can see that 'one of these is ten of those', since one piece can actually be made from ten smaller pieces fitted together. When working with (plastic) token coins, the principle is rather more abstract: 'one of these is *worth* ten of those'. Theoretically one would expect this to be more difficult to grasp, but in practice I find that most pupils in the 8–12 age range (not all, of course: compare the Year 4 pupil, Mark, described in Chapter 2) have enough experience of money in their lives out of school to handle this principle of exchange quite confidently. In fact, I would say that, of all the suggestions I have ever made to those who teach mathematics to low attainers, the simple idea of doing number work practically with plastic token coins, using just ones, tens and pounds, has proved to be the most helpful. Incidentally, when using coins, I switch quite freely between referring to a pound coin as 'a pound' (£1) and calling it 'a hundred' (100p) – and I keep on stressing that 'one of these is worth ten of those' (i.e. ten of the ten-pences).

By contrast, many low-attaining pupils have difficulties handling the less familiar concepts of length and weight, so these are not such useful vehicles for experiencing another difficult concept, that of place value. A similar argument occurs in Chapter 7, in considering the important objective of 'choosing the operation': it is preferable to establish mathematical structures first in contexts which are more familiar to pupils (such as handling money) and then to move these structures into less familiar contexts (such as handling lengths and weights).

Finally, I just do not find abacuses much use at all when working with low attainers. Part of the problem with them is that there seems to be no perceptible reason why ten counters on one peg should be replaced by one counter on the next, other than the fact that the teacher tells you that this is so. My view is that the abacus is an interesting application of the place-value principle, but as a concrete embodiment for teaching purposes it is artificial and ineffective. It seems to me that in order to handle an abacus the pupil actually needs to understand the principle of place value already.

So my proposal is that, in order to develop understanding of place value, we should focus on the connections between the language or symbols of number and these two concrete embodiments of the principle: base-ten blocks and coins (1p, 10p, £1). Activities using these two embodiments should go side by side, so that the pupils experience the same mathematical ideas in the two different experiences. When we are assessing our pupils, if they can demonstrate that they can connect the language and symbols with both these concrete embodiments, then we may be more confident that they are developing some understanding of this key principle of place value.

A note on money notation

When working with coins, pupils will learn to connect, for example, '4 pounds, 5 ten-pences and 3 pennies' with the number '453': they must recognise that they have the equivalent of 453p. But they will also encounter situations where this sum of money is written '£4.53'. This is, in fact, a very useful introduction to the use of decimal notation, arising quite naturally from the pupil's own experience of prices and shopping. We should therefore ensure that pupils develop a facility to translate freely between these two ways of representing a sum of money.

There are some particular aspects of this with which our low attainers may need specific help, mostly associated with zero. For example, there is the convention that 50p is written £0.50 and 5p is written £0.05. Pupils have to be taught this convention of always writing two digits after the point, when writing such sums of money with the £ sign, the first digit indicating the number of ten-pences, the second the number of pennies.

Then, when they are doing calculations with money on their calculators, we need to be aware of some other potential problems. For example, the reader is invited to use a calculator to find:

- the cost of 6 pens at £1.45 each
- the cost per battery if a pack of three costs £2.95

If, for the first problem, you enter '1.45 × 6' the calculator will display the result '8.7'. Pupils need specific help in interpreting this answer, since the obvious interpretation is that it represents 'eight pounds seven pence'. Similarly, they need to learn how to deal with the answer 0.9833333 which arises in the second case. I explain to them that the calculator does not know that you have to have two digits after the point. So in one case we have to put the second digit in ourselves (£8.70), and in the other case (£0.98) we have to throw away the extra digits (which represent little bits of money worth less than a penny).

A note on multi-base work

Another principle for learning mathematics proposed by Dienes is the *mathematical variability principle*. When presenting a mathematical structure to pupils, he argues, we should ensure that we vary the non-essential mathematical variables within the structure as much as possible. There is clearly much common sense in this proposal. For example, if we were teaching some children the addition algorithm with carrying, we obviously would not just use '28 + 45' over and over again, but would vary the digits involved in the two numbers in order to show that the procedure is the same.

Dienes applies this principle to the place-value structure of our number system. He argues that the 'ten' used as the base is arbitrary and not an essential element in the mathematical structure. The same structure would be experienced whatever number is used for the base. For example, we could have a base-three system using 'one of these is three of those' and it would have exactly the same structure as the one based on ten. From this theoretical standpoint Dienes developed his multi-base arithmetic blocks, just like his base-ten blocks shown in Figure 5.1, but using different bases such as 2, 3, 4, 5 and 6. His view was that, by experiencing the same arithmetic concepts and principles through working with the concrete materials in these different bases, the children would develop a much more secure understanding of the underlying mathematical ideas.

As far as I know, there is no convincing research evidence to support this assertion. One study (Biggs, 1967) suggests that there can be some benefit for some pupils in learning arithmetic through a multi-base approach, provided they use the materials consistently over a long period of time, such as two years, but on the whole his results were inconclusive. My personal observations suggest that pupils get more confused than helped by using the multi-base approach, particularly if it is something which teachers dabble in from time to time. Multi-base arithmetic might be an interesting topic for mathematically more able pupils to investigate, but I would not advise teachers to adopt a multi-base approach as a way of helping low attainers to grasp the principles of place value. Rather I would suggest plenty of practical experience with the base-ten blocks, which are an excellent model of the place-value system, supported by similar experiences with coins, which have the advantage of being familiar and meaningful for most children. Since only the base-ten blocks are used it makes more sense to refer to them as units, tens and hundreds, rather than units, longs and flats, which would be appropriate general terminology if a number of different bases were being experienced.

OBJECTIVES FOR UNDERSTANDING PLACE VALUE

Having considered what might be involved in understanding this important principle of place value, I will now propose a set of realistic objectives for low attainers in the age range 8–12 years. Many of these stem directly from the connections model of understanding and focus on behaviours which show that the pupil has formed significant connections between language, symbols, the number line and the two concrete embodiments of base-ten blocks and coins.

I have framed these objectives mainly with three-digit whole numbers in mind. For many of our low attainers, up to the age of 12 years, mastery of three-digit numbers will be a sufficient goal, particularly since they will not often encounter numbers greater than a thousand in their day-to-day lives. If they can achieve these objectives with three-digit numbers then we would feel confident that they have sufficient understanding of the place-value principle to extend it to four or more. (Some objectives related to handling big numbers are included in Chapter 8.)

In working towards these place-value objectives teachers would probably want first of all to specify similar objectives with two-digit numbers. Most of the objectives are easily modified to two- or four-digit numbers, although the use of coins becomes inappropriate beyond three digits.

Each objective should be specific enough to make clear how it would be assessed. In some cases however I give examples of what I have in mind to clarify the objective. We should remember that there is always a danger of using assessment tasks which can justifiably be criticised as being 'disembedded' and may therefore give a less than fair indication of the children's understanding. Teachers may well find that pupils can better demonstrate that some of these objectives have been attained through their performance on some of the place-value games suggested later in the chapter, where the same mathematical tasks are embedded in more purposeful activity.

A set of 25 objectives for place value is given below. My view is that, if we can get our low attainers to succeed on this limited set of objectives, then we will have given them a really good foundation of understanding for further development of number work.

Place-value objectives 1–4

First the focus is on the principle of exchange, using the concrete materials of coins (objectives 1 and 3) and base-ten blocks (objectives 2 and 4). The pupil should be able:

1. *Given a pile of 1p coins (less than a hundred), to reduce this to the smallest number of equivalent coins, using a process of exchange.*
   (For example, given a pile of 67 one-penny coins and a supply of ten-pence coins, the pupil should be able to reduce the pile of 1p coins to 6 tens and 7 ones, by exchanging 10 ones at a time for a ten.)

2. *Given a pile of base-ten units (less than a hundred), to reduce this to the smallest number of equivalent blocks, using a process of exchange.*
   (For example, given a pile of 43 units and a supply of tens, the pupil should be able to reduce the pile of units to 4 tens and 3 units, by exchanging ten units at a time for a ten.)

3. *Given a pile of 1p and 10p coins (less than £10-worth in total), to reduce this to the smallest number of equivalent coins, using a process of exchange.*

(For example, with a supply of 10p and £1 coins available, the pupil should be able to reduce a pile of 35 one-penny coins and 28 ten-pence coins to 3 one-pound, 1 ten-pence and 5 one-penny coins.)

4. *Given a pile of base-ten units and tens (less than the equivalent of a thousand units), to reduce this to the smallest number of equivalent blocks, using a process of exchange.*
(Similar to objective 3: a supply of tens and hundreds blocks should be available for exchange.)

Place-value objectives 5–11

The next group of objectives focuses on connections between symbols and language, between symbols and concrete materials and between language and concrete materials. The teacher should ensure that these objectives are attained particularly in respect of numbers where common confusions arise, e.g. between 471 and 417, or between 417 and 470. Also it is important that the pupil can handle numbers with 0 in either the tens or the units place, and those with 11, 12, 13, 14, 15, 16, 17, 18, or 19 as the last two digits. For all possible three-digit numbers, then, the pupil should be able:

5. *To say in words the name of any written three-digit numeral.*
(For example, the pupil should be able to say the names of 278, 465, 564, 103, 130, 405, 450, 471, 417, 470, 600, 812 . . .)

6. *To write the numeral for any stated three-digit number.*
(This is just the reverse of objective 5: here the number is stated in words and the pupil writes the corresponding numeral. The same range of possibilities needs to be covered.)

7. *To demonstrate the meaning of the digits in a three-digit numeral by selecting appropriate coins from a supply of 1p, 10p and 100p coins.*
(For example, the pupil should be able to show the number '403' by selecting 4 pound-coins and 3 ones.)

8. *To demonstrate the meaning of the digits in a three-digit numeral by selecting appropriate blocks from a supply of base-ten materials (ones, tens and hundreds).*

9. *Given a collection of coins (1p, 10p, 100p: no more than nine of each), to say and write the corresponding number.*

10. *Given a collection of base-ten blocks (ones, tens, hundreds: no more than nine of each), to say and write the corresponding number.*

When these objectives have been attained the pupil should then be able:

11. *To explain the meaning of each digit in a three-digit number.*
    (For example, explain that the '4' in '453' represents '4 hundreds',
    the '5' represents '5 tens' and the '3' represent '3 ones'. Examples
    with zeros are particularly significant in this objective.)

Place-value objectives 12–15

This group refers to the connections between the picture of number in the
number line and the language and symbols of number. As with objectives
5–11 it is important that the pupil attains these objectives in respect of the
full range of possible three-digit numbers, particularly those which give
rise to common misunderstandings and confusions. The word 'approximate' is used in these objectives, thus laying them open to the charge of
being imprecise. However I am confident that most teachers would agree
over what level of accuracy would indicate an acceptable degree of understanding in these tasks. So, the objectives are that the pupil should be
able:

12. *To indicate the approximate position of a three-digit number, given in
    words or symbols, on an appropriate section of a number line marked in
    tens.*
    (For example, the pupil should be able to indicate the approximate
    positions of 305, 352, 399 on the number line shown in Figure 5.2(a).)

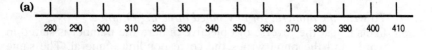

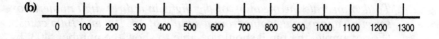

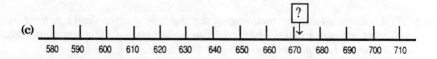

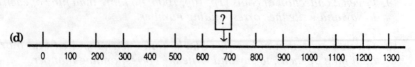

Figure 5.2   Connecting numerals with number-line diagrams

13. *To indicate the approximate position of a three-digit number, given in words or symbols, on a number line marked in hundreds.*
(For example, the pupil should be able to indicate the approximate positions of 305, 450, 790 on the number line shown in Figure 5.2(b).)

14. *To state the approximate number corresponding to a given point on a number line labelled in tens.*
(For example, to recognise that the arrow in Figure 5.2(c) is pointing to about 672.)

15. *To state the approximate number corresponding to a given point on a number line labelled in hundreds.*
(For example, to recognise that the arrow in Figure 5.2(d) is pointing to about 680.)

Place-value objectives 16–17

These objectives refer to the application of the place-value principle to the processes of ordering numbers. The pupil should be able:

16. *To arrange a set of numbers (up to 999) in order (a) from smallest to largest, (b) from largest to smallest.*

17. *To write down a number which comes between two given numbers (up to 999).*

Place-value objectives 18–21

A pupil's understanding of place value can be shown by the facility with which they can target the hundreds, the tens or the ones in a number, when appropriate, in mental arithmetic. The four objectives below therefore look simply for the ability to add or subtract 1, 10, 100, 2, 20, 200, mentally. Of course, we will aim for greater mental facility than this rather limited set of objectives (see Chapter 8), but these are included here specifically as an indication of the pupil's understanding of place value. As part of our goal of developing this understanding it is worthwhile to give pupils activities designed to achieve these particular limited objectives. So, in showing that they can target the appropriate place in a three-digit number mentally, the pupil should be able:

18. *Mentally, to add 1, 10 or 100 to any given three-digit number.*
(Note especially examples containing the digit 9, e.g. to add 10 to 796.)

19. *Mentally, to subtract 1, 10 or 100 from any given three-digit number.*
(Note especially examples containing the digit 0, e.g. to subtract 10 from 804.)

20. *Mentally, to add 2, 20 or 200 to any given three-digit number.*
(Note especially examples containing the digits 8 or 9, e.g. to add 20 to 386.)

21. *Mentally, to subtract 2, 20 or 200 from any given three-digit number.*
(Note especially examples containing the digits 0 or 1, e.g. to subtract 20 from 406.)

Place-value objectives 22–25

It is, of course, in adding and subtracting that we encounter the need for the process of exchange which lies at the heart of the understanding of place value. I include therefore in this section four simple objectives which show that the pupil can use the process of exchange in these contexts. Since this is an objective for understanding place value, and not one related to the ability to perform calculations, I am looking here for no more than the ability to use the process of exchange in adding and subtracting with concrete materials. As with other objectives in this set, two versions are given, one with coins and one with base-ten blocks. So, the pupil should be able:

22. *To perform an addition of two three-digit numbers, by putting out the corresponding two sets of coins (1p, 10p, 100p), combining them, exchanging where necessary, and stating the answer to the sum.*

23. *To perform an addition of two three-digit numbers, by putting out the corresponding two sets of base-ten blocks, combining them, exchanging where necessary, and stating the answer to the sum.*

24. *To perform a subtraction with two three-digit numbers, by putting out the corresponding set of coins (1p, 10p, 100p) for the larger number, taking away the set corresponding to the smaller number, exchanging where necessary, and stating the answer to the sum.*
(For example, given '413 – 275', the pupil would put out 4 hundreds, 1 ten and 3 ones. They would then exchange the ten for 10 ones and take away the required 5 ones, exchange one of the hundreds for 10 tens and take away the required 7 tens, and then take away the required 2 hundreds. This would leave them with 1 hundred, 3 tens and 8 ones, which they would interpret as the answer '138'. This is, of course, the process known formally as *subtraction by decomposition*.)

25. *To perform a subtraction with two three-digit numbers, by putting out the corresponding set of base-ten blocks for the larger number, taking away the set corresponding to the smaller number, exchanging where necessary, and stating the answer to the sum.*

SOME ACTIVITIES FOR ACHIEVING PLACE-VALUE OBJECTIVES

In the remainder of this chapter I suggest a number of games which can be used to provide low-attaining pupils with some purposeful activities, in which the principle of place value can be experienced and the achievement of the objectives outlined above can be pursued. All these games have been used successfully with low attainers, and, in my experience, prove more effective for developing understanding, and in generating commitment, than most work-cards and text-book exercises.

Generating numbers at random

A number of the activities suggested here (and in later chapters) make use of packs of home-made cards as a means of generating numbers at random. Good-quality blank playing cards can be obtained from educational suppliers. It is probably worth the time and expense of preparing some smart sets of these cards for use in the activities proposed below: children seem to be better motivated by good-quality cards than those cut from old cereal boxes. To start with, prepare:

- Pack A: 50 red cards, five each with the digits 0, 1, 2, 3, 4, 5, 6, 7, 8, 9, written on one side
- Pack B: 50 blue cards, five each with the digits 0, 1, 2, 3, 4, 5, 6, 7, 8, 9, written on one side.

Pack A, for example, is used as a simple means of generating single-digit numbers at random for various games. Pack A and Pack B used together can generate two-digit numbers at random, with, say, the blue cards representing tens and the red cards representing ones. I prefer this method to the use of various kinds of dice for generating numbers at random for small-group games, simply because, in my experience, in a classroom setting cards are quieter and less likely to be disruptive.

If dice are to be used, note that ten-faced dice, numbered from 0 to 9, are available from educational suppliers. Alternatively, wooden or plastic

```
10  CLS
20  PRINT RND(10)-1
30  PRINT "PRESS N AND RETURN FOR NEXT NUMBER" N$
40  INPUT N$
50  IF N$ = "N" THEN 10 ELSE 30
```

Figure 5.3   Program for generating random single-digit numbers

cubes with single digits written on them can be used: for example, a blue cube with the digits 1, 2, 4, 5, 6, 9 (representing tens) and a red cube with the digits 0, 3, 5, 7, 8, 9 (representing ones) will generate a good range of two-digit numbers.

An alternative which may appeal to some teachers (and most children) is to use a computer program to generate random numbers. Figure 5.3 provides a (deliberately very-simple) program, written in BBC BASIC, which could be typed into a computer situated next to the group playing the game. This program can then be adapted easily to generate two-digit numbers by replacing line 20 with: PRINT RND(10)-1; RND(10)-1. This adapted program will produce, for example, the output '04' for 'four'. If an output of '4' is preferred, then use: 20 PRINT RND(100)-1. Further modifications for generating numbers with three or more digits are obvious.

Activity 5.1 Race to a pound

Objective This is a small-group game, for up to four players plus a banker. It focuses on *objective 1*, that is, the process of exchanging ten ones for one ten. It is one version of a fairly common game, which I regard as essential experience of handling the basic place-value principle, for all low-attaining pupils.

Materials Pack A (or some other means of generating single-digit numbers) and a supply of 1p and 10p coins.

Rules The pack of cards is shuffled and placed face down in the middle of the table. In turn each player turns over a card. The number revealed indicates their winnings, which are paid to them in pennies by the banker. Used cards are returned to the bottom of the pack.

When any player has ten pennies they must exchange them at the bank for a ten-pence coin before having their next turn. If another player spots that they have failed to do this they must miss a turn. The banker also acts as referee. The first player to get ten ten-pences (i.e. a pound) is the winner. It is not necessary to insist that they finish exactly on a pound.

Variation Exactly the same game can then be played with base-ten blocks, units and tens, thus focusing on *objective 2*.

Activity 5.2 Race to ten pounds

Objectives This is an obvious extension of Activity 5.1, focusing on *objective 3*, and, to some extent, *objective 22*.

Materials Pack A and Pack B (or some other means of generating two-digit numbers) and a supply of 1p, 10p and £1 coins.

Rules The rules are similar to the previous game. Now, however, they use two packs of cards, Pack A (representing ones) and Pack B (representing tens), turning over one card from each to generate two-digit numbers. The banker pays them the appropriate number of tens and ones from the bank.

When any player has ten pennies or ten ten-pences they must exchange them at the bank for a ten-pence coin or a pound coin respectively, before having their next turn. As above, failure to exchange results in a turn being missed. The first player to get ten pounds (or more) is the winner.

Variation Obviously, exactly the same game can be played with base-ten blocks, units, tens and hundreds, thus focusing on *objective 4*, and, to some extent, *objective 23*.

Activity 5.3 Place-value cards

Objectives This is a simple activity in which two children can practise translating between symbols and words for numbers, thus focusing on

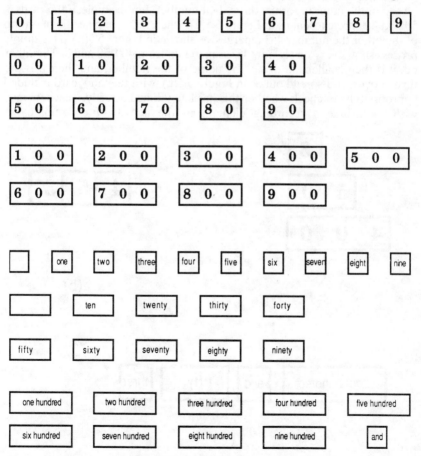

Figure 5.4   Place-value cards

objectives 5 and 6. The activity helps children to learn to recognise, for example, that the 5 in 453 represents 50, and also focuses on the role of zero as a place holder.

Materials A set of cards, as shown in Figure 5.4, with the numerals, shown in the top half of the figure, written on one side, and the corresponding words, shown in the bottom half of the figure, on the other. Notice that the cards with '0' and '00' on one side are blank on the other: this is to emphasise the place-holder function of zero. There is also one other card with just the word 'and' written on it.

Method The cards are arranged on the table, with the numerals face up, in three sets, single-digit numerals in one set, two-digit in the next and three-digit in the next.

One child picks up one card from each of the sets and assembles them one on top of the other to form a three-digit number. For example, if the cards 3, 50 and 400 are chosen, as in Figure 5.5(a), when they are placed one on top of the other the number 453 emerges, as shown in Figure 5.5(b). This simple process shows very nicely how 453 is made up from 400, 50 and 3. The other pupil is then challenged to say the name of the number, and the cards are turned over, and spread out as in Figure 5.5(c), with the 'and' card included appropriately, to check whether this has been done correctly. Teachers may wish to include a recording element in the activity. For example, by

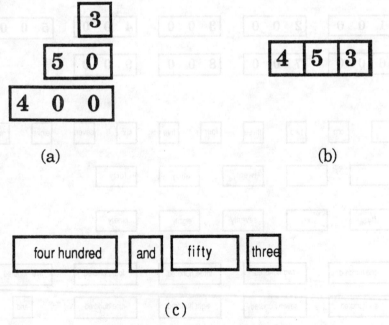

(a)

(b)

(c)

Figure 5.5   Using the place-value cards

copying the symbols and words written on the cards, they might record the above choice as: '400 + 50 + 3 ↔ 453 ↔ four hundred and fifty three'.

Note: it is best initially to remove the 10 (ten) card from the pack for this activity, because of the special names used for numbers with a '1' in the tens position. When the children are confident with using all the other cards, the ten should be put back in and the teacher should discuss with them the conventions for reading numbers like '417' (which will appear as 'four hundred and ten seven').

Variation The activity can then be done in reverse. The cards are spread out in rows with the words shown uppermost. One child writes down in symbols a choice of a three-digit number and the other child is challenged to select the cards required to assemble this number. For example, if one child writes down '207', the other must pick up the card labelled 'two hundred', the card labelled 'and', the blank card from the two-digit row, because there are no tens, and the card labelled 'seven'. This child then turns over the three cards with digits on, places them one on top of the other and confirms the correspondence with the number written down.

Activity 5.4 Place-value connections

Objectives This simple activity for a group of four children aims to develop connections between the numerals, the language, and the two concrete embodiments, coins and base-ten blocks, thus focusing on *objectives 7, 8, 9 and 10*.

Materials Pack A, the place-value cards from Activity 5.3, a set of base-ten materials (ones, tens, hundreds) and a set of coins (1p, 10p, 100p).

Method One child has Pack A, the second child has the place-value cards, the third child has the base-ten materials, and the fourth has the coins. The first child turns over three cards from Pack A to form a three-digit number. The next child assembles this number with the place-value cards and, turning them over, arranges the name of the number on the table. The third child puts out the corresponding blocks, and the fourth puts out the corresponding coins. The first child checks that all the inputs are correct and then calls the teacher over to demonstrate the connections. After a few turns the children all move round one place in the sequence and so are responsible for a different input.

Admittedly, this does not appear to be a very exciting activity, but it can be effective if used for short periods, say, for about fifteen minutes, with children at the younger end of the 8–12 age range.

Activity 5.5 Happy families

Objective This is a small-group game for up to five players, focusing on *objective 11*. Children playing this game have to recognise the meaning of the digits in three-digit numbers.

Materials A calculator for each player.

Rules This is a highly enjoyable game provided the children are able to cooperate with each other and can be trusted to play honestly without cheating. It is useful to have one child acting as an umpire who moves around the group, looking over the shoulders of the players to ensure that they play fair!

Each player enters a three-digit number on their calculator. This is not revealed to other players. The game is then played like the traditional 'Happy Families' card game, with players asking each other in turn whether they have particular digits, and being required to hand them over if they have. The easiest way to explain the game is to give an example:

Three players, A, B, and C, choose the numbers 453, 634, and 135 respectively. A starts the game.

A asks B: 'Have you any fives?'

B (634) responds to A: 'No.' (End of A's turn.)

B asks C: 'Have you any threes?'

C (135) responds to B: 'Yes, three tens.'

(C now 'gives' B the three tens, i.e. C subtracts 30 from his or her number and B adds 30 to his or hers. B now has 664 on display, C has 105. B, having been successful, gets another go and turns to the next player.)

B asks A: 'Have you any sixes?'

A (453) responds to B: 'No.' (End of B's turn.)

C asks A: 'Have you any threes?'

A (453) responds to C: 'Yes, three ones.'

(A subtracts 3, leaving 450 on display; C adds 3, getting 108 on display.)

C asks B: 'Have you any sixes?'

B (664) responds to C: 'Yes, six hundreds and six tens!'

(B must now give both the 600 and the 60 to C. So, B subtracts 600 and 60 in turn from his or her number, leaving him or her with just 4 on display. C adds 600 and 60 to his or her number, getting a total of 768.)

And so on.

A player is out when their display is reduced to zero. The winning player should end up with the total of all the numbers chosen to start with. The umpire could write these down at the start and the total could be used as a check that the game has been played correctly.

An interesting feature of this game is the children's behaviour when someone gets a total displayed greater than a thousand. Even low-attaining children cotton on very quickly to the idea that asking 'Have you any ones?' is a good tactic for getting a thousand off a player who has recently won a large number of hundreds. Once discovered, the thousand tends to get passed around very rapidly from player to player.

Activity 5.6 Boxes

Objectives This is a small-group game for two, three or four players, focusing on *objective 11* (recognising the meaning of the digits), and also *objective 16* (ordering).

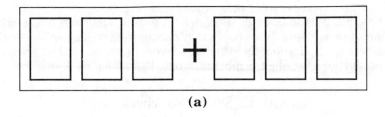

(a)

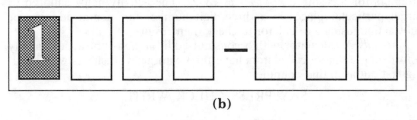

(b)

Figure 5.6   Boxes (Activity 5.6)

Materials Pack A; a strip of card with boxes drawn as shown in Figure 5.6(a) for each player: the boxes should be the same size as the cards in the pack; a calculator for each player.

Rules In turn, each player turns over a card from the pack, thus revealing a single digit. This can be placed in any empty box, either one of their own or one of their opponents. The object is to finish up with the highest total. So, if a player turns over, say, a '7', they may decide to put this in the hundreds box for one of their own numbers. But if they turn over, say, a '2', this might be put in a hundreds box of one of their opponents.

When all the boxes are full, each player finds the total of their two numbers, using their calculator, to determine who has the highest score. I find the game works well if the children play ten rounds, writing down their scores after each round and then using their calculators at the end to add up their overall scores. The game is very popular with children and really helps to focus their attention on the meaning of the digits. They quickly learn that the hundreds are the most significant digits in a three-digit number. Comparing scores at the end of each round and at the end of the game is, of course, an exercise in ordering.

Variations A nice variation of the game is based on subtraction rather than addition. With low attainers I have found it most successful to give each player a strip of card with one thousand already written in the first number, as shown in Figure 5.6(b), thus ensuring the first number is larger than the second. In the subtraction version the children learn that you can do yourself a good turn by putting a small digit in the hundreds box of your

second number, or do your opponent a bad turn by giving them a large
digit in the hundreds box of their second number.

The game can also be easily simplified for two-digit numbers or extended
to four or more digits. Some pupils may benefit from trying versions of the
game with multiplication; for example, a layout of boxes could be given for
the product of a two-digit number by a one-digit number.

Activity 5.7 Say, press, check, write

Objectives This is a simple but effective activity which I have used with low
attainers for focusing on *objectives 18–21*. The activity helps children to
target particular places in a three-digit number for mental addition or
subtraction, using a calculator to check their results.

Materials A calculator with a constant addition and subtraction facility
(most simple school calculators have this); various worksheets with headings set out as in this example:

SAY, PRESS, CHECK, WRITE

SUBTRACT 1	ADD 2	SUBTRACT 100	ADD 20
404	184	901	150

Method Children work in pairs to complete the worksheet, by writing
nine more numbers in each column. So, for example, in the column above
headed SUBTRACT 100 they would finish up writing: 801, 701, 601, 501,
401, 301, 201, 101 and 1. The procedure adopted is as follows.

The first child (A) enters the number at the head of the column on the
calculator, followed by the instruction above it (e.g. '901 – 100'). The
second child (B) *says* what the answer will be, A then *presses* the equals
key and *checks* whether this is correct. Then B *writes* the correct answer in
the column (801). A then *says* what the next number will be, B *presses* the
equals key and *checks* the answer. A *writes* the correct answer in the
column (701). This process goes on until the whole column is complete.
Using a calculator with a constant addition and subtraction facility means
that only the equals key has to be pressed each time once the initial '–100'
has been entered.

Clearly the worksheets can be sequenced to make the tasks gradually
more and more difficult, first of all focusing on adding and subtracting 1,
then 2, then 10, 20, 100, 200. Grading of the worksheets should take into
account the particular examples highlighted in *objectives 18–21* (e.g. adding
20 when the tens digit is 8 or 9).

Activity 5.8 What's on the card?

Objectives This is a game for two players. It focuses again on objectives 18–21.
Materials A calculator, and two packs of cards:

- *Pack C:* 30 cards, five each with +1, +10, +100, −1, −10, −100 written on one side
- *Pack D:* 30 cards, five each with +2, +20, +200, −2, −20, −200 written on one side

Rules Depending on the level of difficulty required, the game can be played with either Pack C or Pack D, or both packs shuffled together. Player A (or the teacher) chooses a three-digit number between 200 and 800, for example 459. This is written down clearly for both players to see and entered on the calculator. A then turns over a card, carries out the instruction written on it, and then hands the calculator to B, who has to say what is written on the card. For example, if the calculator is displaying 461, B should deduce that the card said '+2'. If B is correct and can also get the original number back on display, by applying the inverse operation (e.g. '−2'), they win the card. Otherwise the card goes back in the pack. It is then B's turn to turn over a card and to perform the stated operation, and A must deduce what is on the card. The game proceeds until all the cards are used up. The winner is the player with the most cards.

Activity 5.9 Grids

Objectives This is yet another activity which gives practice in the skills involved in *objectives 18–21*.

Materials Copies of grids like the one shown in Figure 5.7(a).

Method The instructions for moving across and down the grid can be any combination of ADD 1, SUBTRACT 1, ADD 10, SUBTRACT 10, ADD 100, SUBTRACT 100, ADD 2, SUBTRACT 2, ADD 20, SUBTRACT 20, ADD 200, SUBTRACT 200. A starting number is written in the top left hand corner and a finishing number in the bottom right hand corner. These

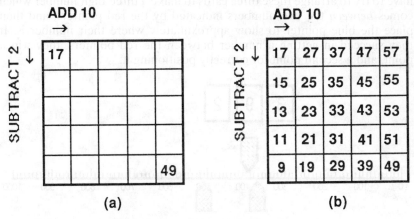

Figure 5.7   Grids (Activity 5.9)

have to be chosen with a little care. For example, with the instructions ADD 10 and SUBTRACT 2, a starting number of 17 must have a finishing number of 49 (17 + 10 + 10 + 10 + 10 – 2 – 2 – 2 – 2). Writing in the finishing number provides both a check and a target for the pupils. It is probably best with low attainers to avoid examples of grids which produce negative numbers.

Children work individually in completing these grids, ensuring that they obey the given instruction for all movements left to right along the rows or down the columns.

Figure 5.7(b) shows the completed versions of the grid given in Figure 5.7(a). When working with low attainers I find it useful to keep a supply of blank grids on which I can quickly write appropriate instructions and numbers. These can then be given to individual children in odd moments when other tasks are completed. They are always very popular.

Activity 5.10 Between the pointers

Objective This is an example of several simple games, for a small group of children, which can be used to focus on *objective 17* (being able to choose a number between two given numbers) and *objectives 12–15* (connecting numbers with the number line).

Materials A number line, labelled in hundreds, subdivided into tens, as shown in Figure 5.8; three coloured pointers, say, two red and one blue; Pack A.

Rules It is probably best to have a child who is fairly confident with the number line to act as an umpire for this game. For each round the umpire places the two red pointers on two marks on the number line. In turn, each player turns over three cards from the pack to reveal three digits. They have to try to arrange these three cards to make a three-digit number which comes *between* the two numbers indicated by the red pointers, and then place the blue pointer to show approximately where their number is. If they succeed in getting a number between the red pointers, they win a point, and a second point for correctly positioning it.

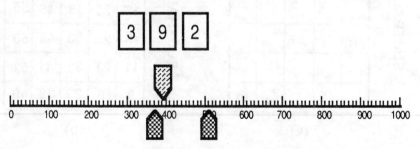

Figure 5.8   Between the pointers: Activity 5.10

In Figure 5.8, the umpire has placed the red pointers at 370 and 510. A player has turned over 2, 3 and 9, rearranged these to form 392 and positioned the blue pointer at about the right point on the number line.

Variation A simpler version with two-digit numbers and a number line marked in tens, subdivided into units, can be played.

Activity 5.11 Win some, lose some

Objectives This is a very popular game for up to four players, plus a banker. It is directed at *objectives 22 and 24*, involving the process of exchanging in adding and subtracting with coins.

Materials Pack A; a supply of 1p, 10p and £1 coins; a calculator; also, a further pack of home-made cards:

Pack E: 25 cards, ten with the symbol '+', and five each with the symbols: '−', '×', '='.

Rules Each player starts with a float of £5 (five one pound coins). The first player to achieve £20 is the winner. In turn they turn over alternately cards from Pack A and Pack E, laying them out in a row on the table, until an equals sign appears. For example, a player might turn up the following sequence:

$$3 + 8 \times 5 - 0 + 2 =$$

The sequence of calculations displayed must then be worked out, either mentally or using a calculator, to determine the player's winnings. In the example above the calculator gives the result '57'; the player is paid five tens and seven ones by the banker. A player must always exchange ten ones for a ten and ten tens for a hundred: failure to do this, if spotted by an opponent, results in a turn being missed.

Sometimes a negative answer is achieved, in which case the player has to pay to the bank, rather than collect. In this case, note that the bank does not give change. The bank however will exchange one ten for ten ones or one hundred for ten tens if asked to do so.

Note that, if, for example, a player turns up '8' and then, immediately, '=', their turn is complete and they just win 8p.

This game has been very successful with low attainers. Players get very excited when they produce a long string of cards before an equals sign appears. Of course, the cards are merely a device to generate numbers at random, but there is a considerable pay-off in terms of incidental learning from the game. Children quickly recognise the significance of multiplying by a large digit; they soon start groaning when they get a subtraction sign; they can discover what happens when you multiply by zero; and they get some surprising insights into negative numbers. But the main purpose of the game is to give practice in the process of exchange in addition and subtraction.

Variations (i) Play the same game with base-ten blocks, to focus on objectives 23 and 25.

(ii) To generate three-digit answers rather more frequently, players can be allowed to turn over two cards at a time from Pack A *once* in each turn. A canny player might wait for a multiplication sign to appear before taking this option, for example, scoring 384 with:

$$3 + 5 \times 48 =$$

Note: Mathematicians talk about something called *precedence of operators*. This refers to certain conventions, which, for example, give multiplication precedence over addition. Using such a convention, '4 + 5 × 2' would be equal to 14 (i.e. '4 + 10'), since the multiplication would be done first. Scientific calculators (ones which use what is called an *algebraic operating system*) use these conventions and will give the answer '14' if the calculation '4 + 5 × 2 =' is keyed in. However the simple calculators normally used with primary and middle-school children do not use these conventions. They simply perform the calculations in the order in which they are entered. So, keying in '4 + 5 × 2 =' on a simple calculator will produce the answer '18' (i.e. 9 × 2), since the addition, entered first, is done first.

The conventions of precedence of operators are really only important when we get on to manipulating algebraic expressions. In practical arithmetic calculations the context always determines in what order the operations should be performed. It would, in my view, be quite inappropriate to raise the question of these conventions with low-attaining pupils in the 8–12 age range. I am therefore quite happy to ignore the conventions in the above game and to follow the logic of the simple calculator which takes the sequence of operations in the order they appear. Calculators which use the algebraic operating system should not be used with pupils in the 8–12 age range.

Activity 5.12 Spend ten pounds

Objective This is a small-group game, for up to four players, plus a banker, with a focus on *objective 24*, the process of exchange in subtraction with coins.

Materials Pack A and Pack B (or some other means of generating two-digit numbers) and a supply of 1p, 10p and £1 coins.

Rules This is simply the reverse of the game described in Activity 5.2. Players start with ten pounds and race to be the first to spend all their money. Once again, the bank does not give change, but will exchange ten ones for a ten or ten tens for a hundred, if requested. This ensures that the place-value objective is involved.

Variation Play the same game with base-ten blocks, starting with a thousand block, to focus on *objective 25*.

PLACE-VALUE OBJECTIVES RELATED TO MONEY NOTATION

It is important to include in our work with low attainers some additional objectives related to the specific problems of money notation, allowing the principles of place value to be extended to this first important experience of decimal notation. These include being able to translate freely between the pence notation (235p) and the pound notation (£2.35) and to use the conventions for the latter correctly (e.g. two figures after the point and no 'p').

Place-value objectives 26–31

Activities should therefore be designed to ensure that the pupil is able:

26. *To write a sum of money given in pence correctly with a pound sign, and vice versa.*
(This should include being able to translate, for example, between 25p and £0.25, and between 7p and £0.07.)

27. *Given a collection of coins (1p, 10p, 100p: no more than nine of each) to write down the sum of money using the pound notation.*

28. *Given a sum of money using the pound notation to put out the corresponding collection of coins (1p, 10p, 100p).*

29. *To interpret correctly the sum of money indicated by an answer to a calculation performed on a calculator.*
(In particular, this would include calculator answers such as 8.3, which has to be interpreted as £8.30, and 8.6666666, which has to be interpreted as £8.66.
Note: I would not include a requirement for rounding to the nearest digit as a realistic or necessary target for low attainers in this age range.)

30. *To arrange a set of prices, written in pound notation, in order from (a) lowest to highest, (b) highest to lowest.*
(For example, to order these prices: £4.50, £4.99, £4.05, £5, £0.75, £3.10.)

31. *To write down a sum of money which comes between two given sums of money, expressed in pound notation.*
(For example, to write down an amount between £5.99 and £6.10.)

ACTIVITIES FOR ACHIEVING PLACE-VALUE OBJECTIVES RELATED TO MONEY NOTATION

Activity 5.13 Money notation worksheets

Objective Children should be given some money problems to solve with a calculator which deliberately throw up answers with only one figure after the point, or with more than two figures after the point, thus focusing on *objective 29*. By doing these simultaneously with coins and recording their results, *objectives 26–28* are also involved.

Materials Coins, calculator, worksheets.

Method Using both coins and the calculator, children work through a set of examples focusing on interpreting calculator answers with just one digit after the point, such as:

1. How much altogether for a book costing £3.25 and a pen costing £1.45? (Use +)
2. Share £19.20 between 3 people. How much each? (Use ÷)
3. How much for 5 burgers at £1.22 each? (Use ×)
4. How much change from £5 if you spend £3.70? (Use –)

In the first question, for example, they would put out the two sums of money in coins and establish that the total is £4.70. But when they enter '3.25 + 1.45 =' on the calculator, they get the result '4.7'.

Further examples, using division only, focus on the problem of interpreting calculator answers with more than two digits after the point:

5. Share £4.25 between 3 people. How much each? (Use ÷)

Here the pupils would put out £4.25 in coins, and, exchanging where necessary, share this into three piles of £1.41, with 2p left over. Then they would enter '4.25 ÷ 3 =' on the calculator to get the result 1.4166666. The teacher will have to explain what is going on: the calculator tries to share out the 2p and gives each person some little bits of pennies; we can just give the result as '£1.41 and a little bit.' Usually, of course, '£1.41' would do, since the little bits are not big enough to worry about.

Other activities

To focus further on the objectives for money notation, some of the activities suggested above can be adapted in obvious ways. For example:

- The games described in Activities 5.1, 5.2, 5.11 and 5.12 could all include a recording element, each player being required to keep a written record, using pound-notation, of their winnings (or losses) and remaining balance.

- In Activity 5.6 the boxes could be set out with a £ sign and a point:

$$£ \;\square.\square\square + £ \;\square.\square\square$$

- In Activity 5.7, the say, press, check, write sequences could include instructions to add or subtract 1p, 10p, £1, 2p, 20p, £2, and the results written down in pound notation, for example:

SUBTRACT 1p	ADD 2p	SUBTRACT £1	ADD 20p
£4.04	£1.84	£9.01	£1.50

These suggestions are incorporated in the scheme for teaching money, outlined in Chapter 10.

QUESTIONS FOR FURTHER DISCUSSION

1. What are some of the problems which, in your experience, children have in handling zero? Why does zero cause so many difficulties?
2. Do you agree with my conclusion that dabbling in multi-base number work is likely to confuse rather than help low attainers in mathematics?
3. Is my set of statements of objectives an adequate description of what it means to understand place value? Are these objectives realistic for low attainers up to the age of 12?

6
MEASUREMENT FOR LOW
ATTAINERS

Learning to cope with the measurements which we encounter in everyday life is an essential component of numeracy. This must therefore be a major part of our work in mathematics with low attainers in the 8–12 age range.

A few years ago I observed a lower mathematics set of 11–12-year-olds working on the topic of length. They were struggling with questions like these in their text-book:

$$
\begin{array}{r}
1 \text{ m } 55 \text{ cm} \\
+ \ 2 \text{ m } 48 \text{ cm} \\
\hline
\end{array}
$$

At the same time, the school buildings were undergoing some major alterations. Workmen were taking down internal walls and putting in alcoves and bookcases for a library. These men were clearly experts at linear measurement, using tape-measures, rulers, spirit levels and set squares with great accuracy and confidence. I was struck by the enormous gulf between the purposeless tasks in which the pupils were engaged and the purposeful applications of the concepts of length demonstrated by the workmen around us. Out of interest I asked one of the workmen to try some of the questions in the pupils' text-book. This expert at measurement struggled as much as some of the pupils: a salutary lesson for those of us committed to making mathematics for low attainers more relevant and purposeful.

In this chapter I lay out what I consider to be a set of realistic and relevant objectives for teaching measurement to such pupils. For each aspect of measurement the set of objectives are designed to include the four categories described in Chapter 4:

- knowledge of terms, facts, definitions, principles
- mastery of techniques and manipulative skills
- understanding of concepts, procedures, principles
- application of knowledge, skills and understanding

As far as possible I have aimed for the objectives to emphasise understanding as much as skills and knowledge. Even where I have deliberately limited the objectives on the basis of what might be realistic for low attainers, it is important also that each set of objectives gets the pupils far enough on to be able to use the skills and concepts of measurement in some purposeful applications. The suggestions given in the second half of the chapter for activities suitable for low-attaining pupils in the 8–12 age range include some examples of such purposeful applications.

MEASURES

Four aspects of measures are considered suitable for work with low attainers:

- length and distance
- weight
- capacity and liquid volume
- time

Competence and confidence in these measures is essential for making sense of the world in which we live. Understanding of how time is measured and recorded is clearly necessary for organising one's life, for catching buses and trains, and for following any sort of timetable. This should be a major focus of our work with low attainers, especially because of the complications of the non-decimal system of measuring and recording time. Length and distance are the easiest measuring concepts for children to grasp, and provide a useful and accessible experience of the basic principles of measurement. Weight is encountered in both shopping and cooking, as are capacity and liquid volume.

I have excluded area and solid volume from the list of measures for low-attaining pupils in the 8–12 age range. Apart from some preliminary experiences, such as filling spaces with tiles and building solids with cubes, there is not much work which is suitable for low-attaining pupils in these aspects of measurement. Children find the concepts difficult to handle, and they frequently confuse them with other concepts, such as perimeter. Furthermore, there are not actually many direct practical applications of area and solid volume which are relevant for these pupils. It is much better for us to focus on developing confidence in a limited number of aspects of measuring, and it would seem that the four aspects listed above are the most relevant and important.

DEVELOPING UNDERSTANDING AND SKILLS OF MEASUREMENT

Comparison and ordering

The first stages of learning to measure in any of the four aspects being considered is to be able to compare two things directly and to determine which is the greater or smaller according to the attribute in question. To make these comparisons the pupil will need to use the important language of comparison. So, for example, they might place two pupils side by side and determine which is the taller and which the shorter; or they might place two objects in the pans of a balance and determine which is the heavier and which the lighter; or they might pour water from one container into another and decide which holds more and which holds less; or two pupils might undertake a task and discover which takes longer and which takes a shorter time to complete it.

From direct comparison of two things, the pupils should then move on to order a set of three or more things, according to the attribute being measured. Again this is done by direct comparison, at this stage without any units being involved.

Conservation

It is generally agreed that an important component of understanding of length, weight and liquid volume is that the pupil should grasp the principle of *conservation*. This refers to the fact that the attribute in question is unchanged when the object being measured is subjected to certain transformations. For example, the length of an object is unchanged when the object is moved to a new position, the weight of a lump of Plasticine is unchanged when it is broken up into a number of smaller pieces, or the volume of the water in a container is unchanged when it is poured into a differently shaped container.

What is not generally agreed is how the child's grasp of these ideas might be recognised. A pupil's response to some questions might indicate that they have not grasped the principle, whereas their response to other questions or behaviour in other situations might indicate that they have. For example, a number of 10-year-olds in one low-attaining mathematics set failed on one of the standard tests of conservation of volume. When the water in containers A and B, shown in Figure 6.1, was poured into containers C and D respectively, they gave the response that C had more water in it than D. The orthodox interpretation of this response is that the pupil is focusing on the height of the water rather than the volume, although there

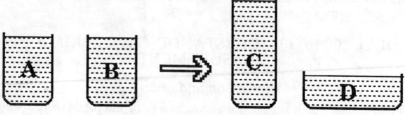

Figure 6.1   Conservation of liquid volume

are other plausible explanations. The following day was very warm and sunny. When the pupils came in, hot and thirsty from morning break, we engaged in some role play, with me playing the part of a father with two children. I filled a glass tumbler with some orange squash and poured this into one container, then did the same with a second, differently shaped container. When I gave the two drinks to my two children, the pupils who the previous day had failed on the conservation test were now quite certain that what I had done was fair. It was clear that they recognised that the two children had received the same amount of orange squash.

Where I have included objectives related to conservation in the sets of objectives given below, it is my intention that teachers should seek to recognise that the principles have or have not been grasped through observation of the pupil's behaviour or responses in situations which have some meaning for them.

Non-standard units

Pupils should begin to measure the attribute concerned using non-standard units. In this stage they get experience of the idea of measuring in units and they develop a clearer idea of what it is that is being measured, using familiar items such as hand spans for length, pebbles for weight, and egg-cups for capacity. Often these non-standard units are more appropriate sizes for measuring the objects in the pupil's environment than the standard units, such as the gram or the millilitre.

Approximation

Even at this early stage, pupils can be introduced to the idea that measurement is always approximate. We can only ever measure something to the nearest unit. The key language to be developed here is 'to the nearest' and 'between . . . and . . . '. For example pupils might record the length of a corridor as being 'nearly 25 paces' or 'between 24 and 25 paces'. These language structures apply equally to other aspects of measurement. They are then developed further through the use of standard units.

Standard units

For each aspect of measurement we must decide which standard units are appropriate for use with our low-attaining pupils. Apart from measuring time, where pupils must learn to use seconds, minutes, hours, days, weeks, months and years, I have found that it is best to limit the number of different units we introduce to these pupils. In this I am guided by the units most frequently used in everyday situations, such as shopping and cookery. So, in the objectives below, I have referred to the following metric units only: centimetre and metre for length, gram and kilogram for weight, and millilitre and litre for capacity and liquid volume. These are sufficient for pupils to develop competence with the measures concerned and to begin to make sense of the information which confronts them in shopping, cooking and other aspects of the world outside of school.

Developing decimal notation

This restriction of the units for measuring makes it possible for our low attainers to have a sound introduction in practical contexts to decimal notation.

They should first have mastered the pound-notation for money, such as £1.75 as an alternative way of writing 175p, as outlined in place-value objectives 26–31 in Chapter 5. Then an exact parallel can be drawn when measuring in centimetres: a length of 175 cm can also be written as 1.75 m. We stress that this works the same way, because there are 100 pence in a pound and there are 100 centimetres in a metre. With low attainers I stick to the same conventions for recording length as we use for money. So, if writing a length, such as 150 cm, in metres, I will have two digits after the point: i.e. 1.50 m rather than 1.5 m. The parallel with 150p = £1.50 is very helpful and should be reinforced as far as possible.

When we move on to measuring weight we have 1000 grams in a kilogram, so now we get three digits after the point. So, a weight of 1550 g can also be written as 1.550 kg. Low-attaining pupils seem to get the idea that this is just the same as pounds and pence, but with three digits rather than two because of the 1000 g in a kilogram. It is not necessary, or realistic, to attempt to explain that the first figure after the point represents tenths of a kilogram, the second hundredths of a kilogram, and the third thousandths of a kilogram. We simply build on and extend the everyday experience of handling money notation. Then, of course, millilitres and litres behave in just the same way as grams and kilograms: 1550 ml = 1.550 litres. So, the pupils have two practical experiences of handling numbers with two figures after the point (money and length) and two with three figures after the point (weight and capacity). This seems to me to be a sufficient competence to aim for with low-attaining pupils up to the age of 12 years, and a sound basis for future development of work with decimal fractions.

Measuring devices

In developing skills of measuring we have to make decisions about which measuring devices pupils should learn to use and in which order.

For length, these could include rulers of various sizes. Many styles are available, but with low attainers I would use just 30-cm and metre rulers, graduated only in centimetres. We will also need to use tape-measures, both metre-length tapes, graduated in centimetres, and 30-metre tapes, graduated in metres, and metre trundle-wheels.

In the early stages of learning about weighing it is most helpful for pupils to use the balance-type weighing-device. If they use just kilogram, 100-gram, 10-gram and 1-gram weights then this experience provides a useful reinforcement of place-value concepts: something that weighs 345 grams, for example, will be balanced by 3 hundreds, 4 tens and 5 units. Later on they should learn to read the scale or digital display on a spring-type weighing-device, such as kitchen scales or bathroom scales.

Measuring jugs and containers of various sorts, graduated in millilitres and litres, will be needed for liquid volume and capacity. Measurement of time intervals necessitates skill in using a stop-clock or stopwatch. The question of different types of watches and clocks for telling the time is considered later in the chapter.

Estimation

In each set of objectives for measurement there is a reference to the pupil being able to estimate a quantity, such as the length or weight of an object, the capacity of a container, or the length of a time interval. Each of these objectives specifies what I would judge, from my experience, to be a reasonable level of accuracy to expect from low-attaining pupils up to the age of 12 years.

I have found that experiences aimed at developing the ability to make reasonable estimates for measurements are some of the most successful and effective ways of building up low-attaining pupils' confidence with the aspect of measurement concerned. Some suggestions for such experiences are given towards the end of the chapter.

Reference items

To assist pupils in making these estimates, and therefore to build up their confidence with the different aspects of measurements, I have found it very helpful to give them some *reference items*. These are simply some familiar objects for which they can memorise a measurement, and then use this for reference in comparisons with other objects. For example, I found that the pupils in one class who made the best progress in the work we were doing on capacity were those who knew that a can of drink was 330 ml, and who were able to use this frequently as a reference item.

Metric and imperial

The Mathematics National Curriculum (Attainment Target 8) rightly asserts that pupils should be able to 'use imperial units still in daily use.' If we aim to make mathematics relevant then we cannot ignore the fact that many such units have survived attempts to metricate the United Kingdom. But there are difficult decisions involved here. We aim for relevant objectives, but we must also be realistic about what can be achieved. We cannot really expect our low attainers to cope with all the units which they might hear people using outside of school:

- just a couple of *inches* wide of the off-stump
- he's nearly six *feet* tall
- the ball is on the 10-*yard* line
- it's 119 *miles* to London
- a *pound* of apples, please
- my weight's gone up to nearly 12 *stones*
- four *ounces* of ham, please
- add 15 *fluid ounces* of water
- go to the shop and buy a *pint* of milk
- my car does about 35 miles to the *gallon*

In the objectives below I have referred only to miles, pounds, ounces and pints, as the most frequently used and most relevant of these imperial units. Teachers may well question this limited reference to imperial units and may find that many low attainers, because of their practical experience outside of school, may be able to cope confidently with more than I have suggested.

OBJECTIVES FOR LENGTH AND DISTANCE

Units for length and distance

As has been suggested above, it is quite unrealistic to expect our low-attaining pupils to handle all the possible units of length which are around: metric units such as metres, kilometres, decimetres, centimetres and milli-metres, and imperial units such as inches, feet, yards and miles. In fact, most linear measurements are now metric. In their day-to-day experience of shopping, children will not encounter many items which are actually sold by length, but those they do come across, such as wood, carpet, ribbon, curtains and dress material, will normally be sold by the metre. One case where imperial units of length are most often used is in giving people's heights. But, in general, I reckon that we can dispense with inches, feet and yards in the classroom in our work with low attainers and concentrate on metres and centimetres.

I have excluded millimetres (1000 mm = 1 m), partly because they are small and fiddly, and partly because of the complications for low attainers of handling the extra relationships involved, such as 135 mm = 13.5 cm = 0.135 m. However, provided the pupils are confident with centimetres and metres, it may be useful to introduce millimetres towards the end of the 8–12 age range if a greater degree of accuracy is required in practical tasks, especially since millimetres are used so extensively in many trades. I have also excluded kilometres, but included miles. This is simply a recognition that all road distances in Britain are – and, no doubt, will for some years continue to be – given in miles. Since pupils obviously cannot have any direct practical experience of measuring distances in kilometres, any mathematical activities based on these will inevitably be too artificial to be acceptable.

Reference items for length

In helping low-attaining pupils to develop a sense of the size of the units we use for measuring length, I have found some useful reference items to be: (a) a child's finger is about 1 cm wide; (b) the pupils' rulers are 30 cm long; (c) a metre stick, used for pointing, is 100 cm long; (d) the classroom door is about 200 cm or 2 metres high. These facts can be referred to repeatedly for comparison with other objects in the classroom, when the topic of length is being taught. Children should memorise them. For measuring longer distances, athletics track-events provide obvious reference items. Important aspects of language here and throughout this topic are the words used for comparison: longer, shorter, taller, higher, lower, wider, narrower, further, nearer.

Applications

I have included some objectives below in the category of application. One of these is the use of scale-drawings. This is potentially a difficult aspect of mathematics, but, provided a one-to-one scale is employed, low-attaining pupils towards the end of the 8–12 age range can use this idea to tackle some interesting and purposeful problems. It is important to plan carefully in advance the size of grid on the squared paper which pupils will use for their scale-drawings, in order that, say, one metre measured can be represented by one unit on the scale-drawing. The concepts, skills and knowledge of length measurement can also be applied to various construction tasks. An important associated skill here is the use of a set square for drawing right angles.

Realistic and relevant objectives for length and distance

Pupils will, therefore, have a basic competence in handling the concepts of length and distance if they are able:

1. *To order a set of two or three objects by length, height or width, using the language 'longer than', 'taller than', 'shorter than', 'wider than', 'narrower than' correctly to describe the ordering.*
   (No units at this stage: comparisons are made directly placing objects side by side.)

2. *To choose and use an appropriate non-standard unit of length (from digit, span or cubit) to measure the length of an object.*

3. *To state the results of 2 using the language 'is about . . . units' and 'is between . . . and . . . units'.*

(For example, 'the length of the desk is about 8 spans' or 'the length of the desk is between 8 and 9 spans'.)

4. *To measure and compare distances, using paces and the language 'further than' and 'nearer than'.*
(For example, it is 90 paces to the front entrance, and 55 paces to the hall; the front entrance is further away than the hall.)

5. *To recognise that the length of a given object is unchanged when it is moved to a new position.*
(This is the idea of conservation of length.)

6. *To measure the length of a room, a corridor, or a distance in the playground in metres, using a metre stick, or a trundle wheel.*

7. *To measure the linear dimensions of an object to the nearest centimetre, using a 30-cm ruler, a metre ruler or a tape measure.*

8. *To recall that 1 metre is 100 cm.*

9. *To draw a line or to measure out a distance of a given length in centimetres or metres, using appropriate measuring devices.*

10. *To measure and compare the lengths, widths or heights of two objects, and, using a calculator if necessary, to formulate statements using the appropriate language of comparison.*
(For example, if person A is 125 cm tall, and person B is 143 cm tall, to state that A is 18 cm shorter than B.)

11. *To recall the lengths of some specific objects or distances, used as reference items, including a 30-cm ruler and a metre stick.*
(See comments above: the approximate width of a child's finger, the height of the classroom door, a circuit of the school running-track might be used.)

12. *To estimate, by eye, the length of an object in centimetres, up to 200 cm, to within 25% either way.*
(For example, given a length of 80 cm, any estimate between 60 cm and 100 cm would be acceptable.)

13. *To recall approximately how far it is in miles to significant places from their home.*
(For example, how far to school, how far to London or Newcastle upon Tyne.)

14. *To translate correctly between centimetres and metres.*
    (For example, 185 cm = 1.85 m.)

15. *Use a simple one-to-one scale to make scale-drawings.*

16. *Follow instructions for construction tasks involving measurements in centimetres, including the use of a set square for making right angles.*

OBJECTIVES FOR WEIGHT

Weight and mass

Strictly, we should not say that the *weight* of an apple is 300 grams, but that the *mass* of the apple is 300 grams, or that the apple *weighs the same as* 300 grams. This is because grams (kilograms, pounds, ounces etc.) are actually units of mass. The weight of an object is strictly the force of gravity acting on it, and should therefore be measured in the units of force, such as newtons. (See Haylock and Cockburn, 1989, for a fuller discussion of this issue.) I have not maintained the distinction between mass and weight in my work with low attainers on this topic simply because in practice most people talk about weight, where they mean mass. To be pedantic about the language here will confuse unnecessarily pupils who often have special deficiencies in language anyway, and we must therefore just concede to the colloquial usage.

Units for weight

Imperial units continue to cause confusion here. Most pre-packed produce is sold in metric units of weight, but fruit and vegetables from a market stall are likely to be sold by the pound, and it is common to buy, for example, half a pound of cheese or six ounces of ham from the delicatessen counter in the supermarket. Although most recipes in cookery give the weights of ingredients in grams, many give them in ounces as well. We cannot ignore in the classroom the pupil's experience of weight measurements outside of it, so some limited recognition of these continuing uses of imperial units must be made. It is particularly important for low-attaining pupils to build on their day-to-day experiences and to relate what we do in mathematics lessons to the real world, so the case for some concessions to the continuing use of imperial units is even stronger for them. I have therefore included some objectives related to pounds and ounces.

Reference items for weight

In helping low-attaining pupils to develop a sense of the size of the units we use for measuring weight, I have found some useful reference items to be:

(a) an individual packet of crisps weighs 30 grams; (b) a standard packet of tea weighs 125 grams; (c) a standard size tin of baked beans weighs about 500 grams (including the tin); (d) a litre of water weighs a kilogram (1000 grams). A set of such items as these can be made available for comparison in the classroom when the topic of weight is being taught. Children should memorise their weights. Important aspects of language here and throughout this topic are the words used for comparison: 'heavier than' and 'lighter than'.

Realistic and relevant objectives for weight

To have a basic competence in handling the concept of weight in practical situations, the low-attaining pupil, by the age of 12 years, should therefore be able:

1. *To order a set of two or three objects by weight, using a simple balance, and to use the language 'is heavier than' and 'is lighter than' correctly to describe the ordering.*
   (No units at this stage: comparisons are made directly by balancing one object against another.)

2. *To choose and use an appropriate non-standard unit of weight and a simple balance to weigh an object.*

3. *To state the results of 2 using the language 'weighs about the same as' and 'weighs between . . . and . . .'.*
   (For example, 'the book weighs about the same as 9 pebbles' or 'the book weighs between 9 and 10 pebbles'.)

4. *To recognise that the weight of a given object is unchanged when its shape is transformed or when it is reassembled in some way.*
   (This is the idea of conservation of weight.)

5. *To use a simple balance and 1-gram, 10-gram, 100-gram and 1-kilogram weights to weigh an object.*

6. *To recall that 1 kilogram is 1000 g, that a half-kilogram is 500 g, that a quarter-kilogram is 250 g.*

7. *Use a spring-type weighing device to weigh an object.*
   (For example, to use kitchen scales to determine that a book weighs 350 g.)

8. *To follow the instructions in a recipe (or science experiment) to measure out a given weight of some substance, in grams, or ounces, using a balance-type or a spring-type weighing device.*
   (For example, to measure out 250 g of flour for a recipe in cookery.)

9. *To measure and compare the weights of two objects and, using a calculator if necessary, to formulate statements using 'is . . . heavier than' or 'is . . . lighter than'.*
(For example, if object A is found to weigh 250 g and object B to weigh 750 g, to state that A is 500 g lighter than B.)

10. *To recall the weights in grams of some reference items, including a litre of water (1000 g).*
(See comments above: these items might be a 30-gram packet of crisps, a 125-gram packet of tea, and a 500-gram tin of baked beans.)

11. *To estimate, by holding in the hand, the weight of an object in grams, up to 1000 g, to within 40% either way.*
(For example, given a container holding 100 g, any estimate between 60 g and 140 g would be acceptable.)

12. *To determine, by holding in the hand, whether a given object has a weight which is less than, about equal to, or more than (a) a kilogram, (b) 100 g, (c) a pound, (d) half a pound.*
(In fairly obvious cases: for example, a book might be recognised as weighing less than a kilogram but more than 100 g.)

13. *To translate correctly between grams and kilograms.*
(For example, 750 g = 0.750 kg.)

14. *To use conversion charts between imperial and metric units which occur in cookery.*
(This might involve, for example, conversion between grams and ounces.)

OBJECTIVES FOR CAPACITY AND LIQUID VOLUME

Units for capacity and liquid volume

Capacity refers to the volume of water (or other liquid) which can be held by a container. In the metric system, liquid volume and capacities are both usually measured in litres or millilitres (1 litre = 1000 ml). Cubic centimetres and cubic metres are also units for measuring volume, but the convention is that these are reserved for volumes of solids. One cubic centimetre is actually the same volume as one millilitre.

Most produce sold by volume in supermarkets is measured in litres or millilitres, although some are marked in centilitres (1 cl = 10 ml) or even decilitres (1 dl = 100 ml). With low attainers we should use just millilitres and litres, to avoid the confusion caused by too many different units.

There are some difficult decisions to be made concerning the use of the imperial units for liquid volume which continue in use in everyday life. With one group of low-attaining 10–11-year-olds, I found the most common reference point they used for discussing and comparing volumes was a 'pint of milk'. In fact they nearly all referred to a half-litre carton as 'a pint of milk', although it is actually about 0.88 of a pint. Some drinks are also still sold by the pint or half pint, and pints and half pints occur in many recipes. It seems appropriate, therefore, to include some reference to pints in our work in school.

Fluid ounces (20 to the pint) occur only in recipes: to my knowledge, nothing is sold in fluid ounces, although some 500-ml cartons of milk, for example, have the equivalent in fluid ounces (17.6) marked on them. Since all recipes which children encounter which give liquid volumes in fluid ounces will also give them in millilitres, I would propose that we exclude fluid ounces from their experience in school. Petrol is now sold in litres, even though many people continue to think in terms of gallons. We will not do our low attainers a serious disservice by also excluding reference to gallons.

Reference items for capacity and liquid volume

Helpful reference items for developing pupils' sense of the size of the metric units for capacity and liquid volume are: (a) a standard can of drink, 330 ml; (b) a wine bottle, 750 ml; (c) a one-litre carton of milk or fruit juice. Children should memorise the capacities of these specific items. They should be available in the classroom and referred to repeatedly, comparing them with other containers. The key language for comparison here is 'holds more than' and 'holds less than'.

Realistic and relevant objectives for capacity and liquid volume

To have a basic competence in handling the concepts of capacity and liquid volume in practical situations, the low-attaining pupil, by the age of 12, should therefore be able:

1. *To order a set of two or three containers for capacity by pouring from one to the other*.

2. *To choose an appropriate non-standard unit (teaspoon, egg-cup etc.) to measure and compare the capacities of two given containers*.

3. *To recognise that a given volume of water is unchanged when poured from one container to another*.
   (This is the idea of conservation of volume.)

4. *To use a litre container or a pint container to measure the approximate capacity of a larger container.*
(For example, to measure the capacity of a bucket by filling it with litres of water.)

5. *To use a calibrated measuring jug or container to measure the capacity of a container in millilitres.*

6. *To follow the instructions in a recipe (or a science experiment) to measure out a given quantity of liquid in millilitres.*
(For example, to measure out 250 ml of milk for a recipe in cookery.)

7. *To recall that 1 litre is 1000 ml, that a half litre is 500 ml, that a quarter litre is 250 ml.*

8. *To measure and compare the capacities of two containers and, using a calculator if necessary, to formulate statements using 'holds ... more than' or 'holds ... less than'.*
(For example, if container A is found to hold 250 ml and container B to hold 750 ml, to state that A holds 500 ml less than B.)

9. *To recall the capacity in millilitres of a can of drink (330 ml), a wine bottle (750 ml) and a litre carton of drink (1000 ml).*

10. *To estimate the capacity of a container in millilitres, up to 1000 ml, to within 40% either way.*
(For example, given a container holding 100 ml, any estimate between 60 ml and 140 ml would be acceptable.)

11. *To determine, by eye, whether a given container has a capacity which is less than, about equal to, or more than a litre, or a pint.*
(In fairly obvious cases: for example, a wine bottle should be recognised as having a capacity more than a pint.)

12. *To translate correctly between millilitres and litres.*
(For example, 750 ml = 0.750 litres.)

OBJECTIVES FOR TIME

Time intervals and recorded time

There are two aspects of time to be developed, both very important components of numeracy, necessary for coping confidently with the demands of everyday life.

First there is the notion of a *time interval*, the length of time which passes between two instants, the amount of time that an event or activity takes.

For example, we might say that the mathematics lesson lasts for one hour. Then there is the idea of *recorded time*, the time at which an event occurs. So, we might say that the mathematics lesson begins at 9:20 am. The idea of recorded time can include days of the week, dates and years: we could say, for example, that the mathematics lesson begins at 9:20 am on Wednesday 3rd February 1993. Children have to learn both how to measure and manipulate time intervals and how to tell and record the time.

Digital or dial?

A major problem in teaching children to tell the time is that many children have digital watches and first learn to tell the time with reference to these, whereas others have the conventional dial watch. A further complication is that some children have digital watches which use the 24-hour system. Classroom clocks tend to be the dial type and most schemes seem to concentrate on telling the time from dial clocks first. We have to decide how best to build on the children's first-hand experience of telling the time. So, what is the actual situation with regard to children's personal watches? Teachers should determine how far the following data is typical of their own teaching situations.

In a recent survey of about 1000 children in the 8–12 age range in a variety of local schools, I found that only 32% were actually wearing a watch to school. Of those wearing watches, there was a slightly greater proportion with digital displays:

- 45% were wearing dial watches with hands (no digital display)
- 50% were wearing watches with digital displays only
- 5% were wearing watches with both digital and dial displays

Of those watches with digital displays, 45% could give the time in the 24-hour system. (Some digital watches give both the 12-hour and the 24-hour time.) There was, as would be expected, a tendency for more of the older pupils to have watches. There was also a marked tendency for more girls than boys to wear dial watches, and vice versa for digital watches.

It is, of course, actually easier to read the time from a digital display than it is to read it from a dial clock. It is the connection between the different forms of stating the time which is especially difficult. This, combined with the data about children's own watches, suggests that we might give more prominence in the early stages to telling the time by digital displays, thus using times in the form '3:45' before learning to read 'quarter-to-four' from a conventional dial clock. This reverses the normal order used in many schools for developing the skills of telling the time. We should also ensure that our classrooms have digital clocks on the wall as well as dial clocks: this obvious suggestion is probably one of the most effective ways of contributing to the achievement of many of the objectives below.

The 24-hour system

This then leaves the question of what to do about the 24-hour system with our low attainers. I would like to be able to omit this, because it does seem to cause considerable difficulties. We already have two ways of giving the time, with, for example, '3:40 pm' and 'twenty-to-four in the afternoon'. To add to this '15:40' is to increase the complications. But a significant number of pupils have 24-hour digital watches. Furthermore, bus and train timetables use the 24-hour system, as do many automatic timing devices such as video-recorders. The relevance criterion for objectives for low attainers makes the case for including a facility with the 24-hour system a strong one.

Some comments on the objectives for time

The first group of objectives for time focus on measuring time intervals. They progress from comparison, through measuring time intervals with non-standard units, to measuring and estimating time intervals in seconds. The obvious problem about actually measuring longer time intervals is that it takes a long time! But, through explicit discussion of the events of their lives, pupils should develop some awareness of what ten minutes, an hour, and so on, feel like. The next group of objectives focuses on recorded time using a digital display, first the 12-hour system and then the 24-hour.

If the pupils have a grasp of time intervals and can also tell the time from a digital display they can then move on to calculating time intervals, preferably in practical and realistic problems. Having seen some low-attaining pupils struggling needlessly with formal calculations of this kind, I would assert that these should definitely not be set out with one time written above the other and a subtraction algorithm being applied. This is a clear case where adhocorithms are superior and would be used by most people in practice.

Objectives related to telling the time from a conventional dial clock include the important ideas of 'nearly' and 'just after'. This set of objectives also includes the ability to translate between the different ways of recording time of day. I have *not* included here that the pupil should be able to draw the hands on a drawing of a clock-face to show a given time of day. This is a quite pointless skill.

Objectives for recorded time also include the use and understanding of a calendar. Finally, I have included three important applications of the knowledge, skills and concepts of time.

Because of the variety of experiences of clocks and watches which children will bring to this work, it is, of course, quite impossible to pre-ordain the order in which the objectives below will be achieved for any given pupil.

Realistic and relevant objectives for time

To have a basic competence in handling the concepts of time intervals and recorded time in practical situations, the low-attaining pupil, by the age of 12 years, should therefore be able:

1. *To make sensible statements about which of two familiar events takes a longer or a shorter time.*
   (For example, which takes the shorter time, school assembly or a football match?)

2. *To time activities or events using non-standard units, such as a pendulum or a tap dripping.*

3. *To time activities or events in seconds using the second counter of a digital watch, starting from zero, or a simple stop clock or stopwatch.*

4. *To make sensible statements about what they could do in one minute, two minutes, five minutes, ten minutes.*
   (For example, about how many pages of their reading book could they read in ten minutes?)

5. *To estimate a time interval in seconds, by counting, up to a minute, to within 25% either way.*
   (For example, given an interval of 45 seconds, any estimate between 34 seconds and 56 seconds would be acceptable.)

6. *To make sensible statements about how long events within their experience take, in minutes up to an hour, and in hours up to a day.*
   (For example, to state that walking to school takes about ten minutes; that they spend about six hours in school each day.)

7. *To state the number of seconds in a minute, the number of minutes in an hour, the number of hours in a day, and the number of days in a week.*

8. *To state the number of minutes in a quarter of an hour, half an hour, three-quarters of an hour.*

9. *To convert a time interval related to their experience (up to 5 hours) from hours and minutes to minutes, and vice versa.*
   (For example, a football match lasts 1 hour 30 minutes = 90 minutes.)

10. *To use correctly the notions of morning, midday, noon, afternoon, evening, night-time, midnight, and the o'clocks, in describing events of their day.*

(For example, to say what they will be doing at six o'clock in the evening.)

11. *To state what would be displayed on a 12-hour digital watch at significant times of the day.*
(For example, at the start of school, end of school, bed-time.)

12. *To describe what happens on a 12-hour digital watch display from one minute to the next, from one hour to the next, and in the course of a day.*
(For example, when the watch shows 3:59 what will it show next? What will it show one hour later?)

13. *To distinguish between am and pm.*

14. *To reset a 12-hour digital watch or clock to the correct time.*

15. *As for objectives 11, 12 and 14 using the 24-hour system.*

16. *To calculate how many minutes must pass from any given time on a 12-hour digital display to the next o'clock.*
(For example, if the watch now shows 3:48 how many minutes till 4 o'clock?)

17. *To calculate, by an informal adding-on process, the time interval from one digital time (12-hour) to another.*
(For example, to find the time for a train journey starting at 3:45 pm and arriving at 5:25 pm, the pupil could count 15 minutes to 4 pm, then an hour to 5 pm, then a further 25 minutes, giving a total of 1 hour 40 minutes. Note especially problems with events starting before noon and finishing after noon.)

18. *As for objectives 16 and 17 using the 24-hour system.*

19. *To read a conventional dial clock for o'clocks, half past, quarter past, quarter to.*

20. *To describe how the hands of a dial clock behave in one hour, two hours, 12 hours, a day, half an hour, quarter of an hour.*

21. *To tell the time to the nearest five minutes from a dial clock or watch, giving the answer in the colloquial form.*
(For example, 'twenty to four'.)

22. *To use the expressions 'nearly' and 'just after' appropriately when reading the time from a dial clock.*

23. *To reset a dial clock to the correct time.*
    (Preferable to drawing hands on clock faces!)

24. *To translate between times from a dial clock and the digital equivalents in the 12-hour and 24-hour systems.*
    (For example, to read a time of 'half past two in the afternoon' and to convert this to '2:30 pm' or '14:30'.)

25. *To order a set of times of the day given in a variety of forms, from earliest to latest.*
    (For example, to order: 3:40 pm, 12 noon, twenty to four in the morning, 18:00.)

26. *To recite the names of the days of the week, the months of the year and the seasons, in order, starting from any day, any month or any season.*

27. *To state the number of days in each month, the number of days in a year and a leap year.*

28. *To use a calendar to find and record the date, using the two common systems.*
    (For example, 3rd February 1993 or 03-02-93.)

29. *To use a calendar to find the number of days or weeks from one given date to another.*

30. *Explain the relationships between the earth's rotation and a day, and the earth's orbit round the sun and a year.*

31. *To compile a timetable for an event, given constraints of starting time, finishing time, number and length of time for various activities.*

32. *To set automatic timing devices.*
    (For example, time switches and electric cookers.)

33. *To programme a video recorder to record a sequence of television programmes.*

ESTIMATION CLASS-CHALLENGE (Activity 6.1)

This is an activity for use with a class of children which can always be included in the programme of activities, whatever aspect of measurement is being considered. In focusing on the measurement objectives related to estimation, it aims to develop the pupils' sense of what it is that is being measured and the size of the units concerned. If structured very carefully, it can also give low attainers in mathematics some successful experience of collecting and organising a set of data, displaying it in graphical form and interpreting the results.

Estimating length (length objectives 11 and 12)

The beginning of each mathematics lesson for a period of, say, eight days focusing on the topic of length measurement, is used for the class to make their estimates for some length. For the first four days the lesson should begin with a quick revision of the lengths of the reference items for length, the children being encouraged to memorise these and to use them for comparison. For the second four days the children may not need to be reminded of the reference items.

The teacher indicates or shows to the children an item for which they each must write down their estimate for its length on a slip of paper. These lengths should be up to 200 cm. Over a period of eight days with one low-attaining set I used, for example, the distance from my nose to my outstretched finger tip (101 cm), the length of my brief-case (43 cm), my height (183 cm), a pupil's height (142 cm), the width of a window-pane (50 cm), the height of the chalk-board (114 cm), the width of the door (84 cm) and the height of a desk (63 cm). The challenge to the class is to see if we can gradually get better and better at making estimates of length.

Handling the data

The slips of paper with the estimates are collected. I always make a point of not disclosing the actual measurement at this stage, keeping the class in some suspense. A group of three children is then given the responsibility of organising and presenting today's data in graphical form.

With low attainers this process should be very carefully structured. First, they put the slips of paper into piles, to determine how many estimates are in single figures, how many in the tens, how many in the twenties, the thirties, the forties and so on. I would advise against attempting any more complicated groupings of the data than this.

The graphs drawn each day should then follow a prescribed model: I actually provide the group on the first day with an example of what a finished graph should look like. Here is a simple suggestion for enabling low-attaining pupils to produce fairly quickly an effective and satisfying bar-chart.

Give the group a large sheet of 2-cm squared paper, a metre ruler for drawing axes, 2-cm-wide strips of coloured paper, a pair of scissors and a glue-stick. The horizontal axis is labelled 'estimates' and the vertical axis 'number of children'. The vertical axis can then be labelled from 0 to 20, and the horizontal axis labelled in tens, covering the range of estimates made by the class. Then, to represent on the graph the number of children in each group, they simply place a strip of coloured paper along the vertical axis, mark off carefully the length required, cut off this length and glue it onto the chart. This technique produces a colourful bar-chart in a way which is undoubtedly preferable to the children drawing the columns and then spending hours colouring them with felt-tip pens.

How did we do?

When the group has finished representing the data they are then allowed to measure the actual length of the item concerned. This is shown by an arrow on the graph. At the end of the lesson the teacher should show the graph to the class and discuss with them how well they have done today in their estimating. Over the course of eight lessons we can expect to see the children gradually getting better at estimating, and a wall display of the bar-charts produced each day (see Figure 6.2) should demonstrate this. The class should be challenged to get everybody giving an estimate within two groups either side of the actual length.

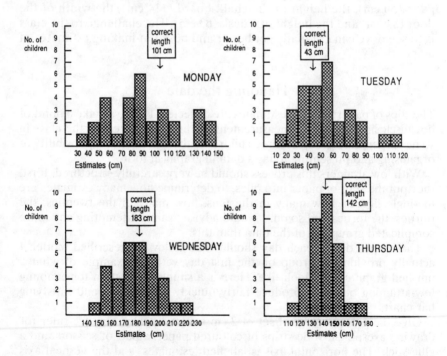

Figure 6.2   Bar-charts showing improvement in estimating lengths (Activity 6.1)

Estimating weight (weight objectives 10 and 11)

Exactly the same estimation project can later be repeated for the topic of weight. This time the teacher presents each day an object which is passed round the class for the children to handle and to estimate the weight. It is useful to have several identical objects, otherwise it may take most of the lesson for the children to make their estimates. The weights should be up to 1000 g. Examples might be: a text-book (240 g), a can of drink (360 g), a National Curriculum document (870 g), a lump of Plasticine (550 g), a half-litre carton of milk (450 g), and so on. The revision and handling of reference items is again important in the early stages of the project.

As with length, I would propose that the handling of the data is tightly structured for low-attaining pupils. The estimates should be grouped simply in hundreds: those up to a hundred, those in the one hundreds, the two hundreds, and so on. Once again, when the bar-chart is completed the children concerned can weigh the object to determine the actual weight, and then indicate this on their graph. The challenge could again be to get all the class within two groups either side of the actual weight.

Estimating capacity (capacity objectives 9 and 10)

This follows exactly the same pattern as the weight project. A range of containers (bottles, cans, jars, vases, jugs) is used, with the teacher each day showing one of them clearly to the class for them to estimate the capacity. The reference items – a can of drink (330 ml), a wine bottle (750 ml) and a litre carton (1000 ml) – again play an important part in the process of estimating. As with weight, the estimates can just be grouped in hundreds.

Estimating time (time objective 5)

A similar project can be run on the topic of time. Since we do not have reference items for time available for direct comparison in the same way as we do for length, weight and capacity, I would start the first few lessons of the topic by getting pupils to count out loud, together with me, in seconds. Then each day they are required to write down their estimates for a time interval in seconds, up to a minute. I do this by asking them to close their eyes and then, in silence, to estimate the number of seconds which passes between my clapping my hands once and my clapping them a second time. Using the second-counter on my watch, I give them a range of time intervals, such as 23 seconds, 48 seconds, 37 seconds, and so on. For grouping the data here it is probably necessary to use a smaller interval size than 10 seconds, in order to distribute the children's estimates across a number of groups. Five-second intervals (0–4, 5–9, 10–14, 15–19, . . .) are usually appropriate.

SOME MEASUREMENT GAMES

In this section I give some examples of games, all of which have been used successfully with low attainers for developing skills and concepts related to the objectives for measurement. These may be useful to supplement the more conventional activities of measuring which are implied by and necessary for the objectives specified above.

Activity 6.2 Estimation challenge

Objectives This small-group game focuses on *weight objectives 5 and 11*.

Materials Two balance-type weighing devices, a supply of 100-g weights, a supply of Plasticine, wood-shavings, ball-bearings, etc., some light plastic jars.

Rules Two pairs of children play against each other. Behind a screen, each pair measures out a quantity of some of the material available, into one of the jars. The weight of material should be approximately a multiple of 100 grams. For example, one pair might choose to measure out 200 g of Plasticine, while the other might measure out 800 g of ball-bearings. Each team then has to estimate the weight of the contents of their opponent's jar. One point for getting within 100 g, two points for getting it correct.

Variation For *length objectives 9 and 12*, the children could use a metre ruler to draw lines of a length of their choosing. The opposing team has to estimate the length of the line.

Activity 6.3 Kilogram challenge

Objectives This is another estimation game for a small group of children, focusing on *weight objectives 5, 6 and 11*, and also giving experience of multiplication in the context of weight (see Chapter 7). Teachers may be surprised at how quickly even low-attaining pupils develop the ability to make the estimates required for this game.

Materials Players need access to various objects for weighing, a balance-type weighing device, with a supply of 1-g, 10-g and 100-g weights, a calculator each.

Rules It is useful to have one child acting as umpire for this game. One of the players chooses an object. Each player then estimates how many of these would be needed to weigh a kilogram or more. Their estimates are written down by the umpire, who then weighs the object. If it is less than 50 g then all the other players automatically win a point: this rule is to discourage players from choosing very light objects. Provided this is not the case, the players then use their calculators to determine the minimum number of the object needed to weigh 1 kg or more. A point is awarded to any player getting this right.

For example, a paperback book, which is found to weigh about 225 g, might be chosen. A player might estimate that four of these would be needed to weigh more than 1 kg. When they check this on their calculator they find that $225 \times 4 = 900$. Then they try 225×5 and from the result (1125) decide that five of the books would be required.

Variation A messier version of the game, using the context of capacity and liquid volume, can be played with water and a supply of containers. Players estimate how many of these would be required to exceed a litre.

Activity 6.4 Time-cards

Objectives This activity for a small group of pupils relates to a number of *time objectives*, for example, *10, 11, 13, 24 and 25*, in the area of recorded time. There is also opportunity for practice of timing an activity, using a stop-clock (*time objective 3*).

Materials The children themselves should prepare a frieze on card, showing significant events in their day. They could do this individually, or as a group. Figure 6.3 is an example of what might be done, using 12-hour digital times and the corresponding colloquial versions. The 24-hour equivalents could be added if appropriate. Some children will prefer to draw the events of the day rather than write them. The frieze can then be cut up into cards and used in various activities for practising the ordering of times of the day. The frieze shown in Figure 6.3 produces 24 cards, for example. A stop clock or stopwatch may also be required.

Method The cards are muddled up and the children should be challenged to re-assemble the frieze. This can be done one at time with pupils timing each other, using a stop clock.

One pupil can then be given cards for the events of the day, another the digital times and a third the colloquial equivalents. They re-assemble these separately and then check to see if the three lines correspond.

Variations Two rows of cards are removed from the frieze, turned face down and muddled up. Pupils take it in turns to turn over two cards. If these give the same time of day the pupil wins a point, the cards are placed

asleep in bed	arrive at school	assembly	play time	having lunch	end of school	watching TV	going to bed
5:00 am	8:30 am	9:15 am	10:30 am	12:30 pm	3:45 pm	6:30 pm	9:00 pm
5 o'clock in the morning	half past 8 in the morning	quarter past 9 in the morning	half past 10 in the morning	half past 12 in the afternoon	quarter to 4 in the afternoon	half past 6 in the evening	9 o'clock in the evening

Figure 6.3   Example of frieze for Activity 6.4: Time-cards

back in their positions in the frieze and the player gets another turn. If they do not match they are turned face down again.

Activity 6.5 Messages to order

Objective More practice of ordering times of day, as in *time objective 25.*

Materials A set of cards with times of the day written on one side and letters, spelling out a message, written on the other. Figure 6.4 is an example.

Method The cards are muddled up and given to a pupil, or pair of pupils, who must arrange them to show the times in the correct order. When this is done they turn them over to reveal a message. For example, the cards in Figure 6.4 give the message 'GENIUS!'

Variations Pupils enjoy making their own set of these cards to give to other pupils to find the message.

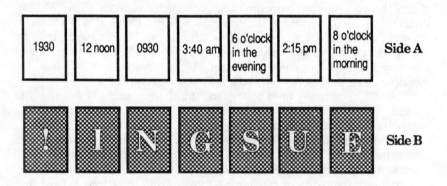

Figure 6.4   Example of cards for messages to order (Activity 6.5)

Activity 6.6 Timing calculations

Objective Practice in timing events, using a stop clock (*time objective 3*) as well as useful practice in key-pressing and reading answers on a calculator.

Materials Two calculators and a stop clock; pencil and paper.

Method Pupils work in pairs. Each pupil, using a calculator, prepares a two-option multi-choice test for the other. This is just a list of ten sums, two-digit numbers only, with a choice of a correct answer or an incorrect answer. The incorrect answer should always use the same digits, but with the last two reversed. This forces the pupils to take great care in reading the digits on display in their calculator results. It will be necessary, of course, for the teacher to give the pupils an example of what is required to get them started. For instance, one player's test might begin:

23 × 59	1357	1375
48 + 67	151	115
76 ÷ 43	1.7674418	1.7674481

They then use the stop clock, in turn, to time each pupil in answering the other's questions on their calculators, ringing the correct option each time. A simple way of scoring is to add on an extra ten seconds for each incorrect answer.

Activity 6.7 Calendar puzzle

Objective This puzzle is a very good way of assessing pupils' grasp of the structure of a calendar (*time objectives 26 and 27*).

Materials An old calendar, with the months cut out separately and the names of the months removed.

Rules The problem is simply to re-assemble the calendar – to decide which month is January, which is February, etc., and to arrange them in order. Pupils normally need a hint that they should start by identifying February.

Before they tackle this they need to revise the order of the months, and the number of days in each month.

Activity 6.8 Watch the clock

Objective To develop pupils' ability to tell the time (*time objectives 11, 12, 13, 15, 19, 20, 21, etc.*). Pupils are simply encouraged to keep their eye on the classroom clock and to become aware of the time of day.

Materials The classroom clock (dial or digital, preferably both) and a set of cards with times of the day written on them. Some small rewards, such as chocolate buttons.

Method At the start of the school day (or a mathematics lesson), give each child a card with a time of day written on it. This could be at whatever level or in whatever form is appropriate to the individual child. For example, some pupils may be given something as simple as '10 o'clock', whereas others might be given '14:30'. The normal lessons then just continue for the day. However, the pupils are expected to keep an eye on the clock and when it gets to the time on their card they should hand the card to the teacher and collect their reward. If they miss their time, they miss the reward, but should get some appropriate explanation from the teacher. It is amazing how quickly pupils in this informal way will pick up the skills of telling the time, which we struggle to teach them through more formal exercises. Try this for a week and see the improvement.

Activity 6.9 Reading a scale

Objective This is a suggestion for a simple but effective model for enabling pupils to practise reading a scale for liquid volume (*capacity objective 5*)

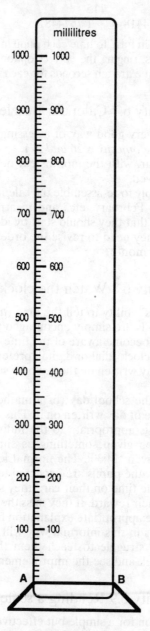

Figure 6.5   Model for practice in reading a scale

without the practical difficulties involved in having pupils pouring water all round the classroom.

Materials A photo-copy of the picture shown in Figure 6.5 is required for each pupil. A slit is cut in the picture along line AB. A strip of coloured paper, the same width as AB, is passed through the slit. This can then be moved up and down to represent water or other liquid in the container. Various games can be devised to enable pupils to practise reading off the level shown on the scale.

Game Each round of this game begins with each pupil in a small group setting their 'water levels' to whatever point on the scale they wish, and writing down the volume. One more capable pupil, acting as umpire, checks these. There are two packs of cards: the cards in one pack have various volumes written on them (e.g. 450 ml); those in the other have either 'more than' or 'less than'. The umpire turns over a card from each pack, to reveal, for example, 'less than 450 ml'. In this case each pupil who has set their water level to less than 450 ml wins a point.

SOME PURPOSEFUL ACTIVITIES IN MEASURING CONTEXTS

Low attainers, who find many of the exercises in the school mathematics scheme to be confusing and purposeless, stand their best chance of developing the knowledge, skills and concepts of measurement through their application to purposeful activities. Following the instructions for measuring out ingredients in a recipe in cookery is the best example of a purposeful activity for achieving many of the objectives listed in this chapter for weight and liquid volume. My view is that practical cookery should be regarded as part of the mathematics curriculum, especially for low-attaining pupils. Two examples of activities with some genuine purpose, involving each of length measurement and time measurement, are given below.

Activity 6.10 Make a box (length objectives 7, 9 and 16)

Identify some materials in the classroom for which a storage-box is required, such as a set of calculators or a set of text-books. A box to hold the plastic token-coins, with separate compartments for 1p, 10p and £1 coins would also be very useful. Pupils, working in pairs, undertake to make the various boxes. When completed, the best ones should actually be used, so that the activity is genuinely purposeful.

Pupils have to make a number of mathematical decisions, both spatial and numerical. For example, they must decide on the layout of the materials in the box (are the 24 calculators stacked in 4 rows of 6, or 3 rows of 8, or how?) and the positioning of flaps. To get some ideas about how boxes are made, the pupils could take a few boxes apart and examine their nets.

The pupils should start by making a prototype from paper and Sellotape.

This will involve measuring the dimensions of the materials, drawing lines and right angles accurately, deciding on flaps, and possibly doing some calculations. One group of low attainers, making a box for a class set of calculators, measured the width of one calculator to be 7 cm, then used the calculator to multiply 7 by 24 and decided that the box had to be 168 cm long. They did not get far with their prototype before deciding that this was not actually the best solution. Once the prototype is found to be successful or modified appropriately, the plan can be transferred and the box constructed from card and glue.

Activity 6.11 Arranging the classroom (length objectives 6, 9 and 15)

What is the best way of arranging the furniture in the classroom? Pupils can be asked to work in groups to solve this problem, with the best arrangements to be accepted and tried out for a day or two, so that the activity is genuinely purposeful. The problem will be solved by the pupils producing a scale-drawing of the classroom showing the fixed positions of doors and windows and their proposals for the arrangement of the furniture.

To be suitable for low attainers this activity will have to be structured carefully. If a scale of 1:10 is used, for a classroom 6 metres by 8 metres, pupils will require a piece of paper 60 cm by 80 cm. This is larger than the normal large-size squared paper, so the children will need to stick two pieces together. (A scale of 1:100 would be too small.) So, the decision might be to work on squared paper where 10 cm on the paper represents 1 metre in the room. This is a bit complicated: note that objective 15 talks about simple one-to-one scales. However we can use squared paper marked in centimetres, with larger 10-cm squares highlighted. The children are then told to use the length of one of these larger squares to represent one metre in the room. If they are using 30-metre tape-measures marked in metres and tenths of a metre, they may also be able to cope with the idea that each extra little bit of a metre is represented by the length of one of the smaller squares on the squared paper.

They can then make scale-drawings to represent tables (or other furniture), again using a simplified version of the 1:10 scale. They measure the tables in centimetres (e.g. 60 cm by 80 cm) and then draw these on millimetre-squared paper. They do not have to know how to handle millimetres, just to use the idea that one centimetre of table length is represented by the length of one of the little squares on the paper.

Clearly, there are also some important spatial concepts involved in the final process of deciding how to fit the scale-drawings of the furniture into the plan of the room.

Activity 6.12 Timetables (several time objectives)

Many situations arise in schools and classrooms where teachers have to devise timetables for pupils. We can look for opportunities to hand these over to our pupils. With low attainers it will be necessary to prepare for and structure this task carefully to allow for their limitations.

A useful preparatory activity is for each pupil to keep a personal record of how they spend their time at school for a week, using a chart like the one shown in Figure 6.6. Every fifteen minutes the teacher can stop the class and get them to fill in an entry on the chart.

This may sound tedious, but by the end of a week the children will have developed a surprising confidence in handling time concepts. They will also have become clock-watchers, which, as far as attaining the objectives for time is concerned, is no bad thing. Some pupils may then be able to extend the activity to keeping a record of how they spend their time out of school as well.

After a week of time-recording like this they can then tackle problems of timetabling. For example, working in pairs, using the same kind of structured grid as in Figure 6.3, they could devise the timetable for a day (or several days) at school, given whatever constraints the teacher wishes to impose: these timetables could be put on display and the whole class could vote on which one to adopt. They could devise the timetable for a sports event, an entertainment or a class trip.

	Monday	Tuesday	Wednesday	Thursday	Friday
9:15 am					
9:30 am					
9:45 am					
10:00 am					
10:15 am					
10:30 am					
10:45 am					
11:00 am					
11:15 am					
11:30 am					
11:45 am					
12 noon					

Figure 6.6   Chart for personal timetable (Activity 6.12)

Activity 6.13 Programming a video (time objective 33)

One group of teachers who worked with me on the problems of low attainers

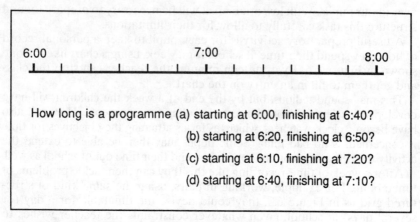

How long is a programme (a) starting at 6:00, finishing at 6:40?

(b) starting at 6:20, finishing at 6:50?

(c) starting at 6:10, finishing at 7:20?

(d) starting at 6:40, finishing at 7:10?

Figure 6.7   Preparation for programming a video (Activity 6.13)

in mathematics decided that this is the ultimate objective for teaching time. If the pupil can successfully programme a video to record a sequence of programmes, transmitted over several days, then a large proportion of the objectives for time will have been achieved. If there are programmes which we want recorded for use in school in a particular week, then setting the video recorder is a job for our low-attaining pupils, not one for the school secretary. Teaching them to do this, using the information in the published TV schedules, will be the most useful learning experience we could possibly give them in this aspect of measurement.

To lead up to this facility, one teacher found it helpful to give a group of low-attaining pupils a worksheet like the one shown in Figure 6.7. This was then followed by worksheets with other time lines marked in ten-minute intervals, and extended to lines marked in five-minute intervals. Before setting the video, the pupils recorded their plans in a table with these headings:

Programme title   Day   Start time   Finish time   Length in minutes

QUESTIONS FOR FURTHER DISCUSSION

1. Can you improve on my suggestions for reference items for length, weight and capacity?
2. What other explanations might there be of a pupil's incorrect response to the conservation of volume task shown in Figure 6.1? How might a pupil's grasp of the principles of conservation of length, weight and liquid volume be recognised through activities embedded in more meaningful contexts?
3. How could Activity 6.2 be adapted for capacity and liquid volume, and Activity 6.3 for length?
4. Can you devise some other games using calendars (see Activity 6.7) which could be used to help pupils achieve time objectives 26–29?

7

CHOOSING THE OPERATION

A PRIMARY OBJECTIVE FOR NUMERACY

The objective

In this chapter I consider in detail what I referred to in Chapter 4 as 'the most basic and important objective for numeracy'. In a technological, calculator age, more important than being able to do the actual calculations is that the pupil should be able:

- to state what calculation should be entered on a calculator in order to solve a practical problem, for each of the operations, addition, subtraction, multiplication, division, using any of the models of the operation, and in any appropriate context, and to be able to interpret the answer.

This objective is seen as crucial for two reasons: (a) because it is useful, and (b) because it forms an important component in the development of the pupil's understanding of number operations.

Knowing what calculation to do and which keys to enter on the calculator in all the different practical situations one might encounter is surely a fundamental component of numeracy, enabling pupils to cope confidently with the numerical demands of everyday life. It is also an indication of real understanding, since choosing the operation involves a direct connection between the symbols of arithmetic and the corresponding concrete situations. In my work with low attainers I have made this my primary objective. Far from being a trivial exercise, this has always proved to be a major undertaking. But it seems to me to be so important that as much time as is necessary must be given to it.

The problem is that, although many teachers would accept that 'knowing what sum to do' is an important objective, particularly for low attainers, it is very rare for a teacher (or a scheme) to tackle this in a systematic way. So I have tried in writing this chapter to work out precisely what is involved in the objective: in precisely what situations pupils might be called on to choose the operation. To analyse the task facing us as teachers in working towards this objective, I outline below what I mean here by *contexts* and *models*, and then describe how they relate to each other in *classes of problems*. I will then provide examples of the kinds of practical problems which come into each of these classes, where the pupil could be required to determine what calculation should be entered on the calculator to solve the problem.

Contexts

First, notice that the objective refers to 'any appropriate context'. There are many contexts in which calculations may need to be done, such as those aspects of pupils' lives identified in Figure 4.2 as 'meaningful contexts'. The numbers which turn up in these situations will usually be attached to a set of things, or, most frequently, to money, or sometimes to a measurement of some kind. It is helpful, therefore, to analyse this question of choosing the operation in terms of the following categories of contexts:

- sets of things
- money
- length and distance
- weight
- capacity and liquid volume
- time

In the present analysis I am concerned only with developing the pupil's ability to choose the appropriate operation for a calculation which might arise in these contexts. This assumes the availability of relevant knowledge, skills and concepts associated with the aspects of measurement which are listed above which have been considered in Chapter 6. Two aspects of measurement normally included in the mathematics syllabus for 8–12-year-olds, namely, area and solid volume, have again been deliberately excluded from the list of contexts above. There are not many practical situations in which calculations with areas or volumes of solids would actually be required. In practice, problems about area, such as those associated with fitting carpets, are often solved by manipulating lengths.

Models

Part of the difficulty here, as has been highlighted already in Chapter 3, is that the pupil has to learn to connect the same mathematical symbol (+, −, × or ÷) to a great variety of different situations. These situations vary not just in terms of the contexts, but also in the actual mathematical structure of the problem and the logical relationships between its numerical components. There are different *models* for each operation. The models which will be considered in the following analysis are:

- the *aggregation* model of addition
- the *augmentation* model of addition

- the *partitioning* model of subtraction
- the *reduction* model of subtraction
- the *comparison* model of subtraction
- the *inverse-of-addition* model of subtraction

- the *repeated-aggregation* model of multiplication

- the *equal-sharing* model of division
- the *inverse-of-multiplication* model of division

Each of these models is explained and illustrated later in the chapter.

Classes of problems: addition and subtraction

The above analysis suggests that just the two models of addition and the four models of subtraction operating in the six contexts (sets, money, etc) could generate thirty-six different kinds of situations in which the pupil might be required to choose the correct operation to enter on a calculator. These *classes of problems* are represented by the cells in the grid shown in Figure 7.1. (Multiplication and division are considered later in the chapter.) The intersections of the augmentation and reduction models with the

CONTEXTS

MODELS	Sets	Money	Length	Weight	Capacity	Time
Aggregation	+	+	+	+	+	+
Augmentation	✕	+	+	+	+	+
Partitioning	−	−	−	−	−	−
Reduction	✕	−	−	−	−	−
Comparison	−	−	−	−	−	−
Inverse of addition	−	−	−	−	−	−

Figure 7.1 Classes of addition and subtraction problems

context of sets have been crossed through because these operations are not appropriate to this context.

The classes of problems indicated in Figure 7.1 vary greatly in the extent to which they are realistic and purposeful. Some classes contain problems which are genuine, can be presented in a practical mode and which are likely to be meaningful to pupils. But in other cases the kinds of problem which could be presented to pupils are rather artificial, or can only be presented in story mode, or are likely to be not as purposeful for the pupils as one might hope. However, even the less purposeful or artificial problems contribute to the building up of connections between the symbols, the associated language and the classes of problems, which are so important in the development of the pupil's *understanding* of the operations of addition, subtraction, multiplication and division.

Examples of the kinds of problem which might be generated within each class shown in Figure 7.1 are given in the next two sections, where each model of addition and subtraction is considered in turn. In each example the question presented to pupils would be:

what calculation do you enter on your calculator to solve this problem?

The extent to which the class generates genuine, relevant and purposeful problems will be an important consideration in determining the priority to be given to that class in our work with low attainers. However, if a pupil were able to choose the appropriate operation for all these classes of problems then I would feel fairly confident in asserting that they had a good level of understanding of addition and subtraction. The questions given below also vary in terms of the complexity of the numbers involved, from two-digit whole numbers to measurements to two decimal places. Teachers would obviously adapt the questions in this respect to suit the children concerned. Clearly the structure of the problem is not affected by the actual numbers used, though the interpretation of the result obtained on the calculator may be a more difficult task in some cases.

ADDITION MODELS

The following section attempts to illustrate all the kinds of situations in which the two models of addition might occur: situations in which pupils would have to recognise that the operation to be entered on their calculator to solve the problem is addition. Since addition is a *commutative* operation ('a + b' is always equal to 'b + a') the numbers in the calculator key sequences can, of course, be entered in either order.

The aggregation model of addition

The *aggregation model* would include all situations in which two (or more) quantities are combined into a single quantity and addition is required to find the total number or measurement. Examples of the kinds of questions pupils should be able to answer with their calculators, to show that this model of addition is recognised, are given below for each context in turn.

Aggregation: sets

This is the basic class of addition problems which most pupils would associate with the operation. Examples of problems using the aggregation model in the context of sets of things could be fairly realistic and related to the pupils' immediate surroundings:

- a pupil first determines how many children in each of two classes; how many pupils altogether?
- to find out if there are enough pencils to go round, one pupil counts the number of pencils in one pot, another the number in a second pot; how many altogether?

Aggregation: money

This class of problems has a high degree of relevance and meaning for pupils. Plenty of situations arise in which a pupil would need to add prices or amounts of money together to find the total:

- to find out the total cost of a number of purchases on a shopping list
- to find the total money raised by two classes in a fund-raising event, if one raised £5.95 and the other raised £3.27

Aggregation: length and distance, weight, capacity and liquid volume

Although pupils are likely to recognise the need for addition when two measurements are aggregated, these class of problems are likely to be fairly artificial or lacking in immediacy:

- to make curtains for the living-room we need 6.50 m of material, and for the dining-room we need 4.75 m; what length is needed altogether?
- the distance from Norwich to Edinburgh by road is 369 miles, and from Edinburgh to Aberdeen is 127 miles; how far from Norwich to Aberdeen, via Edinburgh?
- if you buy 280 g of cheese and 250 g of butter what weight do you have to carry?

However, a pupil's understanding of the aggregation model could clearly be assessed through practical experiences of measuring weight and capacity:

- the pupil weighs separately two objects in grams and then calculates the total weight, before checking this by a further weighing
- the pupil measures separately the capacities of two containers in millilitres, then calculates the total capacity before checking this by a further measurement

Aggregation: time

Most real-life problems about time are likely to be solved by informal methods, rather than by entering a calculation on a calculator. This is because of the mixed and non-metric units involved. Problems involving the aggregation of time intervals are again likely to be fairly artificial and have to be expressed in terms of a single unit (e.g. minutes) before a calculator could be used:

- it takes 115 minutes by train from Norwich to Liverpool Street, and then a further 45 minutes to get to South Harrow on the Underground; how long for the whole journey?
- in planning a school event of some kind, pupils might have to aggregate the times required for various activities within the programme

The augmentation model of addition

The *augmentation model* refers to situations where a quantity is increased by some amount, such as a price increase or a weight increase, and addition is required to find the augmented or increased value. The distinction between augmentation and aggregation is not always easy to maintain, but it is essentially that in aggregation two (or more) things are combined, whereas in augmentation one thing is expanded or increased by a transformation of some kind being applied to it.

The augmentation model does not really apply in the context of sets of things. The model does, however, apply to numbers used in their ordinal sense, such as labels on a number line. This is an important part of the pupil's understanding of number, providing a useful model for mental manipulation. For example, when we calculate something like 68 + 7 mentally, many of us would use a spatial image and a process of adding on along an imaginary number line, 68 . . . 70 . . . 75, rather than thinking of this as two sets being put together.

The one genuine example of augmentation which pupils will encounter and need to recognise is in the context of money.

Augmentation: money

The particular application of the augmentation model in the context of money is that of price increases:

- the price of an article costing £6.95 is increased by £1.45; what is the new price?

Augmentation: measurements

In practice, the situations in which we have to recognise the augmentation model as requiring the operation of addition in the contexts of measuring are rather artificial. However, we could assess the pupil's understanding of the augmentation model in these contexts by seeing if he or she can indicate what should be entered on a calculator in order to answer questions about length increase, weight increase, etc:

- in a science experiment a piece of elastic of length 125 cm is stretched by a further 35 cm; what is the length now?
- the mileage shown on my car is 8549 miles; if I drive a further 280 miles today what will the mileage be then?
- a pupil stands on some bathroom scales and records their weight; if they put on another 28 pounds, what would they weigh then?
- the pupil indicates how old their mother is; how old will she be in 38 years' time?

Theoretically the augmentation model of addition applies also to problems where a starting time and the length of time for some event are given and you are then required to find the finishing time; for example, finding what time a train will arrive if it leaves at 14:25 and the journey takes 1 hour 45 minutes. This is clearly an example of addition, but not one where the numbers involved would be entered on a calculator.

SUBTRACTION MODELS

In this section I aim to illustrate all the kinds of situations in which the various models of subtraction might occur: situations in which pupils would have to recognise that the subtraction key on their calculator must be selected to solve the problem. It is clear from the following analysis that subtraction is a far more complex operation for pupils to understand than addition. It involves learning to connect the symbol with a wide range of classes of problems; and this is where a calculator, in enabling the pupil to focus on the structure of the problems rather than the mechanics of the arithmetic, is a real aid to the development of understanding. We should note also that, since subtraction is a *non-commutative* operation ('a – b' is not the same thing as 'b – a'), pupils must learn to enter the numbers in the correct order in the calculator key sequence. In most practical problems this means entering the larger number first.

The partitioning model of subtraction

The *partitioning* model applies to situations where a quantity has a certain amount partitioned off in some way, and subtraction is required to calculate the remaining quantity. This is often the model of subtraction most frequently used by teachers; it is reinforced by the association of the words 'take away . . . . how many/much left?' with the subtraction sign.

Partitioning: sets

Any situation, presented either practically or in story form, where a subset is taken away (removed, destroyed, eaten, killed, lost etc.) from a given set, can be used here:

- a pile of 56 counters is on the table; take away 39, how many left?
- 218 children in the school, 49 have gone on the school trip; how many left?

I include in this class examples which use the notion of the *complement of a set*. This is where a subset with a given attribute is identified and the question is how many do *not* have the attribute. This could have been identified as a separate model for subtraction, but since it is only relevant to the context of sets I have included it under the heading of partitioning.

- There are 218 children in the school; if 126 have school lunches, how many do not have school lunches?

Partitioning: money

This class of problem includes the familiar situations of spending money; many of these can be simulated in the classroom through various shopping games.

- I go to the shop with £25 and spend £18.75; how much do I have left?
- If I give a ten-pound note for something costing £7.85 how much change should I get?

Partitioning: length and distance

Here we would be looking for examples where a length of some material is cut off or removed from a given length:

- a roll of curtain material contains 50 m; if you cut off 6.50 m what length is left?
- the pupil saws a length of 38 cm from a 100-cm rod and must calculate what length remains, before measuring it and checking

Partitioning: weight , capacity and liquid volume

Problems in these classes might arise in a cookery context:

- from a 250-g packet of sugar, use 75 g in a recipe; how much left?
- pour off 150 ml from a 500-ml carton of milk; how much does this leave?

Partitioning: time

Problems in this class arise in situations where a section of a given length of time is devoted to some event and the requirement is to calculate how much time remains for other things.

- Grandma is 82 years old; she has been married for 57 years: how long was she single?
- we have 75 minutes for a maths lesson, but spend 28 minutes playing a game; how much time is left for other activities?

The reduction model of subtraction

The *reduction* model is similar to partitioning, but refers specifically to the reverse of the process of the augmentation model of addition. Here you start with a given quantity and count back or reduce it by a given amount.

The reduction model does not really apply in the context of sets of things. The model applies to situations where numbers are used in their ordinal sense, such as labels on a number line, where the process employed in the early stages is that of counting back. It also applies to situations where numbers are used as measurements and a quantity is reduced by a transformation of some kind. The most significant example of this model is a price reduction; other examples, such as weight reduction, are perhaps not very realistic.

Reduction: money

Some low-attaining pupils, even at the upper end of the 8–12 age range, do not appear to understand the words 'reduce' and 'reduction'. Help with this specific piece of language might be required.

- the price of an article costing £7.25 is reduced by £1.85; what is the new price?

Reduction: measurements

In practice the situations in which we have to recognise the reduction model as requiring the operation of subtraction in the contexts of measuring are not very realistic or relevant. However, we could assess the pupil's understanding of the model in these contexts by asking him or her to indicate what would be entered on a calculator in order to answer questions such as:

- the teacher stands on some bathroom scales and records his or her weight; if they were to lose 28 pounds, what would they weigh then?
- it is now 1992 and I was born 47 years ago; in which year was I born?

Theoretically the reduction model of subtraction applies also to problems where you are given a finishing time and the length of time for some event and then are required to find the starting time; for example, finding what time a train left if it arrives at 16:10 and the journey took 1 hour 45 minutes. This is strictly an example of subtraction, but not one where the numbers involved would be entered on a calculator.

The comparison model of subtraction

The *comparison* model of subtraction is particularly significant in measuring contexts, especially because of all the associated language. This is where subtraction is used to compare two quantities or measurements to find out how many more or how many less, how much heavier or how much lighter, how much dearer or how much cheaper, and so on. In any given situation where two quantities have to be compared by subtraction, there are two questions which can be asked: one referring to the greater quantity (e.g. how much longer?), and one to the lesser quantity (e.g. how much shorter?). I make a point always of stressing the second of these questions as much as the first, especially since the language related to the lesser quantity is often less accessible to pupils. Additionally, the problem might be posed in terms of finding the *difference* between the two quantities. This phrase is particularly appropriate when pupils have made *estimates* of various measurements and are then required to calculate the difference between their estimate and the actual measurement. Part of understanding this model of the operation of subtraction must involve connecting all these aspects of language with the symbol and the corresponding practical situations. Many pupils will therefore require specific help in establishing these rather complex language patterns in each of the contexts.

Since comparison is such a fundamental process by which we make sense of our experiences, all the contexts generate interesting problems. It could be argued, therefore, that this is the most significant model of subtraction and should be given greater emphasis than the others.

Comparison: sets

Many examples of comparing sets by subtraction are readily available. Some teachers may prefer to ask 'how many fewer?' where I have asked 'how many less?' My view is that the fine distinction between 'less' (referring to continuous quantities, used in the phrase 'how much less') and 'fewer' (referring to discrete quantities, used in the phrase 'how many fewer') is disappearing from contemporary language usage.

- two pupils compare their collections of marbles, e.g. Jo has 29, Pat has 54; how many more does Pat have than Jo? How many less does Jo have than Pat?
- pupils determine how many boys and girls in the school; how many more boys than girls? How many less girls than boys?

Comparison: money

The important language here is: more expensive, less expensive, costs more, costs less, cheaper, dearer. Pupils could compare prices of articles from catalogues:

- model A video recorder costs £429, model B costs £385. How much cheaper is model B? How much dearer is model A?
- one brand of trainers is priced at £5.99 a pair, another at £7.25 a pair. How much more expensive is the second brand? How much less expensive is the first brand?

Comparison: length and distance

There is a wide range of important language to be developed in this context, including: shorter, longer, taller, nearer, further, higher, lower, wider, narrower. Some examples of problems in this class:

- a pupil's height and the teacher's height are measured in centimetres. How much shorter is the pupil? How much taller is the teacher?
- the distance from Norwich to London is 119 miles and the distance from Norwich to Birmingham is 164 miles. How much further is Birmingham than London? How much nearer is London than Birmingham?
- the school hall doorway is 150 cm wide, the classroom doorway is 83 cm wide; how much wider is the hall doorway? How much narrower is the classroom doorway?
- a pupil estimates the width of the classroom door to be 100 cm; what is the difference between the estimate and the actual width?

Comparison: weight

In this context, particular attention should be paid to statements using the phrase 'lighter than', which are less readily understood by pupils than the corresponding statements using 'heavier than'.

- a pupil and the teacher record their weights using some bathroom scales. How much lighter than the teacher is the pupil? How much heavier than the pupil is the teacher?
- a pupil weighs two objects on some scales. How much lighter is the first than the second? How much heavier is the second than the first?
- a pupil estimates that a book weighing 620 g weighs about 450 g. What is the difference between the estimate and the actual weight?

Comparison: capacity and liquid volume

Here the key phrases are 'holds more than' and 'holds less than' when comparing containers.

- a pupil measures the capacity of a medicine bottle and a drink can. How much more does the can hold than the bottle? How much less does the bottle hold than the can?
- the Ford's petrol tank holds 38 litres, the Toyota's holds 52 litres. How much more petrol does the Toyota hold? How much less does the Ford hold?
- a pupil estimates that a 450-ml container holds 520 ml. What is the difference between the estimate and the actual capacity?

Comparison: time

Only very occasionally are the numbers in this context in a form suitable for entry on a calculator, since, as has been mentioned above, calculations with time are more amenable to informal manipulations, because of the mixed units often involved. This is particularly the case when comparing the times at which two events occur, using the phrases 'how much earlier' or 'how much later'. There are some examples, however, when we could use subtraction to compare the times of two events:

- a journey takes 48 minutes by train and 65 minutes by bus. How much longer is the journey by bus? How much quicker is it by train?

One familiar aspect of time where the comparison model of subtraction occurs is, of course, in comparing ages:

- I am 48 and you are 11. How much younger are you than me? How much older am I than you?

The inverse-of-addition model of subtraction

Finally, the *inverse-of-addition* model of subtraction refers to situations where the problem is to find what must be added to one quantity in order to reach some target, such as calculating how much more money is needed to buy an item if I have a certain amount already saved.

Of the four models of subtraction identified in this section, this is the one which pupils find the most difficult to recognise. This is because the problems posed here often contain words or phrases (such as, 'how much more is needed') which signal 'addition' rather than 'subtraction'. It certainly seems odd that to find what must be added we have to press the subtraction key on the calculator. A similar difficulty occurs with the comparison model of subtraction, where words such as 'more than', 'longer than', 'heavier than', will often prompt the child to select the addition key. The problem is that children tend to respond in a stimulus-response fashion to key words in questions rather than to the logical structure (see: Nesher and Teubal, 1975). This is precisely why so much emphasis is being given to the objective stated at the start of this chapter. With a calculator available there is more opportunity for pupils to focus on the logical structure of the problem because they are not distracted by the complexity of the arithmetic involved.

Some examples of problems illustrating the inverse-of-addition model of subtraction are given for each of the contexts below. In all these examples, I have found that the low attainer's first inclination is to add the two numbers in the problem.

Inverse-of-addition: sets

The question to be asked here is 'how many more do we need to reach a particular target?'

- a pupil counts the number of pencils in a pot. If we need 140 pencils for the whole school, how many more must we buy?

Inverse-of-addition: money

Here we would be concerned with how much more money is required for a purchase:

- Cathy has £27 in her savings, but a bike costs £95; how much must her parents give her so that she can buy the bike?

Inverse-of-addition: length and distance, weight, capacity and liquid volume

Problems about reaching a target length, height, weight, volume are likely to be a little artificial, even though the inverse-of-addition model of subtraction is clearly embodied in such examples:

- a pupil measures his or her height. How much more must he or she grow to be 180 cm tall?
- London to Norwich is 119 miles. If you've driven 75 miles, how much further do you have to drive?
- an oarsman wants to reach his target weight of 196 pounds. If he now weighs 179 pounds, how much weight must he put on?
- a pupil puts an object weighing 450 g in one pan of a balance and another object weighing 380 g in the other. How much must be added to this pan to make it balance?
- the recipe calls for 500 g of flour, but only 275 g is available. How much more is needed?
- a pupil pours 350 ml of water into an 800-ml container. How much more water must be added to fill the container?

. Inverse-of-addition: time

Here we would look for situations where the requirement is to calculate how much more time is required, or how much time must pass, to reach a target:

- if you are 11 years old, how many more years until you are 50?
- I have to wait 28 days for the books to arrive, and so far I've waited for 15 days. How much longer must I wait?

Problems about time of day which potentially use the inverse-of-addition structure (such as finding the time that passes from 7:25 to 9:15) would almost certainly be tackled by an informal adding-on process. Attempting to use a calculator here would not be an aid to developing the pupil's understanding of this model of subtraction.

A STRATEGY FOR ADDITION AND SUBTRACTION

Priorities

The analysis above has identified thirty-four classes of problems in which pupils might be required to choose the operations of addition and subtraction. Although all classes of problems have a part to play in developing the pupil's understanding of the number operations, it is clear from the examples provided that some of these classes generate more purposeful, relevant, genuine and practical problems than others.

For example, it is clear that problems in the context of money are generally more accessible and relevant than those in the other contexts of measuring. It also seems that practical problems in weight, and then those in capacity and liquid volume, seem less artificial than those in the contexts of length and distance, and time. Furthermore the comparison model of subtraction has emerged as a very significant component of the pupil's understanding and one that merits high priority.

An important principle

Alongside these considerations is an important teaching principle, which was mentioned in Chapter 5 in the discussion of embodiments of the place-value principle:

> mathematical structures should first be established in contexts with which the pupils are more familiar, before being moved into less familiar contexts.

The simple point here is that we should not try to establish a particular mathematical structure in the pupil's understanding through experiences in contexts where they are hesitant about or unfamiliar with the concepts and criteria involved. So, since the contexts of sets and money in our analysis of number operations are undoubtedly the most familiar for most pupils we should first establish the models of addition and subtraction in these contexts. Using the two contexts side by side ensures that the multi-embodiment principle (see Chapter 5) is at work to some extent. Once the pupils are thoroughly confident about choosing the operation for each model of addition and subtraction within these two contexts, we could then move these operations into the less familiar measuring contexts, using the priorities identified above as a guide, in order to deepen or extend their understanding. The second anecdote about 'groans' in Chapter 1 is an illustration of this principle at work.

A possible strategy

These considerations lead me to propose the following as a possible strategy for tackling the classes of problems for addition and subtraction:

1. Establish aggregation model of addition in contexts of sets and money.
2. Establish partitioning model of subtraction in contexts of sets and money.
3. Establish comparison model of subtraction in contexts of sets and money.
4. Establish augmentation model of addition and reduction model of subtraction in the context of money.
5. Establish inverse-of-addition model of subtraction in the contexts of sets and money.
6. Develop comparison model of subtraction through application to the contexts of length, weight, and capacity and liquid volume.
7. Develop aggregation model of addition and the partitioning and inverse-of-addition models of subtraction through application to the context of weight.
8. Further develop the partitioning and inverse-of-addition models of subtraction through application to the context of capacity.
9. Assess understanding of all the models of addition and subtraction by application to some other classes of problems in various measuring contexts.

MULTIPLICATION

Models of multiplication

The *repeated-aggregation* model refers to those situations where multiplication is used to calculate 'so many lots of so many'. This is an extension of the aggregation model of addition and would include, for example, the cost of a number of articles at a given price. There is a second model of multiplication, the *scaling* model, which should be mentioned. This is an extension of the augmentation model of addition. It is the idea that we use when we talk about 'doubling' or 'trebling' a quantity. In this structure a given quantity is increased by a *scale factor*. For example, to increase the price of an article by 20, multiplication by the scale factor 1.20 is required. The practical problems using this model, although important for numeracy, are usually too difficult for low-attaining pupils in this age range, so the model has been omitted from this analysis.

Pairs of contexts

In identifying the classes of problems for multiplication we should note that the two numbers in a multiplication statement cannot refer to the same kind of thing. This is in contrast to addition and subtraction, where, in fact, they must. For example, you can only add a weight to a weight. It would be meaningless to add the weight of an article to the price of it! But it would be equally meaningless to multiply a weight by a weight, or the number in one set of counters by the number in another set.

So, if we consider a multiplication statement, such as '3 × 4', if the '3' refers to the number of apples in a bag, the '4' cannot also refer to a number of apples. It must refer to something else, such as the number of bags, the price of an apple or the weight of an apple. This leads to the idea that to classify multiplication problems we need to consider *pairs of contexts*. The pairs of contexts which would appear to have potential for generating appropriate multiplication problems are as follows:

- sets × sets
- sets × money
- sets × length and distance, weight, volume and capacity, or time
- money × length and distance, weight, volume and capacity, or time
- distance × time

Some pairs of contexts are excluded simply because they do not generate meaningful multiplication problems. The class 'length × length' contains one familiar situation in which we multiply a length by a length, that is, when finding the area of a rectangle. But, as indicated earlier, my view is that area is probably not an appropriate concept to emphasise with low attainers in the 8–12 age range, so this class is not included in the discussion which follows.

Examples to illustrate the classes of multiplication problems are given below. Once again, the question to be asked for each problem is: what is the calculation to be entered on the calculator? The pupil must recognise the logical structure of the problem as requiring the selection of the multiplication key. Since multiplication, like addition, is a commutative operation ('a × b' gives the same result as 'b × a') the order in which the two numbers are entered in the calculator key sequence does not matter.

As with addition and subtraction, there is variation in the degree to which these classes generate purposeful, relevant, genuine and practical problems, and this will be taken into account in determining the priorities to be given to the various classes.

Repeated aggregation: sets × sets

In this class of problems one of the numbers represents a set of things and the other a set of sets. The word 'altogether' is a key piece of language here:

- there are 12 sets of reading books in the classroom, with 24 books in each set. How many books altogether?

Repeated aggregation: sets × money

This is a very relevant class of problems, where one of the numbers might represent a *unit cost* and the other the number of units being purchased. The key word 'each' is used here. We can also introduce in this context the

important little word 'per', meaning 'for each': this is to be a very significant word in the development of multiplication and division.

- how much to buy 12 marker pens at £1.45 each?
- how much will it cost to take 25 children to the safari park if it costs £2.50 per child?

Repeated aggregation: sets × measurements

Here are included problems where a set of equal lengths, distances,
weights, liquid volumes, or times are to be aggregated. Cookery might
provide some situations where a set of equal weights or liquid volumes
must be aggregated. Alternatively, some rather artificial, but practical,
problems can be posed. There may be some special difficulties in interpreting the results, because of the units involved (e.g. a result of 3500 when
working in grams may need to be interpreted as 3.500 kg).

- my journey to work and home again each day is 28 miles. How many miles do I travel in 20 days?
- the pupil measures the length of a pencil (18 cm). How long would a line of 25 pencils be?
- the cake recipe calls for 125 g of sugar. How much sugar do we need altogether for each child in the class of 28 children to make a cake?
- the pupil weighs a book and must work out the total weight of a set of 28 books.
- each of 28 pupils needs 150 ml of milk for their recipes. How much altogether?
- one bottle of drink holds 1.5 litres. How much in 12 bottles?
- one beaker holds 250 ml of cola. How much cola is needed for 25 beakers?
- each football match in the tournament must last 25 minutes. How long is needed for 12 matches?

Repeated aggregation: money × measurements

These classes of problems include cases where a product is sold by length,
weight, or volume or a service is sold by time. One number in the multiplication might represent the quantity purchased and the other number is the *cost
per unit of measurement*. The idea of price per unit is an important notion to
be developed, occurring in all measuring contexts, as well as in division
examples. Pupils could check the unit prices quoted in supermarkets, although this is often complicated by the tendency to give cost per hundred
grams because the gram is such a small unit. More straightforward examples
are provided by heavy items where the cost per kilogram (or cost per pound)
can be used. The same comments apply to drinks sold by volume, since the
millilitre is also a very small unit, although fewer items are sold by volume
than by weight. Petrol purchases are the most realistic problems here.

- curtain material costs £6.49 a metre. How much for 8 m?
- potatoes are 18p a pound. How much for a sack of 28 pounds?
- unleaded petrol costs £0.49 per litre. How much for 40 litres?

- you can earn £1.45 an hour delivering newspapers. How much can you earn in 5 hours?
- if I save £3.50 a month, how much can I save in 12 months?

Repeated aggregation: distance × time

Strictly, this class should be labelled 'average speed × time'. An average speed of 40 miles per hour (i.e. 40 miles for each hour), for example, can loosely be thought of as meaning that you travel a distance of about 40 miles in each hour. To work out about how far you can travel in so many hours, you multiply this distance of 40 miles by the number of hours. Simple problems presented in this form can be readily understood even by low-attaining pupils:

- I can drive a distance of about 45 miles per hour in my car; about how far can I get in 6 hours?

DIVISION MODELS

The equal-sharing model of division

Equal-sharing refers to situations where the problem is to find how many or how much each portion contains when a quantity is shared out into a number of equal portions. So, in this model, '12 ÷ 4' means basically '12 shared between 4'. Since division is non-commutative ('a ÷ b' is not the same thing as 'b ÷ a') pupils must learn to enter the numbers in the correct order in the calculator key sequence. Also, they will have to learn how to interpret a calculator answer which is not a whole number.

As with multiplication, two contexts are involved. The pairs of contexts appropriate to this model are as follows:

- sets ÷ sets
- money ÷ sets
- sets ÷ money
- length and distance, weight, volume and capacity, or time ÷ sets
- money ÷ length and distance, weight, volume and capacity, or time
- length and distance, weight, volume and capacity, or time ÷ money
- distance ÷ time

Other pairs of contexts, not included here, have no meaning for this model (or, at least, are not appropriate for this level). The category of 'distance ÷ time' is included because of the important concept of average speed involved here.

For all the pairs of contexts indicated above, examples are given below of the kinds of equal-sharing problems which the pupil must recognise as requiring a division calculation. They must also be able to enter the numbers in the correct order on their calculator. Once again, the word 'per' is an important piece of language to be developed in this model.

Equal-sharing: sets ÷ sets

This is where a set of items is shared equally into a number of subsets. The first number entered is the total available, and the second is the number of subsets into which it is shared. The result is the number in each subset. A calculator result with digits after the decimal point must be interpreted as meaning that there are some items left over: the calculator has shared these out as well, into little bits of items; the little bits can (usually) be ignored. The key language is 'how many each?'

- 60 children are put into 5 teams; how many in each team?
- 100 marbles to be shared between 7 children; how many marbles each do they get? (Calculator result: $100 \div 7 = 14.285714$; answer is '14 each with some left over'.)

Equal-sharing: money ÷ sets

Here a sum of money is shared out into a number of equal portions and the problem is to find how much each gets. Once again extra digits in the calculator result must be ignored.

- 6 children share a prize of £2; how much each? (Calculator result: $2 \div 6 = 0.3333333$; answer is '£0.33 each with a little bit left over'.)
- it costs £30.48 for a meal for 4 people; how much is this per person?

This class of problems then extends naturally to the idea of *unit cost*. This important and useful concept is used when comparing prices of items sold in multiples.

- 6 batteries in a pack cost £5.10; how much is this per battery? Compare this with 8 batteries in a pack costing £6.50

Equal-sharing: sets ÷ money

The reverse problem to the previous examples is to find how many items can be purchased per unit of money, given the cost of a number of items. This time the number in the set is entered first and the sum of money entered second. Problems in this class are less common than those of the preceding class.

- you can buy 1000 cards for £20; how many cards is this per pound?

Equal-sharing: measurements ÷ sets

In these classes problems are posed in which a given quantity is shared out into a number of equal portions and the size of the portion is to be determined:

- the pupil measures a length of wood and calculates the length of each piece if required to cut it into 5 equal pieces
- a bar of chocolate with 12 squares weighs 200 g; what is the weight of each square?
- share a 1500-ml bottle of lemonade equally between 12 children
- how long should each match be if we want to fit 8 football matches into 200 minutes?

Equal-sharing: money ÷ measurements

The idea of unit cost is here extended to finding the cost per unit of measurement. The pupil has to learn to divide the total cost by the number of units, so that the cost is shared out equally across each unit. For example:

- find the cost per gram for a 250-g packet of cornflakes at £0.80
- compare this with the cost per gram for a 750-g packet of cornflakes at £1.80

A difficulty here is that the cost per gram (or per ml) is nearly always less than a penny, so that interpretation of the results (such as 0.0032 for '0.80 ÷ 250') is very difficult. In practice I find it is often best to tell the pupils to multiply the result by 100 (e.g. $0.0032 \times 100 = 0.32$, i.e. 32p) and thus find the cost per 100 g (or per 100 ml). In doing this pupils have to make use of the repeated-aggregation model of multiplication, so this must be established first.

Also in this group are problems where a sum of money is shared over a number of time intervals:

- £480 is to be repaid in 12 monthly instalments; how much per month?

Equal-sharing: measurements ÷ money

This class includes the reverse of the problems of the previous class and extends the idea used in the 'sets ÷ money' class of problems. Here the problem is to find how much (length, weight, liquid volume) per unit of money is being purchased:

- find how many grams of cornflakes you get per penny if a 250-g packet costs 80p; compare this with how many grams per penny you get in a 750-g packet costing 180p

This is a less frequently used, but acceptable, way of making comparisons, which sometimes makes more sense than comparing the cost per unit of measurement.

Equal-sharing: distance ÷ time

This class of problems is included because it contains questions about finding the average speed for a journey:

- it takes me 4 hours to travel the 164 miles from Norwich to Birmingham; about how many miles per hour do I travel?

To recognise this as requiring a division we imagine that we have to share out the distance travelled equally between each of the hours taken.

The inverse-of-multiplication model of division

The *inverse-of-multiplication* model is involved when division is used to find the number of portions of a given size which can be obtained from a given quantity. So, in this model, '12 ÷ 4' means essentially: 'to find how many 4s make 12'. This is a very important component of a pupil's understanding of division and should not be ignored at the expense of too much emphasis on the idea of equal-sharing. Clearly, in this model, the portions and the total quantity are the same kind of thing, so the two numbers in this model of division will be from the same context. If one is a length, the other is a length, for example. So, in contrast to the previous model of division, the analysis here is by one context at a time.

In each case the pupil has to learn to recognise the following kinds of problems as requiring a division calculation to be entered on the calculator. At this level, with this model, it will always be the number representing the larger quantity which is entered first.

Inverse-of-multiplication: sets

Plenty of genuine, practical problems with sets using this model are encountered:

- there are 200 children in the school to be put into classes of 25; how many classes?
- there are 1000 books in the school library; if we can get 50 on a shelf, how many shelves are needed?

Inverse-of-multiplication: money

Some familiar situations use the inverse-of-multiplication model of division in the context of money:

- how many chocolate bars costing £0.25 can I buy with £2?
- how many contributions of £0.50 are needed to raise £100?

Inverse-of-multiplication: measurements

These classes of problems tend to be more artificial, but, nevertheless, offer opportunities for practical experience of the inverse-of-multiplication model of division:

- how many lengths of 25 cm can be cut from a 200-cm length of wood?
- how many portions of 50 g can be obtained from a packet of 450 g?
- how many 5-ml doses of medicine are there in a 150-ml bottle?
- how many periods of 40 minutes can be fitted into a 320-minute timetable?

Further examples of inverse-of-multiplication using 'per'

In all the above examples of problems using the inverse-of-multiplication model, the answer represents the number of portions which are obtained. In other words, the answer represents a set of portions. There are some situations, however, using essentially the same idea of division, where the answer represents a measurement. These are cases where one of the two numbers in the problem is attached to the word 'per' (or some equivalent phrase).

Each of the classes of multiplication problems which do not use the context 'sets' produces inverse problems of this kind, requiring division. The following problems, for example, are the inverses-of-multiplication problems given above under the heading 'repeated aggregation: money × measurements':

- potatoes are £0.18 per pound weight; how many pounds of potatoes do I buy if I spend £5.04?
  (here money is divided by money, and the result represents a weight)
- petrol is £0.45 per litre; how much petrol can I buy with £18?
  (here money is divided by money, and the result represents a volume)
- how long will it take me to save £42 if I can save £3.50 per month?
  (here money is divided by money, and the answer represents a time)

The answers here represent a weight, a volume and a length of time, respectively, because the second numbers in the calculation have 'per pound weight', 'per litre' and 'per month' attached to them.

Inverse-of-multiplication: finding journey times

The same mathematical structure which occurs in the problems above is involved in the inverse of problems in the 'distance × time' class of multiplication. Here the second number in the calculation, actually representing an average speed, will be given as the distance travelled 'per hour'. For example, this is the inverse of the question given in the corresponding multiplication class:

- how long will it take me to travel 270 miles if I can do about 45 miles per hour?
  (here distance is divided by distance, and the answer represents a time)

Other models of division

I have not specifically mentioned the *repeated-subtraction* model of division. This refers to situations where '12 ÷ 4' would be interpreted as meaning: 'to find how many times 4 can be taken away from 12 until there's nothing left'. Since this has a very similar logical structure to the inverse-of-multiplication model, with just a slightly different question being asked, I have not included it in the analysis here.

There is, however, one further important model of division: the *ratio* model. This is where division is used to compare two quantities, not to find the difference between them (as in the comparison model of subtraction) but to find their ratio. For example, we might compare the salaries of two people earning £12,000 and £15,000 respectively, by dividing one by the other (15,000 ÷ 12,000) to determine the ratio of their salaries (1.25). We would say that one person earns 1.25 times as much as the other. This is a difficult model of division, using a rather abstract notion, and one which causes considerable problems for many adults. Even though it is essentially just a further extension of the inverse-of-multiplication model, specifically the inverse of the scaling model, my judgement is that it is probably too complex to be tackled systematically with low attainers in the 8–12 age range. With the range of problems already identified in which the pupil has to learn to recognise the operation required, we have more than enough to be going on with.

MULTIPLICATION, DIVISION AND RELATIONSHIPS BETWEEN UNITS

There is a case for helping pupils to recognise the need for multiplication and division when faced with problems involving relationships between units in a given context, particularly everyday situations where non-metric units are encountered. The most important class of problems here are in the context of time. So, for example, pupils should recognise that the following problems require a multiplication:

- how many days in 12 weeks?
- how many hours in 3 days?
- how many minutes in 24 hours?

Here multiplication is required because each problem can be interpreted as a kind of repeated aggregation. For example, '12 weeks' is thought of as '12 lots of 7 days'. Then, using the inverse-of-multiplication model, the pupil should recognise the following as requiring a division:

- how many weeks in 350 days?
- how many hours in 240 minutes?
- how many minutes in 3000 seconds?

Finally, in this category, there are the difficult problems of converting units between the imperial and metric systems, such as converting a weight from pounds to kilograms, or a volume of petrol from litres to gallons. Similarly, there are problems of currency exchange, such as converting a sum of

money from pounds Sterling to Deutschmarks. I would not normally expect to include problems of these kinds with low attainers in the 8–12 age
range, although they should be able to make use of conversion charts in
practical situations.

A STRATEGY FOR MULTIPLICATION AND DIVISION

Clearly, there is a considerable agenda before us in helping low-attaining
pupils to learn to choose the operations of multiplication and division in all
the classes of problems outlined above. It is also clear that we will want to
determine priorities for these as has been done above for addition and
subtraction, because some classes are more significant than others. Also, I
would advocate again the usefulness of establishing the structures of the
various models first in the more familiar contexts of sets and money, before
moving them into the less familiar measuring contexts. Furthermore, since
there is evidence that many children actually find the equal-sharing model
of division more meaningful and accessible than multiplication (Brown,
1981), there is a good case for reversing the usual order for introducing the
operations. We can also then establish multiplication and the inverse-of-
multiplication model of division side by side in the various contexts.

These considerations lead me to propose the following as a possible
strategy for tackling the classes of problems for division and multiplication:

1. Establish the equal-sharing model of division in the classes of 'sets ÷
   sets' and 'money ÷ sets'.
2. Introduce multiplication using problems in the class 'sets × sets' and
   the corresponding problems using the inverse-of-multiplication
   model of division in the context of sets.
3. Reinforce multiplication with problems in the class 'sets × money',
   introducing the word 'per', and the corresponding problems using
   the inverse-of-multiplication model of division in the context of
   money.
4. Reinforce the equal-sharing model of division in the class 'measurements ÷ sets'.
5. Reinforce multiplication through problems in the class 'sets × measurements' and corresponding problems using the inverse-of-
   multiplication model of division in measurement contexts.
6. Apply multiplication and division to problems involving the relationships between units of time.
7. Extend the equal-sharing model of division to problems of unit cost in
   the context of 'money ÷ sets', making further use of the word 'per'.
8. Extend the idea of unit cost to cost per unit of measurement, through
   the equal-sharing model of division in the class 'money ÷
   measurements'.

9. Further develop the equal-sharing model through application to the class 'measurements ÷ money'.
10. Develop multiplication and the inverse-of-multiplication model of division through application to the class 'money × measurements' and the inverse problems of division using the word 'per'.
11. Introduce average speed using the equal-sharing model of division in the class 'distance ÷ time'.
12. Apply multiplication to problems of average speed in the class 'distance × time' and to the inverse problems using division.

FUZZY REGIONS

David, aged 10, a low attainer in mathematics, was able to write the correct answer in the first of the following two questions, but he was defeated by the second, even with a calculator available:

- Jim has 3p. The book costs 5p. Jim needs — p more
- Jim has 59p. The book costs 147p. Jim needs — p more

Although he can use the relationship between 3 and 5 and his understanding of the structure of the problem to answer the first question, he does not actually recognise what he is doing as subtraction. Indeed, since David answers the question by counting on from 3 to 5 on his fingers, he appears to be doing an addition. But the structure of the problem is, nevertheless, the inverse-of-addition model of subtraction in the context of money. He is therefore unable, given the larger numbers of the second problem, to recognise that a subtraction is required. He actually presses the addition key on his calculator and looks puzzled by the result.

This is a familiar scenario. Children can often solve small-number problems whose structures are from any of the different models of the operations delineated in this chapter, without explicitly being aware of the operation concerned. Somewhere between the small-number problem which they can solve and the large-number problem which, even with a calculator available, they cannot solve, lies what I call the *fuzzy region*.

David was given the following series of graded problems, all with the same inverse-of-addition structure. He had a calculator and knew that he could use it whenever he wanted to.

1. Jim has 3p. The book costs 5p. Jim needs — p more
2. Jim has 3p. The book costs 7p. Jim needs — p more
3. Jim has 5p. The book costs 8p. Jim needs — p more
4. Jim has 13p. The book costs 17p. Jim needs — p more
5. Jim has 13p. The book costs 27p. Jim needs — p more
6. Jim has 32p. The book costs 47p. Jim needs — p more
7. Jim has 38p. The book costs 71p. Jim needs — p more

8. Jim has 23p. The book costs 61p. Jim needs — p more
9. Jim has 53p. The book costs 92p. Jim needs — p more
10. Jim has 59p. The book costs 147p. Jim needs — p more

David's fuzzy region was around questions 4 and 5. Questions 1, 2 and 3 he could answer from his knowledge of the number relationships or just by counting on his fingers. Clearly, he understood the logic of the questions, but did not associate their structure with subtraction. As he got into the fuzzy region, where he could not quite cope with the numbers involved, he took the calculator and started exploring various possibilities. Because the numbers were almost within his grasp he soon recognised which sequence of keys gave the right answer. So he actually discovered for himself that the operation of subtraction was appropriate to this structure, and he quickly applied this to the remaining questions. It is, of course, important that this learning is reinforced by articulating what he has discovered in conversation with his teacher, otherwise the experience is unlikely to be connected to any coherent network of understanding.

Helen, age 11, was working on the inverse-of-multiplication model of division in the context of money. She had a calculator available to help answer the following series of graded questions:

1. How many pens costing 2p can I buy with 8p?
2. How many pens costing 3p can I buy with 9p?
3. How many pens costing 5p can I buy with 10p?
4. How many pens costing 10p can I buy with 40p?
5. How many pens costing 5p can I buy with 20p?
6. How many pens costing 4p can I buy with 12p?
7. How many pens costing 6p can I buy with 24p?
8. How many pens costing 8p can I buy with 40p?
9. How many pens costing 8p can I buy with 64p?
10. How many pens costing 12p can I buy with 96p?

Helen could answer the earlier questions, but did not associate them with division. So she did not know what calculation to enter for question 10. Her fuzzy region was around questions 5 and 6. This was the stage at which she turned to the calculator, discovered for herself that '20 ÷ 5' and '12 ÷ 4' gave what she could recognise as correct answers, and then went on to apply division to the remaining questions correctly. It was helpful then for Helen's teacher to show her the relationship between the division and the multiplication involved. So, for example, having entered '12 ÷ 4 =' to determine how many 4s make 12, you can then enter 'x 4 =' to show that you do actually get back to 12.

Teachers can make use of series of graded examples like these for any of the classes of problems outlined in this chapter, with calculators available for when the numbers get too big to handle easily. Sometimes these will assist pupils to move from their confidence with small numbers, through the fuzzy region, into the realms of uncertainty, on the way discovering for themselves, then articulating and making explicit the mathematical structure involved.

CALCULATOR SENTENCES

Finally, here is a suggestion for a simple activity which I have found useful for reinforcing the mathematical structures of the classes of problems discussed in this chapter.

Write on a large sheet of card a standard sentence incorporating the structure in question, leaving blank boxes for the numbers involved. The boxes should be about the size of a calculator. Here are some examples of sentences from various classes of problems, which the reader should now be able to identify:

- if a price of £ — is increased by £ — the new price is £ —
- the cost of — metres at £ — per metre is £ —
- £ — shared between — is £ — each

Packs of cards with various appropriate numbers written on them are placed in two of the boxes. Children, preferably working in pairs with a calculator between them, turn over one card from each pack. They then

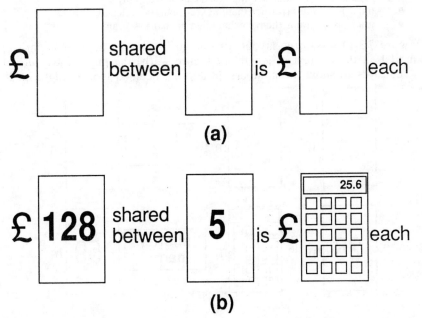

Figure 7.2 *Calculator sentences for equal-sharing*

have to enter the appropriate calculation onto their calculator and place the calculator, with the answer on display, in the remaining empty box to complete the sentence. This is the step which, for some reason, children often find particularly satisfying. They can then copy the completed sentence into their books. Working with one class of low attainers over a period of some weeks, I found that their understanding developed considerably through doing just ten of these sentences each day at the start of their mathematics lesson. Figure 7.2(a) shows the layout for a sentence using the equal-sharing model of division and Figure 7.2(b) is an example where the children have turned over cards to display the numbers '128' and '5', have entered '128 ÷ 5 =' on the calculator, and then placed the calculator in the final box to complete the sentence.

The activity is especially good for establishing important words and language patterns. In the above examples, note the use of 'increased', 'per', 'shared between' and 'each'. When focusing on the language of the comparison model of subtraction another blank box should be incorporated in the sentence. In this box is placed a card which has 'more than' on one side and 'less than' on the other, or the corresponding language for each context (e.g. 'longer than' and 'shorter than', 'heavier than' and 'lighter than'). Sentences such as these use important language patterns:

- — is — (more than/ less than) —
- £ — is £ — (more expensive than/ less expensive than) £ —
- — miles is — miles (further than/ nearer than) — miles
- — grams is — grams (heavier than/ lighter than) — grams

Figure 7.3(a) shows the layout for one such example of the comparison model, in the context of length. In Figure 7.3(b) the pupils have turned over cards to show the numbers 28 and 59, decided that a length of 28

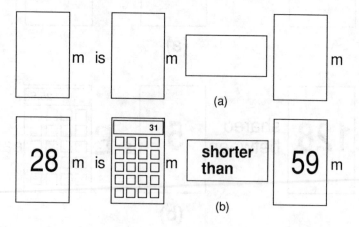

Figure 7.3   Calculator sentences for comparison of length

metres is less than 59 metres, and set the card in the third box to display 'shorter than'. Then they have entered '59 − 28 =' on their calculators and placed the calculator in the remaining box to complete the sentence.

When doing subtraction sentences pupils will, in the early stages, often enter the numbers in the wrong order. When they do this they will get on display the answer to the question, but with a minus sign showing (e.g. '28 − 59 =' gives '−31'). I have found that it is sufficient simply to say to the pupil that when the calculator displays the minus sign this means that they have put the smaller number in first and subtracted the larger number. When this happens they should do it again the right way round and make sure they get an answer without the minus sign.

QUESTIONS FOR FURTHER DISCUSSION

1. Are there more important numeracy objectives than the one considered in this chapter?
2. Can you come up with examples in the various classes of problems described in this chapter which are more practical, genuine and purposeful than some of those given here?
3. Do you agree with my suggested priorities for establishing the different models of the operations?
4. How can a teacher best help a pupil to internalise a mathematical structure which they have discovered through using a calculator in the fuzzy zone of a series of graded examples?

8
CONFIDENCE WITH NUMBER

Confidence with number is a key component of numeracy and will necessarily be an important focus of our work with low attainers. In this chapter I consider four aspects of number work which might be especially emphasised:

- understanding number operations
- number knowledge and mental arithmetic
- calculation skills
- handling big numbers

For each of these aspects I specify in this chapter some objectives for low attainers up to the age of 12 years. The last three of these headings are concerned essentially with the manipulation of numbers. Clearly, none of these objectives is any use unless the pupil learns to connect this number knowledge and skill in calculation to real situations.

So, as a starting point for all the work on manipulating numbers, it is important to include objectives which indicate that the pupil is developing a network of understanding of number operations. I take this to mean that they are learning to make connections between the manipulation of the symbols and the corresponding pictures, language and concrete situations, using the model given in Figure 4.1 in Chapter 4. It is only this basis of understanding of number operations which gives any meaning to the knowledge and skills of arithmetic.

UNDERSTANDING NUMBER OPERATIONS

The primary objectives here are those already described in detail in Chapter 7: the pupil's understanding of the meaning of each operation is best shown by his or her ability to choose the appropriate key sequence to enter on a calculator in the whole range of situations outlined in that analysis. In addition, we can specify as objectives other behaviours which would indicate that the pupil is making connections, bearing in mind the different *models* for each operation discussed in Chapter 7. Some examples of such objectives are given below for each of addition, subtraction, multiplication and division.

Objectives for understanding addition

First, a pupil will have a secure basis of understanding on which to build the numerical skills of addition, if, for example, they are able:

1. *To interpret an addition-fact written in symbols by putting out two sets of objects and combining them.*
   (Connecting symbols with manipulation of concrete materials, using the aggregation model.)

2. *To interpret an addition-fact stated in words, as a movement on the number line.*
   (Connecting language with a picture, using the augmentation model.)

3. *To make up a story to fit a given addition-fact in the context of shopping, using the language of price increase.*
   (Connecting symbols with language and a concrete situation, using the augmentation model.)

Objectives for understanding subtraction

Likewise, the pupil will have a secure basis of understanding on which to build the numerical skills of subtraction, if, for example, they are able:

4. *To interpret a subtraction-fact written in symbols by putting out a set of objects and taking some away.*
   (Connecting symbols with manipulation of concrete materials, using the partitioning model.)

5. *To interpret a subtraction-fact written in symbols by putting out two sets of objects and comparing them.*
   (Connecting symbols with manipulation of concrete materials, using the comparison model.)

6. *To interpret a subtraction-fact stated in words, as a movement on the number line.*
   (Connecting language with a picture, using the reduction model.)

7. *To make up a story to fit a given subtraction-fact in the context of shopping, using the language of comparison, e.g. 'dearer' or 'cheaper'.*

(Connecting symbols with language and a concrete situation, using the comparison model.)

Objectives for understanding multiplication

Similarly, the pupil will have a secure basis of understanding on which to build the numerical skills of multiplication, if, for example, they are able:

8. *To interpret a multiplication-fact written in symbols by putting out the corresponding number of sets of objects.*
   (Connecting symbols with manipulation of concrete materials.)

9. *To interpret a multiplication-fact (using small numbers only) written in symbols, as a number of steps along a number line.*
   (Connecting symbols with a picture: for example '3 × 4' might be interpreted as '3 steps of 4'.)

10. *Given a rectangular array of objects, to state the corresponding multiplication-fact.*
    (Connecting a picture of multiplication with the symbols: for example, given 3 rows of 4 counters, the pupil should recognise this as a picture of '3 × 4' or '4 × 3'.)

11. *To make up a story to fit a given multiplication-fact in the context of shopping.*
    (Connecting symbols with language and a concrete situation, using the repeated-aggregation model: for example, a story for '3 × 4' might be about purchasing 4 items at £3 each.)

Objectives for understanding division

Finally, the pupil will have a secure basis of understanding on which to build the numerical skills of division, if, for example, they are able:

12. *To interpret a division-fact written in symbols by sharing a set of objects into a number of equal subsets and determining how many in each subset.*
    (Connecting symbols with manipulation of concrete materials, using the equal-sharing model: for example, to interpret '12 ÷ 3' by sharing 12 counters between 3 people.)

13. *To interpret a division-fact written in symbols by sorting a set of objects into a number of subsets of a given size and determining the number of subsets.*
    (Connecting symbols with manipulation of concrete materials, using the inverse-of-multiplication model: for example, to interpret '12 ÷

3' by putting 12 counters into groups of 3 and counting the number of groups obtained.)

14. *To make up a story to fit a given division-fact, using the language of 'shared between'.*
(Connecting symbols with language and a concrete situation, using the equal-sharing model.)

NUMBER KNOWLEDGE AND MENTAL ARITHMETIC

It cannot be disputed that the more knowledge of number facts that a person has instantly available the more they will be able to cope with the numerical situations we encounter in everyday life. Knowing by heart the 16-times table, for example, may not be essential for numeracy, but there are times when it is undoubtedly useful. The point I am making is that the more number knowledge we can enable our low-attaining pupils to have at their finger-tips the better. All number knowledge is potentially relevant and useful, and contributes to our confidence in manipulating the numbers which arise in practical problems. So, even though we must be realistic in setting objectives for low attainers, I would put a great emphasis on these pupils actually acquiring as much number knowledge as possible and being able to perform simple calculations mentally. This should include knowledge of addition-facts and the corresponding subtraction-facts (see Figure 8.1), multiplication-facts and the corresponding division-facts (see Figure 8.2). Frequent, short mental arithmetic tests, set at an appropriate level for the pupils concerned, should not be ruled out. Many low attainers have particular difficulty in retaining these number-facts (see, for example, Biggs, 1985); frequent reinforcement is essential, as is an overt emphasis on the importance and value for the children themselves in committing these facts to memory. Many low attainers will respond very positively to the patterns which can be discovered in the tables shown in Figures 8.1 and 8.2.

The suggestions in this section should also be seen as building on the foundation of the place-value work outlined in Chapter 5.

Objectives for number knowledge and mental arithmetic

I would propose, therefore, that it would be realistic and worthwhile for us to aim for low attainers up to the age of 12 years to be able:

15. *To recall, or to evaluate mentally, all the addition-facts given in Figure 8.1.*

16. *To recall, or to evaluate mentally, all the corresponding subtraction-facts arising from Figure 8.1.*

10	10	11	12	13	14	15	16	17	18	19	20
9	9	10	11	12	13	14	15	16	17	18	19
8	8	9	10	11	12	13	14	15	16	17	18
7	7	8	9	10	11	12	13	14	15	16	17
6	6	7	8	9	10	11	12	13	14	15	16
5	5	6	7	8	9	10	11	12	13	14	15
4	4	5	6	7	8	9	10	11	12	13	14
3	3	4	5	6	7	8	9	10	11	12	13
2	2	3	4	5	6	7	8	9	10	11	12
1	1	2	3	4	5	6	7	8	9	10	11
0	0	1	2	3	4	5	6	7	8	9	10
+	0	1	2	3	4	5	6	7	8	9	10

100	100	110	120	130	140	150	160	170	180	190	200
90	90	100	110	120	130	140	150	160	170	180	190
80	80	90	100	110	120	130	140	150	160	170	180
70	70	80	90	100	110	120	130	140	150	160	170
60	60	70	80	90	100	110	120	130	140	150	160
50	50	60	70	80	90	100	110	120	130	140	150
40	40	50	60	70	80	90	100	110	120	130	140
30	30	40	50	60	70	80	90	100	110	120	130
20	20	30	40	50	60	70	80	90	100	110	120
10	10	20	30	40	50	60	70	80	90	100	110
0	0	10	20	30	40	50	60	70	80	90	100
+	0	10	20	30	40	50	60	70	80	90	100

Figure 8.1   Addition-facts

(For example, corresponding to '3 + 8 = 11' are the two subtraction-facts: '11 – 8 = 3' and '11 – 3 = 8'.)

17. *To add mentally a single-digit number to any 2- or 3-digit number.*
    (This is an extension of *place-value objectives 18 and 20* given in
    Chapter 5; note especially examples where the units add up to more
    than 10, e.g. '145 + 8', '193 + 9'.)

18. *To subtract mentally a single-digit number from any 2- or 3-digit
    number.*
    (This is an extension of *place-value objectives* 19 and 21 given in
    Chapter 5; note especially examples like '153 – 8' and '202 – 9'.)

10	0	10	20	30	40	50	60	70	80	90	100
9	0	9	18	27	36	45	54	63	72	81	90
8	0	8	16	24	32	40	48	56	64	72	80
7	0	7	14	21	28	35	42	49	56	63	70
6	0	6	12	18	24	30	36	42	48	54	60
5	0	5	10	15	20	25	30	35	40	45	50
4	0	4	8	12	16	20	24	28	32	36	40
3	0	3	6	9	12	15	18	21	24	27	30
2	0	2	4	6	8	10	12	14	16	18	20
1	0	1	2	3	4	5	6	7	8	9	10
0	0	0	0	0	0	0	0	0	0	0	0
x	0	1	2	3	4	5	6	7	8	9	10

Figure 8.2   Multiplication-facts

19. *To recall, or to evaluate mentally, all the multiplication-facts given in Figure 8.2.*

20. *To recall, or to evaluate mentally, all the corresponding division-facts arising from Figure 8.2.*
    (For example, corresponding to '4 × 8 = 32' are the two division-facts: '32 ÷ 8', '32 ÷ 4'.)

21. *Mentally to multiply any single-digit or two-digit number by 10 or 100, and to state the corresponding division result.*

CALCULATION SKILLS

Calculators, adhocorithms, algorithms

In this section I will outline what I judge to be a realistic and useful set of calculation skills for low attainers up to the age of 12 years. This is a fairly limited set of objectives, since, as has been repeated often in this book, in practice most calculations are carried out nowadays by electronic machines. Because of this, I have emphasised throughout – and repeat again here – that our primary objective must be that the pupil should know what calculation to enter on a calculator to solve problems across the range of different situations which might be encountered in everyday life. This must be more important than the pupil's facility in written calculations. Furthermore, when it comes to doing calculations without a calculator, I have stressed earlier – for example, in Chapter 3 – the importance of giving credence to the use of informal methods, what I call *adhocorithms*, as opposed to the formal *algorithms* of arithmetic. Some low-attaining pupils will need the security of an algorithm, but, in my experience, many are more competent in dealing with calculations when encouraged to use whatever methods make sense to them. These informal methods are always based upon the individual's own repertoire of number knowledge and make use of relationships with which they are familiar and confident. Often they will be related to the pupil's experience of handling money.

Sean, a low attainer in mathematics, aged 11 years, was taking part in a game called *Shopkeeper* (see Activity 10.7 in Chapter 10). He needed to work out the cost of 5 articles at 12p each. In his head, talking out loud, he reasoned: 'Five tens, that's 50p, and five twos, that's ten. That's 60p.' His next problem was to work out the cost of 5 articles at 17p each. He started off in the same way, found that the problem was too complex, turned to his calculator and entered '5 × 17 ='.

This seems to me to illustrate the right balance for which we should be aiming in our work with low attainers. First, encourage them to use their own methods that make sense to them: it really would not help Sean to teach him to set out his calculation for '5 × 12' in the conventional way. Secondly, allow them to turn to a calculator when their adhocorithms fail them: Sean showed good mathematical thinking by actually recognising the need for a multiplication, and by being able to interpret the answer achieved on the calculator.

Objectives for calculation skills

In the objectives below I have not, therefore, specified that pupils should learn one particular algorithm for any operation. Again it should be noted that the skills outlined below are pointless on their own without the ability to connect them to real situations, to the manipulation of concrete materials and to the corresponding language. I have therefore included the phrase 'arising in a practical situation' in each objective below. Often it is the structure of the practical situation which will prompt a pupil to develop an informal method of solving the problem.

I would be satisfied, therefore, if, by the age of 12 years, many of our low attainers, *using informal methods, written or mental, or a combination of the two, or using a standard algorithm*, were able:

22. *To perform an addition of two numbers with up to three digits, arising in a practical situation.*

23. *To perform a subtraction with numbers up to three digits, arising in a practical situation.*

24. *To perform a multiplication of a 2-digit number by a single-digit number, arising in a practical situation.*

25. *To perform a division of a 2-digit number by a single digit number, arising in a practical situation.*
   (To include examples with a 'remainder'.)

An illustration will clarify objective 25 and also reinforce the importance of our accepting informal methods for calculations. Claire, aged 10 years, in the course of a shopping project, had collected data about prices of packs of chocolate biscuits. One pack of 5 biscuits cost 66p. She realised that she had to find '66 ÷ 5' to work out the cost per biscuit. Not knowing an algorithm, she jotted down a jumble of figures, and came up with the answer. She explained to me how she worked it out:

> 'If they were 10p each, it would be 50p . . . another 2p makes 10 . . . 60p . . . another 1p, that's 5p, so 65p. So it's 10, 12, 13p . . . . 13p and a little bit.'

This process is certainly good enough for me to count as success on objective 25.

It is my view that the two best ways in which we can help our pupils to achieve the objectives stated above are: (a) to provide them with plenty of experience of shopping situations, using 10p and 1p coins to solve problems practically; (b) to engage in much more explicit discussion and validation of informal methods, such as that used in the example above, which arise naturally from the manipulation of the coins.

HANDLING BIG NUMBERS

Using calculators, pupils can explore problems with big numbers which would otherwise be inaccessible to them. I find, in fact, that low attainers get a great boost from being allowed to handle big-number problems.

Big-number objectives

Consequently I would include as an important objective that the pupil, by the age of 12 years, should be able:

26. *To say in words the name of any whole number produced as an answer on a calculator.*
   (In other words being able to interpret numbers up to 99,999,999, i.e. ninety-nine million, nine-hundred and ninety-nine thousand and ninety-nine.)

27. *To enter on a calculator any number, with up to eight digits, given in words.*

28. *To compare two numbers with up to eight digits and determine which is the larger and which the smaller.*

DEVELOPING UNDERSTANDING OF NUMBER OPERATIONS

This section considers ways of contributing to the achievement of objectives 1–14, i.e. the development of understanding of number operations. Having identified the importance of giving our low attainers a secure basis in understanding for their work with number, the teacher will aim to provide them with activities designed to develop the connections between symbols, language, pictures and concrete situations. The activity *Calculator Sentences* at the end of Chapter 7 is useful in this respect, as is *Activity 8.5, Turning the Tables*, described below. One of the most useful ways of getting insights into pupils' understanding of number operations is to get them to make up stories to go with sums. This idea is incorporated into the following activity.

Activity 8.1 Number-operations connections

Objectives Any of the objectives 1–14 listed above: i.e. to help develop connections between the symbols of number operations and language, pictures, concrete materials and real situations.

Materials A sheet of 'sums' using addition, subtraction, multiplication and division, as appropriate, with numbers up to 20 (e.g. $3 + 8$, $14 - 6$, $12 \div 3$, 4×2, etc.); a calculator; a supply of number lines, marked from 0 to 20; supplies of linked cubes and token coins; blank paper or a cassette-recorder.

Method A small group of children work together. For each calculation on the sheet, they must: (i) enter the calculation on the calculator; (ii) work out how it can be shown on the number line; (iii) decide how to show it with linked cubes; (iv) make up a problem with the coins; (v) write a story which corresponds to the calculation (or record it on the cassette-recorder if they have difficulty in writing).

For example, given '$14 - 6$', they might (i) enter this on the calculator to get the result '8'; (ii) count back on a number line 6 steps from 14; (iii) put out a row of 14 linked cubes and another row of 6, and compare them to find the difference; (iv) make up a problem where someone with 14p spends 6p, showing this with the coins; (v) write this story: 'Bill is 14, his brother Ben is 6; how much older is Bill?'

When they have decided on the various responses they call the teacher over to demonstrate the connections they have made. To help develop pupils' ability to make such connections the teacher can give various prompts, for example, 'use a story about ages'.

Variations Instead of starting with a calculation, the teacher can give a number-line diagram or a story as a starting point.

ACTIVITIES FOR DEVELOPING NUMBER KNOWLEDGE AND MENTAL ARITHMETIC

There are numerous simple number games, both for small-group and for whole-class activities, which can be used effectively with low attainers in developing their number knowledge and ability in simple mental arithmetic. In this section I provide just a few examples of such games which I have found to be successful in helping low attainers to progress with objectives 15–21 outlined above. For further ideas, see, for example: ILEA (1985) and Duncan (1978).

Activity 8.2 Four in a line

Objective This game for two players focuses on the development of knowledge of the addition-facts given in objective 15 above.

Materials A board laid out as in Figure 8.3(a); Packs A and B of cards (see Chapter 5 Activities) with extra cards for '10' included, or some other means for generating numbers from 0 to 10; a set of counters for each player, in different colours.

Rules When it is his or her go, a player turns over a card from each pack. He or she may then place one of their coloured counters on a square containing the sum of the two numbers revealed, if one is available. Low attainers should have enough counters available to use them for finding the sums, especially when they are in the early stages of learning these addition-facts. The first player to get four counters in a line (across, down or diagonally) is the winner. (The arrangements of numbers on the boards in Figure 8.3 take into account the expected frequency of various answers.)

Variations (i) Adapt the board and the packs of cards so that pupils can practise additions of multiples of 10: simply replace each number on the cards and on the board by the number multiplied by 10; (ii) for subtraction, use sets of cards labelled up to 20 and the lay-out of board shown in Figure 8.3(b). Pupils have to find the difference of the two numbers displayed, thus focusing on objective 16. (iii) for multiplication practice (objective 19), use the lay-out of board shown in Figure 8.3(c). With low attainers, at least in the early stages, I usually allow them to use calculators for the multiplication version, or a copy of the table in Figure 8.2 for reference.

Activity 8.3 One to twenty

Objectives This is a game for two to four players, plus an umpire. It is designed to strengthen knowledge of addition-facts (objective 15).

Materials Packs A and B, with tens, elevens and twelves added – or some other means, such as dodecahedron (twelve-faced) dice, for generating numbers from 1 to 12; a strip of card (e.g. 30 cm by 6 cm) for each player, marked off in twenty squares and numbered sequentially from 1 to 20; 20

0	18	4	14	13	16	2	1
3	14	7	12	11	6	13	17
15	6	9	10	8	10	9	5
12	11	8	11	10	9	7	15
16	14	9	10	9	6	13	16
5	7	10	8	10	8	11	4
18	12	6	11	12	7	13	3
19	2	4	15	4	5	17	20

(a) Addition

20	14	9	18	13	15	10	19
11	7	2	3	6	3	7	8
16	5	0	4	2	0	5	11
12	3	1	6	3	1	2	17
15	6	4	0	2	4	6	10
9	5	0	2	3	0	1	16
8	7	1	4	1	5	7	13
19	10	14	12	17	9	8	18

(b) Subtraction

1	7	45	56	60	35	21	5
81	100	8	6	12	20	9	25
27	4	18	40	24	18	8	54
50	12	10	20	10	30	6	90
63	16	24	36	12	40	16	48
70	40	20	30	10	18	36	32
64	9	8	24	6	30	4	49
2	14	28	42	72	80	15	3

(c) Multiplication

Figure 8.3   Boards for four in a line (Activity 8.2)

counters for each player, to place in the squares and cover the numbers; possibly a calculator for working out the final scores.

Rules The object of the game is to finish up with the smallest score against you, by covering up the numbers on your strip. In turn, each player is dealt two cards by the umpire, one each from Packs A and B. He or she works out the sum of the two numbers revealed. He or she then uses their counters to cover over any combination of numbers which add up to this total. The umpire checks that this has been done correctly. A player who at any stage cannot make the total given by their cards is out. When all players are out, the numbers not covered are added up for each player (low attainers may need to use a calculator here) and count against them. At any stage a player may decide to be dealt just one card, rather than two.

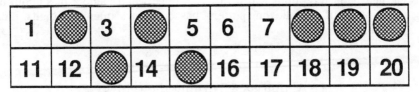

Figure 8.4   One-to-twenty game (Activity 8.3)

In Figure 8.4, if the player is dealt '8' and '5', giving a total of 13, they may choose to put counters on 7, 5 and 1, or on 12 and 1, or on 7 and 6. If however they are dealt '1' and '1', giving a total of 2, they are out, since they do not have numbers totalling 2 remaining on their strip.

Variations For a simplified version, use a strip numbered up to 10, with conventional six-faced dice, and just score the number of squares not covered.

Activity 8.4 Addition and multiplication tables

Objectives To assist pupils in learning the addition-facts and multiplication-facts in Figures 8.1 and 8.2 (*objectives 15 and 19*), and also to enable them to become aware of the patterns within the tables.

Materials A calculator and a blank 11×11 grid for each pupil.

Methods From time to time pupils should make their own copies of Figures 8.1 and 8.2, using a calculator to help them fill in the numbers where necessary. The teacher could engage them in explicit discussion of the patterns they observe as they do this. Each pattern which is observed helps pupils to make sense of the way the numbers are arranged in the table.

I am also not averse to children chanting the multiplication tables as a means of memorising these facts, provided this is not all that they do to learn and understand them. One useful tip, if doing this with a group of children, is to get them to say each result twice, for example: 'one three is three, one three is three, two threes are six, two threes are six, etc.' The value of this approach is that the children who do not get a result the first time do actually say it correctly the second time.

If the teacher is giving regular short tests of these number-facts, pupils can use a copy of each table as a record-sheet. The first time they get a particular result correct they circle it on their copy. The second time, they colour in the square completely, obliterating the number, since they now know this result and do not need to look it up! Each pupil aims eventually to get the whole table coloured in. The teacher can also use the pupils' record-sheets as a guide to which number-facts need special attention.

For example, with one class of 11–12-year-olds, I discovered that no-one had yet encircled the result for '7 × 8'. So we made this a special target. In fact, nearly all the pupils learnt this one, once I had made a fuss about it and pointed out the following pattern, based on the sequence of digits, 1, 2, 3, 4, 5, 6, 7, 8:

$$12 = 3 \times 4 \quad 56 = 7 \times 8$$

Activity 8.5 Turning the tables

Objectives To understand and use the relationships between addition-facts and subtraction-facts (*objective 16*), and between multiplication-facts and division-facts (*objective 20*); also to strengthen the connections between symbols, language and real situations.

Method This is a class activity which can be used regularly and frequently to fill up usefully the odd five minutes at the start or end of a session. One addition-fact, taken from Figure 8.1, is written on the board, for example: '40 + 70 = 110'. The teacher then goes round the class, asking as many questions which can be derived from this fact as possible:

- what is 40 add 70?
- what is 70 add 40?
- what is 110 take away 40?
- what is the total cost of a pen at 70p and a pencil at 40p?
- what is 110 subtract 70?
- what is the difference between 110 and 70?
- how many more than 40 is 110?
- if I am 40 years old, how old will I be in 70 years time?
- if I am 70 years old, how many years until I am 110 years old?
- I am 40, my grand-mother is 110: how much younger than her am I?
- how much left from £1.10 if I spend 40p?

After some experience of doing this, some pupils may be able to make up their own questions, especially if key words or phrases (add, subtract, take away, total cost, older, younger, difference between, etc.) are written on the board.

The same activity can be used with a multiplication-fact. For example, from '7 × 8 = 56', we could derive questions such as:

- what is 7 multiplied by 8?
- what is 8 times 7?
- how many eights in 56?
- how many sevens in 56?
- what is 56 divided by 8?
- what is 56 divided by 7?
- how much for 7 apples at 8p each?
- how much for 8 apples at 7p each?
- share 56 marbles between 8 children: how many each?
- it costs £56 pounds for 7 books: how much for each book?
- my car does 8 miles per litre: how far can I get on 7 litres?

Activity 8.6 Tables jigsaw

Objectives Further awareness of the patterns in the tables in Figures 8.1 and 8.2, as an aid to learning addition- and multiplication-facts (objectives 15 and 19).

Materials A copy of any one of the tables in Figures 8.1.and 8.2, on light card, for each child.

Method The pupil, along the lines of the grid, cuts the table up into a number of pieces to make a jigsaw puzzle. Pupils exchange their puzzles and must reassemble the table. Simple, but effective!

Activity 8.7 What did I do?

Objectives Practice in adding a single-digit number to a two- or three-digit number (objective 17) and subtracting a single-digit number from a two- or three-digit number (objective 18).

Materials One calculator for each pair of pupils; a supply of plastic penny-coins or counters.

Rules A two-digit number is chosen, written down prominently and entered on the calculator. One pupil takes the calculator and may press either '+' or '−' followed by a single digit. The other pupil is then asked, 'what did I do?' If they answer correctly they win a penny. They then take the calculator and must get the starting number back on display, again by pressing either '+' or '−' followed by a single digit. If they can do this they win another penny.

For example, if the starting number is '58' and one pupil presses '+ 7' to get '65' displayed, the other pupil must press '−7' to get back to '58'.

I would suggest that the starting number is changed after each pupil has had five turns. Once pupils are confident with two-digit numbers, the game can be played starting with a three-digit number on display. This is another game where it is useful to have a third pupil available to act as umpire.

Variation Pupils can play the same basic game focusing on objective 21. Now they can choose, if they wish, to multiply by 10 or 100, or they can just add or subtract a single digit as before. If they choose a multiplication, the opponent must undo this with a division by 10 or 100.

Activity 8.8 More grids

Objectives Further practice in adding a single-digit number to a two- or three-digit number (objective 17) and subtracting a single-digit number from a two- or three-digit number (objective 18).

Method Extend Activity 5.9 in Chapter 5, by using instructions for addition and subtraction of any single-digit number along the axes of the grids. For example, with a starting number of 378 in the top left-hand corner of the grid, the instructions ADD 3 and SUBTRACT 8 would lead to a finishing number of 358 in the bottom right-hand corner.

Activity 8.9 I have, who has?

Objectives This small-group activity (2, 3, 4 or 6 players) is a game which I use in many versions, for practising any mathematical skill. Here, for example, it is used for practising recall of multiplication-facts (objective 19). Clearly, it could also be used to practise addition-facts.

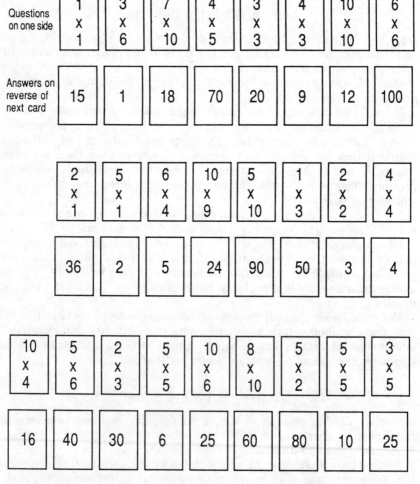

Figure 8.5   'I have, who has?' cards for multiplication-facts (Activity 8.9)

Materials Prepare a set of 25 cards with multiplication 'questions' on one side and 'answers' on the reverse. The answer to one question is written on the back of the card with the next question. The answer to the question on the last card in the set is written on the reverse of the first card. There should be no repeats of answers. Figure 8.5 shows a set of cards designed for practising multiplication-facts up to 6 × 6 and the 10-times table. Note that this arrangement actually makes a cycle of questions and answers, allowing any card to be the starting card in the game described below.

Rules The cards are shuffled and dealt out to the players. The remaining card is placed in the centre of the table, question uppermost. If, for example, this is '5 × 3', the dealer says, 'who has five times three?' Whoever has the card with '15' on the reverse then places it next to the question card, saying, 'I have 15.' When all agree this is correct, the player turns the card over to reveal the next question, and says, 'who has six times four?' Play proceeds like this, the object being to get rid of all the cards in your hand.

Variations (i) Play the game in reverse, starting with the 'answers'. For example, 'who has 15?' is followed by 'I have 5 × 3.' (ii) Play this as a class game. Distribute one card to each member of the class. One person starts, calling out their question. Whoever has the answer calls this out, turns over their card and calls out the next question. One pupil (preferably a low attainer) times the class with a stop clock to determine how long they take to get back to the starting card. Keep a graphical record on display to show the class's times over a number of days, and challenge them to beat their own record.

Activity 8.10 Board games

Objectives To practise any aspect of mental arithmetic and to develop number knowledge.

Materials A board layout, such as the one shown in Figure 8.6; counters and dice.

Rules The example shown in Figure 8.6 is the layout for a simple board game designed to provide a small group of pupils with opportunity to practise adding a single-digit number (up to 6) to a two-digit number (objective 17). In turn each player throws a die and moves their counter the number of places shown on the die. They add the score on the die to the number on the square on which they land. If the answer is larger than the number on the next square they move forward one more square, if it is smaller they move back one square, if it is the same they stay where they are. The game is simply a race from start to finish. The usual rule for such board games about finishing exactly can be employed.

It is clearly important in designing board games like this that the rules are kept simple, so that once one group of pupils has played the game one of them can be responsible for explaining it to the next group.

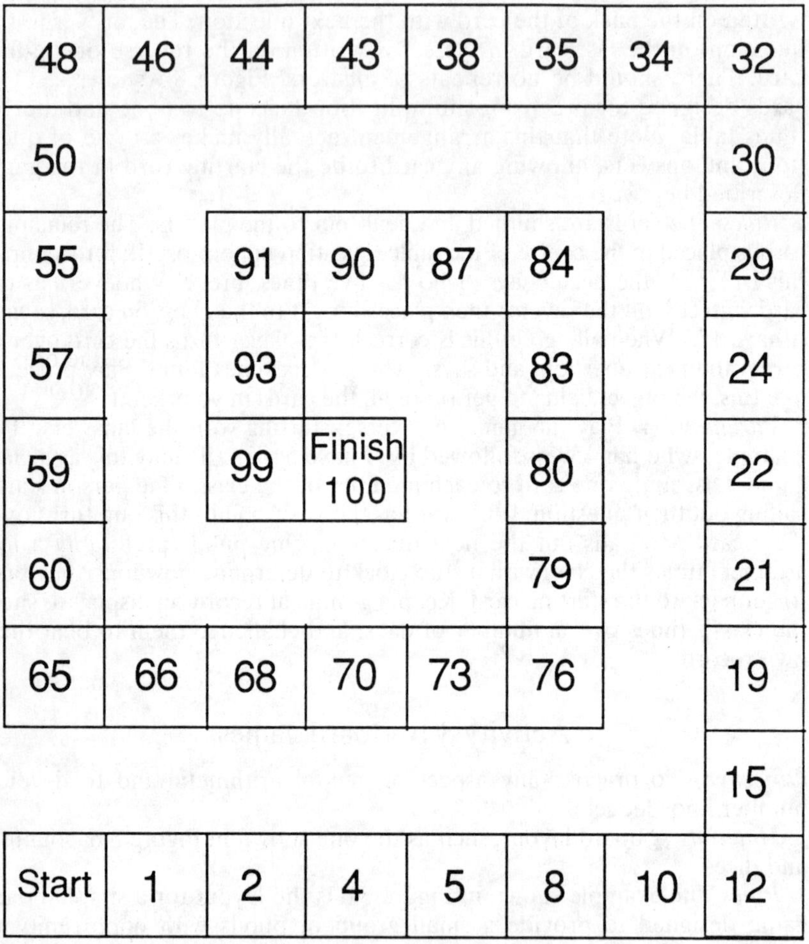

48	46	44	43	38	35	34	32
50							30
55		91	90	87	84		29
57		93			83		24
59		99	Finish 100		80		22
60					79		21
65	66	68	70	73	76		19
							15
Start	1	2	4	5	8	10	12

Figure 8.6 A simple board game (Activity 8.10)

Development Then provide pairs of pupils with appropriate materials, such as a sheet of card, 2-cm squared paper, scissors, glue, colouring pens, a calculator, counters and dice, and get them to invent their own board game to practise a set of appropriate number skills. The teacher could, for example, specify that the game must involve multiplying pairs of numbers from the table in Figure 8.2.

MAKING DRILL ENJOYABLE

Pupils will not master the number knowledge and calculation skills outlined in this chapter, such as those in objectives 22-25, without a considerable component of drill and routine practice. This does not have to be dull and pointless. I will conclude this chapter by suggesting a number of simple ways in which a potentially dull list of arithmetic exercises can be made more enjoyable. The essence of the approach is to provide some form of interesting reward for success, other than just a red tick.

Activity 8.11 Computer drill and practice programs

There is a wide range of computer software available which uses this approach. The pupil is provided with a series of questions for practising some particular skill, such as addition of two numbers. Often there is the option to vary the level of difficulty in these: a computer can, of course, go on and on generating questions at random within a given range. The pupil is then provided with some kind of reward for a correct response, usually associated with some audio-visual display on the computer monitor. This type of software can be very effective with low-attaining pupils, if used to focus particular objectives. Teachers should be wary of any software where the computer's response to an incorrect answer is actually more fun than that for a correct one!

One of the obvious benefits in using a computer to generate questions and to mark, correct and reward pupils' responses is that the activity is low in demand on the teacher. However, it is important that the teacher should give time to supplement the computer's 'rewards' with rewards of their own, such as praise and encouragement. Research into computer-assisted instruction (CAI) with low attainers (Moore, 1988) suggests that the combination of CAI and positive reinforcement from the teacher is significantly more effective than CAI on its own.

Activity 8.12 Picture puzzles

Dot-to-dot puzzles are a familiar and simple technique for providing pupils with a reward for doing a series of arithmetic exercises. Place a sheet of tracing paper over an outline drawing of some familiar object and mark significant points in the outline with dots. Write the answers to the exercises in order next to the dots. Add a few more dots and dummy answers. The puzzle and the set of exercises can then be photocopied for distribution to the class. Pupils answer the questions and join up the corresponding dots to make the picture. It is the gradual emergence of the picture which constitutes the reward for success.

A variation is to make a puzzle in which the picture and the background are divided up into a number of regions. Write the answers to the exercises

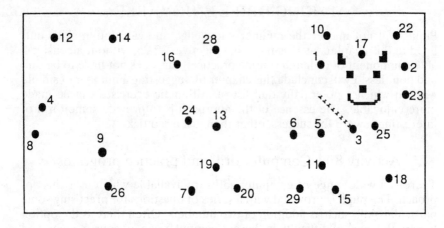

```
2+2   4+5   9+7   20+8   1+0   4+6   10+7   10+12   1+1    20+3   20+5   2+1
3+2   5+6   6+9   9+20   1+5   10+3  9+10   10+10   4+3    20+4   6+20   5+3
```

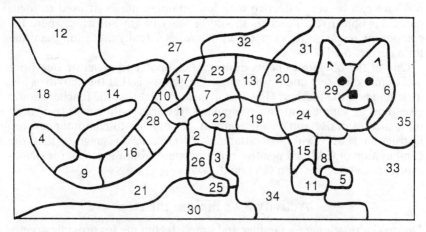

Figure 8.7   Picture puzzles (Activity 8.12)

in the regions within the picture and put some dummy answers in the regions in the background. The picture emerges as the pupils shade in the regions containing the answers to the exercises. Figure 8.7 shows an example of each of these kinds of picture puzzles.

Teachers will probably not have time to prepare more than one each of such puzzles. However, the pupils themselves, once they have the idea, can usefully prepare their own puzzles to give to each other to solve. They could, for example, be required to make a picture puzzle for practising subtraction with two-digit numbers. They would then prepare the series of exercises themselves, using a calculator to ensure that they put the correct answers on the drawing.

Activity 8.13 Calculator marking

Allowing pupils to work in pairs using a calculator to mark each other's answers is a simple technique for enabling them to practise any calculation skill, such as those outlined in objectives 22–25. An enjoyable way of providing the arithmetic exercises is to use packs of cards (e.g. Packs A and B as described in the activities for Chapter 5) or some other means of generating numbers at random.

For example, imagine that two pupils are practising subtraction with two 2-digit numbers (objective 23). Each pupil 'deals' the other two 2-digit numbers. They then work out their answer for the larger number subtract the smaller, without the calculator, using whatever methods they wish. The fun of this is that sometimes they will be dealt an easy question and their opponent a hard one, or vice versa. They then use the calculator to check each other's answers. If the answer is correct they score a point or win a token coin. If a pack of cards is being used to generate the questions, an effective way of rewarding success is for the pupil to retain the cards. In this way the game has a natural ending: i.e. when the supply of cards runs out.

Clearly, this is an activity for two pupils of about the same standard of arithmetic skill. It is a more effective way of engaging them in routine practice of additions, subtractions and multiplications than the conventional approach of giving a page of exercises and having the teacher mark the answers some time later.

EXPLORATIONS WITH BIG NUMBERS

This section suggests a few activities, related to objectives 26–28, enabling pupils to explore big numbers through the use of calculators.

Activity 8.14 Big-number problems

Objectives Using a calculator, pupils should tackle problems with big numbers, extending their experiences of choosing the operation, as analysed in Chapter 7. It is important that they are required to say in words the answers which they get on their calculators (objective 26) and to compare these with answers achieved by other pupils (objective 28).

Method Some examples of problems which pupils enjoy tackling with their calculators are given below. All of these are likely to require some preliminary discussion about the variables involved.

- How many minutes have you lived (approximately)?
- How many cans of drink (chocolate bars, etc.) could you buy with a million pounds?
- How many seconds do you spend in bed in a week?
- If you earn £5 an hour, how much will you earn in a lifetime?
- About how many letters are there in a book?

For this last problem, pupils in a group could each choose a reading book and compare them. The number of letters can be calculated approximately by multiplying the number of pages by the number of lines per page, by the approximate number of letters per line.

Activity 8.15 Big-number challenges

Objectives This is an effective way of enabling pupils to explore big numbers and to put them in situations where they have to compare one big number with another (objectives 26 and 28).

Method Give the pupils a set of cards representing a selection of keys on the calculator. Obviously the level of difficulty can be varied by the selection of cards used. Always include one card with an equals sign. The challenge is to arrange the cards into a key sequence on the calculator, aiming to get the largest possible answer. Several pupils should work individually on the problem, comparing their largest answers so far at each stage. The teacher's interventions should concentrate on getting the pupils to say the numbers out loud.

Figure 8.8 shows an example of a set of these cards, and one pupil's suggestion for arranging them, producing the answer 'seventy-nine thousand and forty-eight'. (Is this, in fact, the biggest possible answer?)

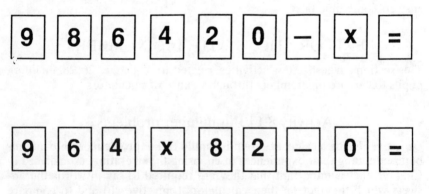

Figure 8.8   Example of cards for Activity 8.15

The note about 'precedence of operators' at the end of Activity 5.11 in Chapter 5 applies again here.

Activity 8.16 Lesser-known facts of the universe

Objectives These are some examples of a set of work-sheets which have proved very popular with all pupils, especially low attainers, who enjoy exploring the absurd suggestions contained within them. (For further ideas for encouraging low attainers to investigate 'amazing facts', see: Womack, 1988.) Each problem involves some practical measurement, relationships between units, a big number given in words, a calculation to be entered on a calculator, and a large number at the end to be interpreted, thus bringing together objectives from Chapters 6 and 7 and objectives 26 and 27 from the present chapter.

● *Lesser-known fact no. 1: hamsters and elephants.*
Use some scales to weigh a hamster.
Write the answer in kg (for example, 125 g = 0.125 kg).

A hamster's weight is — kg.

An adult male African elephant weighs about five thousand kilograms.
About how many hamsters would be needed to balance this elephant?

● *Lesser-known fact no. 2: children laid end to end.*
Measure your height in centimetres.
Change this to metres (for example, 135 cm = 1.35 m)

My height is — m.

It's about two-hundred-and-sixty-four thousand metres from Norwich to Birmingham.
About how many children of your size could be laid end to end along the road from Norwich to Birmingham?

● *Lesser-known fact no. 3: swallowing a swimming-pool.*
Use a large measuring jug to find out how much water you can drink in one go.
Write the answer in litres (for example, 850 ml = 0.850 litres, 1500 ml = 1.500 litres)

I can drink — litres of water in one go.

About how many children would be needed to drink a swimming pool which holds four-hundred-and-fifty thousand litres of water?

Activity 8.17 The E-game

Objectives This game for two players is designed to develop pupils' confidence in handling big numbers, and also gives them experience of the technique of *front-end estimation* in arithmetic. This is the process of making an estimate by recognising that it is the first digit and the number of digits in each number which are the most significant factors in determining the size of the answer.

Materials One calculator and a die. It is assumed that the calculator will display an 'E' (for ERROR) if asked to produce an answer with more than 8 digits.

Rules The die is rolled and the number which appears is the 'target digit'. This target digit is entered on the calculator. Players then take it in turns to add numbers to the number on display. The number entered must have the same number of digits as the current display. Every time a player succeeds in getting the target digit as the first digit in the answer a point is scored. The round ends when an E is displayed. The player who produces the E loses a point. There are some interesting strategies for playing this game to be discovered.

Example The die is rolled and the target digit is found to be '3'. This is entered on the calculator. A and B then might play as follows:

Player	Entry	Display	Score
A	+ 5 =	8	0
B	+ 9 =	17	0
A	+ 20 =	37	1
B	+ 62 =	99	0
A	+ 99 =	198	0
B	+ 150 =	348	1
etc.			

Variation The E-game can then be played using multiplication rather than addition. The rules are the same except that only single-digit numbers (greater than 1) may be entered each time. For example, with '3' as the target digit, a game might proceed like this:

Player	Entry	Display	Score
A	× 5 =	15	0
B	× 2 =	30	1
A	× 9 =	270	0
B	× 4 =	1080	0
A	× 3 =	3240	1
B	× 9 =	29160	0
A	× 4 =	116640	0
B	× 3 =	349920	1
A	× 9 =	3149280	1
B	× 9 =	28343520	0
A	× 2 =	56687040	0
B	× 2 =	E	–1

QUESTIONS FOR FURTHER DISCUSSION

1. What further objectives (see objectives 1–14 in this chapter) might be included under the heading 'understanding number operations'? Use the connections model, given in Figure 4.1 in Chapter 4, and consider the different models of the four operations, as outlined in Chapter 7.

2. Discuss with a group of colleagues how each of you actually calculates the answers to various arithmetical problems, such as finding the cost of 25 articles at 24p each. What is the balance between the use of algorithms and adhocorithms? Do those who use informal methods all do the questions the same way?

3. What is your view on the question of encouraging the use of adhocorithms as opposed to teaching algorithms in working with low attainers in mathematics?

4. What further ideas, in addition to those suggested in this chapter, do you have for rewarding pupils for success in arithmetic drill exercises?

9
USING MATHS TO MAKE THINGS HAPPEN

In this chapter I return to one of the major themes of the book: the importance and value of engaging our low-attaining pupils in purposeful activities in meaningful contexts. This theme is illustrated here by examples where pupils have used and developed their mathematics skills in order to make happen something that matters to them. It is my hope that these examples of what some teachers and pupils have achieved will serve to encourage others to incorporate this kind of activity into their work with pupils who do not otherwise attain very much in mathematics.

RELEVANCE

There seems to be general agreement that mathematics, particularly for low-attaining pupils, must be made more relevant:

> It is of the utmost importance that the mathematical work of children in remedial classes should not consist of the practice of arithmetical skills in isolation, but should be accompanied by discussion of the concepts on which these skills rest and the ways in which they can be used in the children's everyday lives.
>
> (Cockcroft, 1982, paragraph 337)

> Many have urged us to stress that mathematics courses for these [lower-attaining] pupils should be relevant to the requirements of everyday life.
>
> (Cockcroft, 1982, paragraph 459)

> Mathematics is over-concerned with the practice of computational skills, much of which is unrelated to any context that would confer meaning and importance on the work being done.
>
> (HMI, 1984)

> There is abundant evidence that work which is triggered by pupils themselves leads to better motivation and understanding . . . Teachers should have enough flexibility built into their schemes to capitalise on their pupils' interests.
>
> (NCC, 1989)

Pupils, at all stages, need to have experience of tackling 'real life' problems as an integral part of their experience of mathematics.

(NCC, 1989)

It was very common for the schemes of work in the schools visited to refer to the need to relate mathematics taught to the problems of everyday life, but the convincing realisation of this aim was much more rare.

(HMI, 1978)

However, people have different ideas of what is meant by 'relevance'. I would suggest that there are four ways in which this notion is applied in mathematics teaching.

Vicarious relevance

The following mathematical problems might appear to have a kind of relevance to pupils:

- Look at the train timetables for Norwich to Peterborough and Peterborough to York; what time should I catch a train from Norwich to get to York by 12 noon?
- My living-room is 6 metres by 6 metres; what will it cost me to carpet this if the carpet is 4 metres wide and costs £6.75 per square metre?

These are real problems, but they are not the pupil's problems. The pupil is not travelling from Norwich to York, or laying carpet in their living-room. They are being asked to solve someone else's problem. This is what I term *vicarious relevance*. Mathematics text-books are, of course, filled with questions of this kind, where you are asked to solve a problem on behalf of someone else, and I cannot imagine that any mathematics teacher could manage without recourse to them. The mathematics is at least embedded in a meaningful context. But often this type of problem fails to motivate pupils to commit themselves to its solution, because the activity lacks any real purpose for them.

Artificial relevance

A second way of making mathematics relevant is what might be termed *artificial relevance*. This is where the teacher makes use of situations or contexts which are of interest to the pupils as a basis for generating some mathematical activity. This approach, drawing on pupils' interests in such things as sport, television schedules and pop music charts, can be effective. For example, with one group of 9–10-year-olds, I took the idea of 'goal difference' – used in the Football League tables to put in order teams with the same number of points – as a starting point for introducing them to negative numbers. They were motivated by their interest in football to engage in the mathematical activity. The context gave meaning to the mathematical ideas, but once again the problems posed were, to be honest, artificial and lacking in any real purpose. Mathematics is related to real life, but it is not being used to do anything purposeful.

Teachers can sometimes make use of this artificial relevance in incorporating mathematical activity into cross-curricular topic work. Often teachers miss the opportunity to do this, keeping mathematics as an isolated experience unrelated to anything else children do in school. For example, a group doing a cross-curricular project on transport might collect data about the different ways in which pupils in the school come to school, organise this, display it in graphical form and interpret the results. The mathematics is thus relevant, in the sense that it is related to other activities in which the pupil is engaged, but it lacks genuine purpose.

Long-term relevance

A feeble approach to making mathematics relevant is to try to persuade our reluctant learners that the mathematical skills we are trying to teach them will be useful for them when they leave school. Often this is no more than an admission by the teacher that they do not actually know themselves what is the point of the pupils learning the material in question. On the whole an appeal to *long-term relevance* is unsuccessful in motivating pupils. However, recalling an occasion (cited at the beginning of Chapter 6) when we had workmen in the school doing major alterations at the same time as the pupils were trying to learn about length measurement, it did seem to imbue the pupils' own practical work with some degree of relevance when we were able to draw their attention to the way these measurement skills were being used all around them by the workmen.

Immediate and genuine relevance

Undoubtedly, the type of relevance for which we should be aiming is *immediate and genuine*. This is where the pupil is using mathematics to achieve something which matters to them at the present time. There is a considerable body of evidence that pupils will achieve much more and show greater commitment when they are engaged in tasks with immediate and genuine relevance.

One group of low-attaining 14–15 year-olds, for example, used their limited mathematics with unexpected competence and developed a range of new skills, in planning and carrying out a day trip to Boulogne (Bowers, 1981). As is so often the case in such examples of purposeful mathematical activities in meaningful contexts, the teacher was impressed particularly by their commitment to the task, and their growth in self-esteem and self-confidence in mathematics, contrasting markedly with their usual disillusionment and diffidence in mathematics lessons. Even children as young as 9 years, who, for some reason, happen to be involved in everyday commercial transactions, seem to be able to construct quite complex mathematical strategies for solving problems that emerge, and can achieve success where they would fail at the identical mathematical task presented as either a word problem or as a context-free computation (Carraher *et al.*, 1985, 1988).

A mixed ability class of 10–11-year-olds in one middle school, in a project prompted by the Open University course, PME 233, *Mathematics Across the Curriculum*, set out to solve the problem of washing and changing facilities in their school, caused by the failure of the local authority to complete the provision of a shower-unit (Blake, 1985). Their teacher's report of this project provides many examples of pupils' finding genuine and immediate relevance for using and developing mathematical skills: measurement and scale-drawings; surveys and questionnaires; collecting, organising, representing in graphical form and interpreting data; costing; percentages; averages; timetables. Most impressive was the value of the project for the least able child in the class, a boy called Trever (*sic*), who worked with a friend on gathering evidence about washing and changing facilities in other schools:

> Trever may be full of chatter, but he lacks confidence in his ability to contribute anything in a class where everyone is cleverer than he is. The fact that he and his friend were doing an investigation all on their own boosted his morale from the word go . . . Trever gained confidence from the whole exercise because he had contributed something. He learned some specific skills, such as sorting according to given criteria and calculating percentages using a calculator.'

We are probably all familiar with the person who, although a failure in school mathematics, shows a stunning competence in the additions, multiplications and subtractions involved in playing darts or snooker. In a context which makes sense to them and in an activity which has some purpose, they are able to learn and master skills which their teachers failed to teach them in many years of schooling. The challenge for teachers is to try to find ways of giving mathematics in school the same degree of immediate and genuine relevance.

A slogan which I have adopted to describe the approach being advocated here is: *use maths to make things happen*. It is when the pupil is committed to a task in which they have to use mathematics to make something that matters to them happen that the mathematics becomes immediately and genuinely relevant. The pupils who investigated the forgotten shower unit in the example above produced such a convincing case that the PTA donated a large sum of money towards the cost of their recommendation. The pupils had made something happen.

MAKING THINGS HAPPEN

All the categories of purposeful activities identified in Chapter 4 have the potential for pupils to experience mathematics as being immediately and genuinely relevant, as they make something happen. In *solving a real problem* or *planning an event* the pupil is clearly engaged in making something happen and draws upon mathematical skills to achieve this. Even in *role play* or *a simulation* the pupil becomes a participant in an imaginary situation in which they have to use mathematics to solve a problem or achieve some goal. *Design and construction* are clearly activities in which mathematics is used to achieve something definite and, it is to be hoped, useful. An effective *small-group game* is one in which the pupil uses mathematics to try to win the game.

In particular, the two categories of real problem-solving and planning an event prove to be the most effective ways in which pupils can use mathematics to make things happen, and thereby experience mathematics as having immediate and genuine relevance. These two categories are the focus for the remainder of this chapter.

A framework

Some of the components of a project in which pupils use mathematics to make something happen might be as follows:

(a) *Identifying a Situation* This will be a situation which the pupils want to do something about and for which they are prepared to take responsibility to make something happen. In particular, this might be a real problem, raised by the pupils themselves, for which a solution is required, or a school or class event which has to be planned.

(b) *Accepting Responsibility* The teacher will discuss with the group of children what must be done to achieve a solution or to make the event happen. Various components of the problem or event can be mapped out in a large network diagram on the board, showing how they relate to each other. With larger projects, it is often useful for different groups of children to take on responsibility for different aspects.

(c) *Applying Existing Mathematical Skills* As the various groups work on their contributions, inevitably their existing mathematical skills will be called upon and applied to a real situation, thus increasing their confidence in and understanding of these skills. Of course, it is likely that tackling a real-life problem or event will involve many other useful and important skills, for example, in the areas of literacy, oracy, and personal and social development.

(d) *Acquiring New Mathematical Skills* Pupils will themselves become aware at times that they do not have the necessary skills to deal with aspects of their area of responsibility. The problem or event thus provides an immediate and genuine purpose for learning some new mathematics in a meaningful context. The appeal of the desired outcome should be strong enough for the pupils to persist in mastering the mathematics required.

(e) *Making Something Happen* The teacher will have to coordinate the work of the different groups and bring them together at various stages, in order to produce a final solution or plan. The whole point of the project must be that ultimately the pupils do actually make something happen. Often this will involve convincing adults that the solution or plan is acceptable and appropriate, so the pupils will need to assemble evidence to support their proposals.

(f) *Making the Mathematics Explicit* To underline the relevance of mathematics, the teacher will discuss with the pupils what mathematics was used in their work and how this enabled them to achieve the desired outcome. This will also be important for the teacher themselves to justify the time given to the activity against, for example, National Curriculum criteria for programmes of study in mathematics.

Mathematical content

When a teacher embarks on a project of this kind with a group of pupils, they may have in their mind certain mathematical material which might be involved, but it is normally impossible, without first solving the problem or doing all the planning yourself, to predict the mathematical content completely. It will not be possible to set out specific mathematical objectives for the project. The emphasis here is not on objectives and attainment, but on experiencing the use of mathematics to make something happen.

What I am quite certain about, however, is that a rational and systematic approach to solving real problems and planning real events will inevitably involve the application and development of important and useful mathematical knowledge and skills. Teachers who have used this approach have usually found that the mathematical content involved is precisely what would be recognised as some of the important components of numeracy: calculations set in real-life contexts; using calculators and learning to choose the appropriate operation; estimating quantities and measurements; handling money, costing, purchasing, budgeting; practical measurement of length, time, liquid volume and weight; scale-drawing; drawing up timetables and planning; making questionnaires and carrying out surveys; handling data and simple graphs; handling ratios, percentages, and averages in practical contexts.

One of our purposes in this kind of work will be to develop the pupil's ability to make decisions on a rational basis, rather than in a haphazard, unthinking manner. There are many people who leave school without the intellectual skills to make rational decisions in the situations that confront them in adult life. Consequently they make their choices on such shaky premises as their emotions (it feels right), traditions (we've always done it like this), peer pressure (everyone else in my group does this), or on the tacit acceptance of other people's judgements and advice. Such individuals have not been served well by our education system.

These points are illustrated below by detailed accounts of one example of a mixed ability class solving a real problem, and one example of a low-ability mathematics set planning an event.

SOLVING A REAL PROBLEM

The problem identified by one mixed ability class of 10–11-year-old children, in discussion with their teacher, was: *how can we make play-time safer and better?*

After a lively class discussion, it was agreed that, in order to solve this problem, a number of aspects and associated questions would need to be considered:

1. *Safety*. Which games and activities cause minor accidents? How frequently? Is there enough room for all the children? How can safety be improved?
2. *Wet weather*. What are the reasons for dissatisfaction with present arrangements? What do teachers and children think about it? How often do wet play-times happen? What alternative arrangements might be better?
3. *Refreshments*. How much do children spend at the tuck-shop? What do they spend it on? Are the drinking facilities adequate? Any suggestions for improvements?
4. *Tidiness*. What are the main places where litter is dropped? How much is there? How many bins are there? Are they in the right place? Why do children drop litter? How can we improve the look of the playground?
5. *Activities*. What do children actually like to do during play-time? Are they able to do this? What problems are there? Are there ways of making play-time better for more children?
6. *Beginning and ending*. What problems are there at the beginning and end of play-time? How much time is taken up by lining up? Can it be made better?

A group of children took on responsibility for each of these aspects of the problem. All of them were then engaged in using mathematics in an immediate and genuinely relevant way. They formulated their plans, and over a period of about four weeks in which a number of mathematics lessons, most of their play-times, and other odd moments, were given over to the project, they gathered their evidence, clarified the problem and formulated their solutions. The teacher found it best to have only two groups working on the project in any one mathematics lesson, with the rest of the class engaged in more conventional mathematical activity. She also found that it was important to allow pupils to make mistakes, avoiding the temptation to alert them to potential difficulties every time they formulated their own ideas for solving their component of the problem. Any recommendations arrived at by the groups, along with their supporting evidence, were presented to the rest of the class for agreement, before being taken further.

The Safety Group monitored children's activities during play-times over a week, and collected data about the number of children participating in various games. Two of them found the total area of the playground and the maximum number of children using it at a time. They then used a calculator to determine the amount of space per child. The group kept records of the number of occasions in which a child was hurt and the cause of this. This data was then presented graphically with their interpretation. They measured and made a scale-drawing of the playground, showing where various activities took place and the locations of minor accidents. This was a point at which they had to be taught a technique by their teacher, prompted by one mathematically weak boy who announced that he had measured the playground but it was too big to draw on a piece of paper! Their main recommendation was that the netball games which went on during play-time should be restricted to a smaller area. This area was identified on a scale-drawing, submitted to the headteacher as part of their evidence along with the proposal. The recommendation was accepted. The pupils had used mathematics – data-gathering, graphical display, calculations, measurement, scale-drawing – and made something happen.

The Tidiness Group, amongst other activities, determined the extent of the litter problem by gathering data about its distribution and the location of bins, again presenting this on a scale-drawing of the playground. They found out how often the bins were emptied and entered this on a calendar. Since most of the litter was found to be on the ground near one overflowing bin, they were able to put forward a solution, involving the re-siting of some bins, and the more frequent emptying of key bins. This was accepted by the class, and then put to the headteacher and the caretaker. They collected all the litter after one play-time, weighed it, and announced the result to the school at assembly the next day. They were then able to repeat this for subsequent play-times and to demonstrate a marked improvement. They had used mathematics to make something happen.

Two of the children in this group pursued a different line. Some old wooden boxes, once used for flowers, stood in the playground. These children put forward a proposal for the boxes to be repainted and replanted with flowers. They did a survey to find the most popular colour for the boxes and the favourite flowers. They estimated how much compost would be required. Then they costed the whole project. The proposals, along with their evidence and arguments, were put to the PTA and accepted: once again the children had used mathematics to make something happen.

The Refreshments Group gathered data about how much money children spent at the tuck-shop, and were surprised at how much this turned out to be. They learnt and used the concept of average, and how to use a calculator to find the average amount of money spent per child. They discovered that most money was spent on expensive canned drinks and that one reason for this was the inadequacy of the water drinking facilities available at play-time. When they themselves then cleaned up the water-fountains and monitored the effect, they were able to report a significant increase in their use.

A survey of what children actually like to do during play-time, carried out by the Activities Group, revealed that the most popular activity was simply talking to friends. This was part of the evidence they presented in their sensible recommendation that more seating should be available in the playground.

The Wet Weather Group also undertook surveys of opinions. Finding it impossible to ask every child in the school, they were taught about the principles of random sampling. In addition, they set up a long-term record of wet play-times to determine the extent of the problem.

The Beginning and Ending Group undertook timing of journeys and measurement of distances from each classroom to the playground. The lowest-attaining pupil in mathematics in the class was a member of this group. He learnt how to measure distances in metres and centimetres, and, assisted by a more able child, found out how to enter a number of distances onto a calculator in order to add them up. And so on . . . each group was actively committed to their aspect of the problem and were engaged in using mathematics for an immediate and genuine purpose.

What impresses me most in observing projects of this kind is the commitment shown by the less able pupils. They are often boosted by being given genuine responsibility, they surprise their teachers by their mathematical competence when the mathematics arises in a meaningful context, and, because of their commitment to the task, they show an unexpected determination to master new techniques when these become necessary to solving their problem.

PLANNING AN EVENT

Pupils can also have genuine and immediate experience of using mathematics to make something happen if they are encouraged to take on responsibility for planning some of the events which take place as part of school life.

Rational planning inevitably involves mathematical thinking. In particular, pupils will have opportunity to develop their facility in the sequencing of activities, an area of difficulty for some low-attaining pupils in mathematics. Often they will find it helpful to use spatial techniques to lay out their plans, in order to get an overall view of how components fit together, as for example, in drawing up a timetable.

There is a wide range of events which pupils might plan, varying from those which might require as little as one hour's work in a mathematics lesson to substantial projects running for several weeks: for example, a day's timetable for the class; a Christmas party for the class; a class outing; a five-a-side hockey tournament; a fund-raising activity for charity, such as a sponsored multiplication tables test; a school camp; a school concert; a disco; a fete; a school sports day.

The Easter parade

The example to be considered in detail was an event planned by a mathematically low-attaining set of 20 children in the age range 8–9 years (Haylock and Morgans, 1986). They took on the responsibility for planning the school's Easter Bonnet Parade, an event which traditionally took place on the last day of the Spring Term. (The school was actually a primary school on a British military base in Germany; hence the use of Deutschmark (DM) in the following account.)

Again, the project started with a class discussion in which the children expressed their willingness to take on the organisation of this event. The teacher commented that their enthusiasm and commitment were matched only by their disbelief at being given genuine responsibility: there is always the temptation to overlook the least able pupils when teachers are seeking individuals to take responsibility. The class discussion identified what needed to be done in order to make the event happen, and various tasks were allocated to small groups of children: these covered the use of the hall, the prizes, the photographs, the bonnets, the judging, the children taking part, and the timetable. Because of their young age, it was important for the teacher to guide them carefully through the planning, ensuring that groups consulted with each other when necessary. From time to time she called all the groups together to report on progress. This provided good opportunities for the development of communication skills, oral, written and pictorial. So every detail of the event was planned by these low-attaining children, they put their plans into operation, and, on the day, they proudly supervised and organised the Easter Bonnet Parade.

Some examples of the mathematics undertaken by some of the groups of children demonstrate nicely the potential in this kind of project for the development of mathematical skills and concepts.

Two boys were responsible for purchasing prizes, and were given a budget of DM50. Following some initial gathering of information about prices, their report (children's spelling retained) was as follows:

> We will be giving a prise to each class winner. We will need 11 prises for the classes + 2 prise for the judges. We will need 13 prises altogether. We are going to buy 13 Easter bunnies for prises. They cost DM3 each.
> $3 + 3 + 3 + 3 + 3 + 3 + 3 + 3 + 3 + 3 + 3 + 3 + 3 = DM39.$

It was interesting to note that they were unable to use their sketchy knowledge of multiplication by three to solve their problem here, but instead developed an informal method appropriate to the situation. They first laid out ten piles of DM3, counted these, more or less in threes, to get DM30, then added on three more threes, to get 39. They then checked this on a calculator, laboriously entering $3 + 3 + 3 + \ldots$, before recording their work as shown above. The teacher also showed them how you could do this with multiplication, and they were intrigued to get the same answer. Their result was within their budget, and the teacher encouraged them to predict the change they should expect. They were then ready to go to the shop, with a DM50 note, make the purchases, check the change, and have the prizes ready for the great day. In the course of all this they had applied and developed some elementary but important numeracy skills: budgeting, addition-facts, multiplication as repeated aggregation, use of a calculator, coin and note recognition and combinations, addition and subtraction in the context of shopping and giving change. But most significantly, they had actually used their developing mathematical skills to make something happen.

Another example of children being able to solve problems of calculations using their own informal methods appropriate to the context was provided by two pupils who were planning the timing of the actual parade. First they organised one class to do a dummy run, parading round the hall, while they timed them with a stop-watch. They found that 30 seconds would be needed per class for parading in their Easter bonnets. They then estimated that 5 minutes per class would be needed for the judges to discuss and make their judgements. They needed then to work out how long it would take for 11 classes. Initially they were stumped by this, but eventually came up with their solution:

> 30 secs + 5 mins + 30 secs + 5 mins + 30 secs + 5 mins + 30 secs + 5 mins + 30 secs + 5 mins + 30 secs + 5 mins + 30 secs + 5 mins + 30 secs + 5 mins + 30 secs + 5 mins + 30 secs + 5 mins + 30 secs + 5 mins.
> Judgeing time $5 + 5 + 5 + 5 + 5 + 5 + 5 + 5 + 5 + 5 + 5 = 55$ min
> Walking around $30 + 30 + 30 + 30 + 30 + 30 + 30 + 30 + 30 + 30 + 30 = 5\frac{1}{2}$
> Altogether the parade showld last $55 + 5\frac{1}{2} + 4\frac{1}{2} = 65$ minutes.

The first thing to note here is the way they have added the intervals of 30 seconds and those of 5 minutes separately, before combining them: the first bit of good mathematical thinking. They were thus able to devise a method based on something that they had discovered from handling the stop-watch and with which they were confident, i.e. that two lots of 30 seconds made one minute. This is a characteristic of informal methods of doing calculations: the individual will manipulate and transform the data in order to be able to apply knowledge and techniques with which they are confident.

Having got the problem down to '55 minutes plus $5\frac{1}{2}$ minutes' they were again stumped. So, they ingeniously decided to allow an extra $4\frac{1}{2}$ minutes (just to be on the safe side), thus making the awkward $5\frac{1}{2}$ minutes up to a convenient 10 minutes: they could cope with adding 10! How they worked out the $4\frac{1}{2}$ minutes is something of a mystery. This delightful piece of mathematical thinking and problem-solving demonstrates vividly the difference between the *ad hoc* method which makes sense to the individual in a practical context, and the formal methods taught in many mathematics lessons. Giving the pupils the space and freedom to develop their own ways of dealing with the real calculations they encountered enabled them to solve a problem (5½ multiplied by 11) which would have otherwise been judged to be way beyond their ability.

On the day of the parade the two children concerned were on duty with their stop-watches, timing each participating class. They were thrilled to find that they were only two minutes out in their estimate. The teacher identified an impressive range of mathematics with which they had been engaged in their planning. This included important language related to time, such as: morning, afternoon, when, before, after, then, beginning, end, faster, slower, fastest, slowest, takes the same time as. They were involved in ordering and comparing, sequencing of events, estimating time intervals, recording times, using stop-watches and digital clocks, informal methods of calculating, approximating, and using the equivalence between 30 seconds and half a minute.

A third group was responsible for taking polaroid photographs of the participants in the Easter Parade. As part of their rational planning they had to work out how many films to buy. Like most real-life problems, and unlike most text-book problems, it did not work out neatly. This was part of their report:

> We will take 1 photo of the winners from each class + 1 photo of each class.
> 11 classes = × 2 = 22 photos, + 2 photo of the winners together.
> Altogether we will take 22 + 2 = 24 photoes.
> 1 film will take 10 photos.
> So we will need
> 1 film = 10 photos
> 2 film = 20 photos
> 3 film = 30 photos
> so we will need to buy 3 films.

An important point to note here is the way children will often abuse mathematical notation (as these have done above, with the line beginning '11 classes = × 2 = . . . ') when they are tackling a genuine problem. My personal view is that this is quite acceptable. In practice very few people actually use the formal, orthodox methods for recording their everyday calculations. What is important for these low-attaining pupils is that they develop the confidence and competence to cope with the realistic demands of everyday life, not that they learn how to set out mathematical notation in the approved fashion.

The children then went on to calculate the total cost of three films, at DM24, and decided on the notes and coins they would need for the purchase. They bought the films and, on the day, took their photographs: once again mathematics had been used to make something happen.

FURTHER EXAMPLES

There are, of course, many practical difficulties, such as timetable constraints, the need for cooperation of other members of staff and pressures
imposed by National Curriculum assessment requirements, which might
limit the opportunities for teachers to allow their pupils to undertake projects as substantial, in terms of time and resources, as those described
above. However, given the enormous value, particularly for low-attaining
pupils, of experiencing immediate and genuine relevance in learning mathematics, it does not seem unreasonable to propose that, say, once each half-
term they might undertake a small project in which they use maths to make
things happen, and once a year they might be involved in something on a
larger scale. Activities 6.10 (Make a box), 6.11 (Arranging the classroom),
6.12 (Timetables) and 6.13 (Programming a video), described in Chapter 6,
are examples of what I would regard as smaller projects.

Many further examples can be provided of ways in which teachers have
made it possible for their pupils to make things happen with mathematics.
These range from quite small undertakings, lasting possibly for only a lesson
or two, to the more substantial projects, running over several weeks. The
larger projects normally are organised as whole-class activities, with groups
of children taking on responsibility for various components, as in the examples discussed above. Smaller projects might be undertaken by just one
group of children in the class, as one of a number of activities going on in a
mathematics lesson. Alternatively, the whole class might be involved in small
groups working on the same problem, with some means of deciding which
group produces the best solution, and then implementing this.

The examples described briefly below demonstrate the range of projects
in which pupils might use maths to make things happen. All of them are
examples of projects in which I have observed clear benefits for low-
attaining pupils, whether these be pupils in a mixed ability class, or in a
lower mathematics set. In each case, I give some indication of some of the
mathematics developed through the activity.

Display board

One teacher, working with a mixed ability class of 10–11-year-olds, makes a
point of giving a group of children the task of allocating space on the
display board to different groups preparing display material in connection
with the class's topic-work. This involves the application of spatial concepts
and various measurement skills.

Car parking

A group of 10–11-year-olds complained to their teacher that the teachers'
cars parked in the play-ground made it difficult for them to play their

games of football and so on. The teacher asked them to solve the problem. They counted the number of cars, measured their dimensions and estimated the length and width required for parking-spaces. They then produced a simple scale-drawing of the play-ground and on it indicated their solution to the problem. This was put to the school staff and accepted. Mathematics had been used to make something happen.

Book order

One small group of low-attaining pupils, aged 11–12 years, in a mixed ability class, were given the responsibility of dealing with the half-termly order for books from the children's Book Club to which the class belonged. This involved the development of simple accounting skills, handling money, giving change, keeping careful records, filling in the order form, checking the order when it arrived and distributing the books.

Refreshments stall

A group of 9–10-year-olds, including one boy whose attainment in mathematics was poor, took on responsibility for providing refreshments at the school fete. The boy in question discovered that the largest profit could be made by selling orange squash, which could be purchased in large quantities. He organised some 'market research' to determine the necessary level of dilution, thus using simple ideas of ratio. The group used concepts and skills in the area of liquid volume and capacity, estimation, and handling money, in a context which had meaning and genuine relevance.

Tournament

One low-attaining set of 10–11-year-olds organised a hand-ball tournament for their year-group. They developed a mathematical system for allocating individuals to teams, in order to produce a fair distribution of talent, grading each pupil on a scale from 0 to 10, and then trying to achieve teams with approximately the same totals of grades.

They also had to decide whether to have a knock-out tournament or a league. This led to an investigation into how many games would be involved for various numbers of teams. Eventually, with a little help from the teacher in organising their results, they discovered that for a knock-out competition they would need 2 teams, 4 teams, 8 teams or 16 teams, otherwise some teams would have to have a 'bye' in the first round. For a league, in which every team played every other team, the number of games to be organised would follow the pattern 1, 3, 6, 10, 15 . . . for 2 teams, 3 teams, 4 teams, 5 teams, etc.

Having settled on a league, they then had to work out a programme for the event, using and developing their knowledge and skills of handling time of the day and time intervals. They discovered the need for a pictorial representation of the timetable, as a way of getting an overview of what was happening and ensuring that a given team was not scheduled to play two games at the same time.

Write a work-book

One teacher found an effective way of engaging low-attaining 10–11-year-olds in a purposeful activity involving mathematics. She gave each group of children the task of preparing a section of a work-book for 7–8-year-olds, designed to teach them some simple mathematics. As well as making the pupils think about the mathematical ideas themselves, this involved some careful measurement and spatial organisation of the material on each page. They also learnt how to use a photocopier, discovered the relationships between various paper sizes, found out about enlargements and even learned how to use scale factors expressed in percentages.

Welcome to our school

In another British military primary school in Germany, one class of children identified a particular problem: because of the movement of military personnel, there always seemed to be new children arriving and having to settle into the class, the school and the locality. They decided to produce a welcome pack for newcomers. The production of this involved the application of a considerable amount of mathematics in a purposeful and relevant way.

Again, mathematics was involved in designing the layout of the various pages and in learning to use the photocopier. In addition, one group in the class produced information about German currency, for children fresh from the United Kingdom, with diagrams of coins, exchange rate tables and the prices in the local shops of some items of interest to children. One group produced a map of the school, taking numerous measurements and using the idea of scale. Another group produced a map of the local town, showing places of interest and estimating how long it would take to walk from one place to another. Others contributed information about the school timetable, local bus timetables and routes, and the organisation of the school, with ages and numbers of children in each class.

School camp

A mixed ability class of 10–11-year-olds undertook the organisation of the annual school camp, under the guidance of their teacher, who in previous years had done this herself. She had wondered initially whether taking on this responsibility might detract from the pupil's normal excitement about the camp, but what she found, in fact, was that there developed an even greater sense of excitement and anticipation, because the pupils could not wait to see their plans put into effect. Various groups were allocated responsibility for organising transport, planning on-camp activities, planning off-camp activities, arranging the provision of food, planning the lay-out of the site, and working out the overall timetable.

The range of mathematics involved in this project was very impressive. Pupils of varying abilities were engaged, for example, in: estimation and calculations of distance, time and speed; percentages, using a calculator; ideas of proportion; costing and budgeting; map-reading; keeping accounts; drawing graphs; scale-drawings; learning about circles; running opinion surveys; drawing up timetables.

For example, the group organising transport, wrote to and obtained information about seating capacity and estimates for cost from various coach companies. Some of the prices did not include Value Added Tax, whereas others did, so they had to learn how to deal with VAT on a calculator. Another group, preparing a scale-drawing of a possible lay-out for the site, had to learn important ideas about circles, since the children would be sleeping in bell-tents. The food group had information about quantities purchased for the number of children who attended the previous year's camp, and had to find a way of adapting these quantities for a different number attending this year. This involved the development of their own *ad hoc* way of solving proportion problems.

The teacher, in her report on this project, commented on the value of the experience for one low-attaining boy:

> For me it was all worth while when he said that he had done things he never thought he would be able to do, and he was delighted.

QUESTIONS FOR FURTHER DISCUSSION

1. Do you agree with the suggestion that rational problem solving and rational planning must inevitably involve the application of mathematical thinking?
2. What practical difficulties do you foresee in trying to implement the ideas in this chapter in different school situations? If the experience of using mathematics to make things happen is as helpful for low attainers as I suggest, how might these practical difficulties be overcome?
3. In a mixed ability class undertaking a problem solving project or planning an event, where various small groups take on responsibility for different components, should the low-attaining pupils form a separate group, or be integrated into other groups? What are the possible advantages and disadvantages of either policy?

10
MONEY FOR LOW ATTAINERS: A SCHEME OF WORK

Handling money with confidence and accuracy is clearly a key component of numeracy. In this book I have also emphasised the use of money as an effective and meaningful context for low attaining pupils to experience concepts of number and number operations. So, in this final chapter I outline a scheme of work on the topic of money for an imaginary class of mathematical low-attainers in the 9–11 age range. The suggestions here show how some of the principles outlined in this book might be put into practice. Although I have in mind a low-attaining set, it would not be difficult to adapt the procedures for organisation and suggestions for activities given here to a mixed ability class containing a smaller group of pupils whose attainment in mathematics is low.

There is sufficient material in this scheme to cover several weeks' mathematics in a normal school timetable. There is no ideal way of constructing a scheme of work in mathematics. However teachers – and student teachers, in particular – may find the following headings a useful framework:

- *Principles of procedure*: these are the principles which guide the selection of material and the organisation of the children's learning experiences.
- *Objectives*: covering knowledge, skills, understanding and, possibly, application. These should be statements of learning outcomes which can be readily assessed.
- *Activities*: these will be a collection of learning experiences, from which the teacher may select at appropriate times for particular groups of pupils. There will be some whole-class activities, some for small groups and some for individual or paired work. Some may focus on particular objectives, while others may emphasise more the kind of experience of mathematics being provided for the pupil.
- *Materials*: it is important to list the materials required for the planned activities, and to ensure that these are all readily available.
- *Organisation*: some consideration must be given to how the class will be organised in order to participate in the proposed activities.

- *Lesson plans*: it will not be possible to plan more than the first lesson in detail for any scheme, simply because of the obvious fact that plans for subsequent lessons will be dependent on what learning takes place and what difficulties occur in previous lessons.

PRINCIPLES OF PROCEDURE

A common topic

First of all, the scheme is based on the principle of the whole class focusing on the same topic for a number of weeks. Working on a common topic allows for some class-teaching and for some activities involving the whole class. Although whole-class activities inevitably have shortcomings associated with the range of pupil competences, nevertheless there are significant benefits in the opportunities provided for exposition and explanation of important ideas and procedures.

Small-group activities

It is envisaged that the majority of activities undertaken by children will involve them working in small groups. Small-group activities, one of the themes of this book, allow opportunities for pupils to use and develop mathematical language. Many of these activities are simple games, providing both a meaningful context and a purpose for the pupils to engage with mathematics.

Grouping

The way in which the groups are formed will vary from one class to another. If the class has a wide range of mathematical ability then for many activities it may be most appropriate to group children roughly according to ability. With a low-ability set, such as the one envisaged in this scheme, I would propose a flexible grouping system, sometimes grouping children on a friendship basis, sometimes with an eye to their particular mathematical needs. Occasionally, it is helpful for some activities for the less able pupil to work with a more able pupil. Sometimes, where there are some individual pupils whose poor social behaviour is a major consideration, it is important to judge their mood on a particular day to determine which other children they should work with, or even whether it would be more helpful for them to work individually. Teachers should also be on the look-out for the tendency of boys to take control when a mixed-sex group is working with a computer or other technological equipment. If this occurs it would be preferable for single-sex groupings to be used sometimes, for example, for computer based activities.

Individual or paired work

The scheme must also allow opportunity for pupils to engage in individual work to consolidate and practise important skills. However, it is often more effective to have pupils working in pairs, rather than individually, so that they can support each other in interpreting and carrying out their instructions.

Varied demands

It is envisaged that in any lesson there may, at times, be a number of different activities going on in the classroom. It is essential, therefore, that the activities employed are varied in terms of the demands made upon the teacher. In each lesson one group of children should be the main focus of the teacher's attention. While the teacher is aiming to move this group forward in their understanding and mastery of mathematical skills, other groups must be engaged in activities which consolidate and extend previous learning, without the need for very much input from the teacher.

Objectives and assessment

The scheme contains a statement of realistic and relevant objectives, covering knowledge, skills, understanding and, to some extent, application. The teacher should build into lesson plans opportunities for assessing the children in one of the groups against some of these target objectives. This may be done by sitting with them and engaging them in discussion of some mathematical problems. Occasional short written tests of specific knowledge can be used also.

Purposeful activities

The emphasis on objectives and assessment is balanced by an equal emphasis on providing the pupils with purposeful activities in meaningful contexts. The topic of money inevitably provides meaningful contexts for doing mathematics, such as shopping, earning and fund-raising. Within these contexts, some purposeful activities should be developed, such as simulations and role play. If possible, a project in which the pupils can use maths to make something happen, either planning an event or solving a real problem, should be incorporated.

Language development

Some activities are included which focus specifically on the development of important language structures in the context of money. These include particularly the language of comparison (e.g. 'cheaper than', 'dearer than').

OBJECTIVES

Many of the objectives on which I would focus in this topic are already outlined in previous chapters, because money has been identified as an important context for the development of numeracy. So, this scheme will bear in mind many of the place-value objectives outlined in Chapter 5, where it is proposed that the use of 1p, 10p and £1 coins is an important medium for establishing the place-value principle. In particular, there are in that chapter the important objectives (numbers 26–31) related to money notation. In Chapter 7, priority in learning to recognise various models of each of the operations of addition, subtraction, multiplication and division, was given to the context of money. So, within this topic, learning to choose the appropriate operation to enter on a calculator will be an important focus. Then, many of the objectives for developing confidence with number, outlined in Chapter 8, can also be experienced in a meaningful way through activities with money, such as buying and selling.

Additionally, I would include as important objectives, specifically related to handling money in practical, realistic situations, that the pupil should be able:

1. *To recognise and state the values of the coins and notes in common currency: 1p, 2p, 5p, 10p, 20p, 50p, £1, £5, £10, £20.*

2. *To state and show practically the equivalences between each coin or note and smaller denominations.*
   (For example, 10p = two 5p = five 2p = ten 1p.)

3. *To put out in coins, using the smallest possible number of coins, any given sum of money, up to £10.*

4. *To exchange any given collection of coins, up to a value of £10, for the smallest possible number of coins.*

5. *To find, state and record the value of any given collection of coins and notes, up to a value of £100.*

6. *To give change from 10p, 20p, 50p, £1, £2, £5, £10, practically, by adding on.*

7. *To keep an orderly record of income, expenditure and balance.*

WHOLE-CLASS ACTIVITIES

These activities are designed to involve all the children in the class, thus providing opportunity for discussion, explanation and clarification of key ideas within the topic.

Activity 10.1 Estimate cost

Objective To develop the pupil's sense of the value of money. Those low-attaining pupils who are not given much responsibility for handling money outside of school, such as Sharon and Mark in the case studies in Chapter 2, often display very little sense of the value of money and what things cost. Sharon did not know, for example, whether her new bicycle would cost £1, £10 or £100. This activity can help to remedy this deficiency in their understanding, particularly if the teacher engages them in discussion and comparison of the prices of the various items.

Materials Various items, for which the teacher knows the cost. Slips of paper for estimates, materials for graphical display of results.

Method This is the same as Activity 6.1 (Estimation class-challenge), described in Chapter 6 and used there for estimating length, weight, capacity and time, but now adapted to the context of money. For each lesson, over a period of a number of days, the teacher brings in an item for which the pupils must write down their estimate for the cost. These items should be potentially within the pupils' experience, such as some article of children's clothing, a Walkman radio cassette-player, various items of food or drink, a book, or a digital watch. The pupils' estimates are then processed in the same way as their estimates for various measurements in Activity 6.1, with a different group of pupils taking responsibility each day for producing the graph showing the class's estimates.

Activity 10.2 Shopping frieze

Objective This is an activity which can involve the whole class, designed to develop the pupils' sense of the cost of various purchases, and to give them practice in ordering and the correct use of money notation.

Materials Packets and labels from various purchases, with prices shown on them.

Method Various packets and labels are to be mounted on a frieze along one wall of the classroom, with the price written beneath them, along a line labelled: £0.10, £0.20, £0.30, etc. Make a large collection of packets and labels first. Get one group to sort these into ranges of prices, e.g. up to £1, from £1 up to £2. Then give groups of children one of these sets each to prepare a section of the frieze. Pupils are encouraged to bring in packets and labels themselves from home, and challenged to find items to fill in gaps in the display.

Activity 10.3 Best-buy investigation

Objective To practise the use of multiplication and division in the contexts of (a) money and sets, (b) money and weight, or (c) money and liquid volume, for the purpose of determining the best buy. Also, to develop the skill of interpreting answers to money calculations done on a calculator (*objective 29 in Chapter 5*). The investigation provides many useful opportunities for teacher exposition of important ideas, and is therefore an appropriate activity for the whole class to engage in.

Materials Pupils will need information from a supermarket about prices of items (a) bought separately and in multiple packs, or (b) sold by weight in various sizes of packets, or (c) sold by volume in various sizes of containers. It is preferable if they can collect packets from their own family shopping with this kind of information. Each pupil will also need a calculator.

Method Pupils use the information about prices to determine the savings achieved by buying multiple packs or larger quantities. This gives a meaningful context for experiencing division, multiplication and subtraction, and for learning how to enter sums of money on a calculator and how to interpret answers achieved.

For example, one make of battery can be bought for 89p each, or £1.73 for a pack of two, or £3.23 for a pack of four. Pupils should use this information in two ways. First, using the division key on the calculator, they can determine the price per battery in the multiple packs. This requires careful interpretation of the results produced by the calculator: i.e. '1.73 ÷ 2 = 0.865' would be interpreted as a little bit more than £0.86, or about 86p per battery; and then '3.23 ÷ 4 = 0.8075' as a little bit more than £0.80, or about 80p per battery. Secondly, the pupils can use multiplication to find the cost of purchasing the number of items in the multiple packs if bought separately, and compare this with the price of the multiple packs: this last step gives a context for the comparison model of subtraction. For example, for four batteries at 89p each the calculation entered is '0.89 × 4 =', giving the result £3.56; comparing this with £3.23 indicates a saving of £0.33 or 33p if bought in a multiple pack.

One group of low-attaining 11-year-olds doing this investigation were excited to discover that it was actually more expensive to buy a pack of four of a particular kind of chocolate than to buy four separately. On their own initiative, they recorded the savings on the multiple pack as '–2p'.

When exploring best buys for items sold by weight (such as cereals or chocolate) or those sold by volume (such as lemonade or milk), pupils may find it easiest to use their calculators to determine how many grams or millilitres are purchased per penny. For example, given that they can buy a can of lemonade (330 ml) for 29p, and a bottle (1000 ml) for 55p, the pupil might enter on their calculator: '330 ÷ 29 =' and '1000 ÷ 55 ='. They would then be able to read off the results: that the can and the bottle give a little bit more than 11 ml per penny, and a little bit more than 18 ml per penny, respectively. If, however, they wish to explore price per unit weight or per unit volume, they will probably not make sense of the results obtained unless they use the usual supermarket convention of giving 'price per 100 g' or 'price per 100 ml'. For the lemonade example, this would require

---

g' or 'price per 100 ml'. For the lemonade example, this would require entering the following key sequences: '29 ÷ 330 × 100 =' and '55 ÷ 1000 × 100 ='. I have found that, with the calculator doing the arithmetic, many low-attaining pupils can actually make sense of what we are doing here. Sticking with the convention that, because we are working in pence, the digits after the point in the calculator answer just represent 'little bits of pennies', they can interpret the results of '8.7878787' and '5.5' as meaning 'a little bit more than 8p' and 'a little bit more than 5p' per 100 ml.

Activity 10.4 Planning an event: refreshments stall

Objectives To give pupils opportunity to use and develop skills of handling money by using their mathematics to make something happen. This will be a purposeful activity (planning an event) in a meaningful context (fund-raising), probably requiring something like a week's work.

Method The class is invited to take on responsibility for planning and organising the refreshments stall at the school fete. A class discussion will be used to identify what needs to be done and to allocate responsibility for components of the planning to various groups of pupils. Children will be encouraged to take entire responsibility for determining what should be on sale, forecasting numbers and quantities, the purchase and preparation of the items, pricing, negotiating with those organising the fete, setting up and running the stall, determining the float required, handling the sales, giving change, and calculating the profit. It may be helpful to build into the project a dummy run in the classroom, to practise some of the skills of selling and giving change.

Activity 10.5 (Activity 8.5) Turning the tables

This activity, described in Chapter 8, is incorporated in this scheme to strengthen the connections between number-facts and the context of money.

SMALL-GROUP ACTIVITIES

This section includes a number of small-group games described in Chapter 5, as well as three further suggestions.

Activity 10.6 How many ways?

Objectives Practice in recognising values of coins and in using the equivalences between different denominations (objectives 1 and 2).

Materials Plastic token coins.

Method A group of pupils is challenged to find all the possible ways of making a given sum of money, using specified coins. For example:

- Find all the ways of making 19p, using 1p, 2p, 5p, 10p coins.

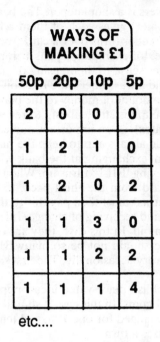

Figure 10.1   Table for Activity 10.6: How many ways?

- Find all the ways of making 35p, using 5p, 10p, 20p coins.
- Find all the ways of making £1, using 5p, 10p, 20p, 50p coins.

Pupils should record their results in a table, showing the numbers of each coins used, as shown, for example, in Figure 10.1.

Activity 10.7 Shopkeeper

Objectives This is a small-group game for up to five players, plus one who acts as the 'bank manager'. Although very simple and obvious, it is very effective, giving opportunity for handling coins in a simulated shopping context (*objectives 1 and 2*), exchanging equivalent coins (*objective 3*) and giving change (*objective 6*). Additionally, pupils experience the operations of addition, subtraction and multiplication in the context of money.

Materials A supply of plastic token coins; a calculator for each player; Pack A of cards (see Chapter 5), or some other way of generating single-digit numbers; a second set of cards on each of which is written an item and a price, for example, 'pens at 15p' – contained in this pack are a number of cards with the word 'BILL' written on them; a third pack with various sums of money written on them, ranging up to £5, representing bills.

Rules Each of the players is a shopkeeper. The bank manager (who also acts as a universal customer) gives each of them a float of £5.55 to begin with. In turn, each shopkeeper turns over a card from each of the first two packs, to represent a sale, for example, '7 pens at 15p'. They work this out, by whatever means makes sense to them, using the calculator if they wish. The bank manager should always check the total on a calculator, and then pay out the appropriate amount of money to the player concerned. Even if a calculator is used, the pupil is still learning to recognise the operation of multiplication in this context, so an important numeracy objective is being developed. Players should always aim to keep the number of coins in their possession to a minimum, exchanging at the bank whenever possible.

Occasionally, a card saying 'BILL' turns up. When this happens the bank manager turns over a card from the third pack, to reveal a bill (such as £1.75). The player concerned must then pay this to the bank. This step will often involve the giving and receiving of change. It is possible that a player might be unable to pay a bill. In this case, they are out of the game, being declared bankrupt: there should not be so many BILLS in the pack that this happens other than very occasionally. The first shopkeeper to accumulate £20 is the winner.

Variations (a) To establish place-value ideas, pupils can play the game using only 1p, 10p and £1 coins. In this case it should be a requirement that ten 1p coins must be exchanged for one 10p, and ten 10p coins for one £1, otherwise the player misses a turn.

(b) An important version of this game, focusing on *objective* 7 above, is played without coins, and without a bank manager. Instead, using a calculator, pupils keep a simple record of sales and bills, using three columns for income, expenditure and balance, like this:

Balance	Income	Expenditure
£5.55	£1.05	nil
£6.60	£1.12	nil
£7.72	nil	£1.75
£5.97	etc.	

In the above example, the shopkeeper has started with a float of £5.55, sold '7 pens at 15p' (£1.05) and '8 chocolate bars at 14p' (£1.12), and then paid out a bill of £1.75. In the process they will have had to recognise the need for entering multiplication, addition and subtraction on their calculators, and been engaged in transforming money notation from pence to pounds.

This version of the game should be used once the pupils have had plenty of experience of the version with coins.

Activity 10.8 I have, who has: change from a pound

Objective This is the small-group game described in Chapter 8 (Activity 8.9) adapted to give practice in working out change from a pound.

Materials The set of cards are prepared as in Activity 8.9, with the 'questions' being various sums of money (e.g. 46p, 35p, 9p, . . .) and the 'answers' being the corresponding change from a pound (i.e. 54p, 65p, 91p, . . .).

Rules See Activity 8.9.

Variations (a) Use pound notation (i.e. £0.46, £0.35. £0.09, . . .). (b) The questions could consist of two prices which must be added together (e.g. 35p, 17p).

Activity 10.9 Role play

This is an example of how role play can be used to give more purpose to doing mathematics. A small group of pupils are given the opening section of a script for a short play and invited to work out the rest of it themselves. It is not necessary to require them to produce a written script. Much of the drama can be improvised, provided they have agreed the framework of the plot. It is important, however, in order to make this a useful mathematical experience, that any financial transactions involved are acted out properly with coins, not just pretended. When they have worked out their scene they can present it to the rest of the class.

> (Tracey is sitting at home, counting her savings: she has £3.76. Mum, Dad, Simon, are sitting reading.)
> *Tracey* One pound, two pounds, three pounds, three pounds fifty, sixty, seventy, seventy-two, seventy-four, seventy-six . . . that's three pounds, seventy-six pence. And I need ten pounds to go on the outing to London next month. I'll never save up enough.
> *Mum* Ooh, that reminds me. Rich Aunt Mabel is calling round later on. Perhaps you'd better drop a hint.
> *Dad* And here's your pocket money, Tracey. (Hands her 50p)
> *Tracey* Thanks, Dad. That's another fifty pence towards the outing.
> *Simon* How much you got saved up now, Trace?
> *Tracey* Er, that's three pounds, seventy-six, plus fifty. Four pounds, and something.
> *Dad* Four pounds, thirty-six, dimwit.
> *Mum* No, George, it's four pounds, twenty-six.
> *Dad* It's thirty-six, I tell you.
> *Mum* It's twenty-six, George.
> *Dad* (Getting angry) Thirty-six!
> *Mum* All right, George, if you say so. (Quietly, to Tracey) It's twenty-six.
> *Dad* Give the money here, Tracey. (He takes the money and counts it.) Now, look. Three pounds, two fifties make a pound, that's four pounds, ten, twenty, twenty-six . . . er, four pounds, twenty-six . . . . (slips another ten pence from his pocket into the pile) There, you are, four pounds, thirty-six pence!
> *Tracey* Thanks, Dad. I knew you were right all along. (Aside) That's another ten pence towards the outing!
> *Simon* So, how much more do you need now, Tracey?
> *Tracey* Well, I've got four pounds, thirty-six, and I need ten pounds altogether . . .

Dad Perhaps this time you'd better use that calculator that Rich Aunt Mabel gave you for your birthday.

Tracey (Picking up the calculator) Right, now let's see, how can I work this out? (There is a knock on the door . . .)

Variation Instead of the opening section of a script, provide the group of children with a brief description of a situation, for which they must improvise and act out their response. For example:

- A customer in a supermarket does not have enough money to pay for all the goods in their trolley.
- A group of children find a lost treasure and get a reward, which they must share between them.
- Some newspaper delivery girls and boys go to their boss to ask for a pay-rise.
- A shop decides to sell off all its toys at half-price.

Again, it is important that each of these role play situations involves children in handling actual coins, albeit plastic tokens, not just imaginary ones.

Activity 10.10 (Activity 5.1) Race to a pound

Activity 10.11 (Activity 5.2) Race to ten pounds

Activity 10.12 (Activity 5.12) Spend ten pounds

These three small-group games from Chapter 5 focus on the processes of addition and subtraction in the context of money, using 1p, 10p and £1 coins to develop place-value concepts.

Activity 10.13 (Activity 5.11) Win some, lose some

This is another small-group game from Chapter 5, developing the principle of exchange using coins.

Activity 10.14 Money-boxes

This activity is the place-value game *Boxes* (Activity 5.6), adapted for use with money notation, as suggested at the end of Chapter 5.

ACTIVITIES FOR INDIVIDUAL OR PAIRED WORK

This section also includes a number of suggestions from previous chapters.

Activity 10.15 Catalogue shopping

Objectives To develop the pupil's ability to recognise the operations of addition and subtraction in the context of money, and to practise the use of

ORDER FORM

Choose [ ] items from the catalogue. You may spend up to £ [ ]

Item	Page	Reference number	Price
		Total spent	
		How much left	

Figure 10.2   Imitation order form for catalogue shopping (Activity 10.15)

money notation in recording purchases. The activity comes in the category of a *simulation* of a real problem.

Materials A collection of mail-order catalogues: pupils will normally be able to bring these in from home; imitation order forms, as shown in Figure 10.2; a calculator for each pupil.

Method Each pupil is given a challenge, set by the teacher at a level of difficulty appropriate to the child. This is done by filling in numbers in the two boxes at the top of the order form. For example, one pupil might be required to buy 5 items, spending up to £50, whereas another might be challenged to buy 12 items, spending up to £200. The challenge is to spend as much of your money as possible. Pupils use their calculators to add up what they have spent so far, and then, by choosing the operation of subtraction, can find out how much they have left to spend at each stage. When they have decided on their purchases they complete their order form.

This is always a very successful activity with low-attaining pupils, giving purposeful experience of addition and subtraction in a meaningful context. They usually get very involved in the simulation, showing great determination to spend as much as they possibly can, while, at the same time, only being prepared to choose things they really want!

```
10   S = 0
20   FOR N = 1 TO 10
30   CLS
40    A = RND(100)*10: B = RND(100)*10
50   C = RND(5)*10+RND(5): D = RND(5)*10+RND(5)
60   PRINT:PRINT:PRINT
70   PRINT N;". CHOOSE EITHER: ":PRINT
80    PRINT "1.  ";A;" g for ";C;"p:PRINT "OR"
90    PRINT "2.  ";B;" g for ";D;"p"
100 INPUT "TYPE 1 OR 2      "X
110 IF X<>1 AND X<>2 THEN 100
120 IF C/A<D/B AND X=1 THEN 150
130 IF C/A>D/B AND X=2 THEN 150
140 PRINT:PRINT "WORST BUY!": GOTO 170
150 PRINT:PRINT "BEST BUY!"
160 S= S+1
170 PRINT:PRINT:PRINT S;"  best buy(s) so far"
180 PRINT:PRINT:PRINT:PRINT"PRESS ANY KEY TO CONTINUE"
190 W=INKEY(32767): NEXT N
200 CLS: PRINT: PRINT
210 PRINT S" BEST BUY(S) OUT OF 10":PRINT
220 IF S>7 THEN PRINT "YOU ARE AN EXCELLENT SHOPPER!":STOP
230 IF S<5 THEN PRINT "I WOULDN'T TRUST YOU WITH MY MONEY!": STOP
240 PRINT "NOT TOO BAD, BUT YOU NEED MORE PRACTICE"
250 END
```

Figure 10.3   Best-buy program

Activity 10.16 Best-buy program

Objective To practise the use of division in the contexts of money and weight, for the purpose of determining the best buy. This would be useful preparation for the *Best-buy investigation* (Activity 10.3).

Materials A microcomputer and a program like the one given in Figure 10.3, written there in BBC-BASIC; a calculator.

Method Experience suggests that the optimum number of pupils working on a microcomputer at the same time is two. This activity is therefore included as individual or paired work. As noted above, under *Principles of Procedure*, it may often be preferable for children working together on a computer to be of the same sex.

The program provides pupils with an opportunity to practise best-buy shopping in the classroom. In each of ten questions they are given a choice of two purchases, presented on the screen like this:

CHOOSE EITHER:

1. 340 g for 58p

OR

2. 250 g for 26p

TYPE 1 OR 2

The computer then responds to the pupil's choice with either 'BEST BUY!' or 'WORST BUY!' A running total of the number of best buys is kept. A person with a score of 8 or more is judged to be an excellent shopper. The low-attaining pupil is expected to use a calculator, paper and pencil, to help make the decisions. This may be done most simply by finding the number of grams purchased per penny, hence gaining experience of choosing the operation of division for an equal-sharing situation in the context of weight divided by money (see Chapter 7).

Variations Some readers will be able to produce more sophisticated versions of the program given here. Even inexperienced programmers will be able to modify it for their own purposes, for example, change the grams in lines 80 and 90 to millilitres for liquid volume rather than weight. Change the criterion for excellence in line 220 from '>7' to '>8', and so on, and write your own messages. Change the 'p' to '£' in lines 80 and 90. To produce different ranges of weights and prices, try putting different numbers in the brackets in the 'RND( )' statements in lines 40 and 50 and see what happens.

Activity 10.17 School cafeteria/tuck-shop

Objective To give pupils real experience of giving change and counting money in a genuine selling situation (objectives 5 and 6).

Method Assuming the school has either a tuck-shop or a lunchtime cafeteria, or both, arrange for two pupils each day to assist in receiving customers' payments, in giving change, and in counting-up the takings at the end of the session. If pupils know that they are preparing for this responsibility their commitment to their work in mathematics lessons will be increased. Some specific training for the job, using role play, dummy items for purchase and plastic token coins, could be given beforehand.

Activity 10.18 Calculator sentences

This is the activity, described in Chapter 7, for developing confidence with important mathematical structures in the context of money, together with the associated language patterns. These would focus particularly on the following language: increased, reduced, costs more than, costs less than, more expensive, less expensive, dearer, cheaper, per, each.

Activity 10.19 Graded exercises: choosing the operation

This refers to work-sheets using a series of graded exercises based on the ideas outlined in Chapter 7 under the heading *Fuzzy Regions*. These are designed to give pupils opportunity to discover for themselves, through exploring keys on their calculators, the mathematical structures of various models of the operations of addition, subtraction, multiplication and division. The work-sheets might focus on the particular models of operations which pupils find difficult, such as the inverse-of-addition model of subtraction, or the inverse-of-multiplication model of division.

Activity 10.20 Money grids

Activity 5.9 (*Grids*) in Chapter 5 (see Figure 5.7) can be adapted for use with money notation, to practise simple additions and subtractions with money. For example, a grid could start with £3.09 in the top left-hand corner and use the two instructions 'EARN 2p' and 'SPEND 10p'. A supply of grids of this sort will be useful for keeping occupied those pupils who finish other activities early.

Activity 10.21 (Activity 5.13) Money notation work-sheets

These work-sheets, described in Chapter 5, focus on the correct use of notation for money, translations between pence and pounds (e.g. 86p = £0.86) and the interpretation of calculator results in money calculations.

Activity 10.22 Say, press, check, write: money

As suggested at the end of Chapter 5, Activity 5.7 (*Say, press, check, write*) can be adapted for use with money notation.

MATERIALS

To employ the activities listed above, the following materials will be required:

- Various items for children to estimate cost (Activity 10.1)
- 12 large sheets of 2-cm squared paper (for graphs, Activity 10.1)
- Metre ruler
- 2-cm-wide strips of coloured paper
- Pair of scissors
- Glue-stick
- Supply of packets and labels with prices shown (Activity 10.2)
- Large supply of plastic token coins, all denominations
- 24 calculators
- 3 sets of Packs A and B cards (generating single-digit numbers)

- Other packs of cards for Activity 10.7
- Account sheets for recording balance, income and expenditure for Activity 10.7, variation (b)
- Cards for *I have, who has games* (Activity 10.8, including variations)
- Copy of script for role play in Activity 10.8
- Copies of statements of situations for Activity 10.8 variation
- Pack E: cards for *Win some, lose some* (Activity 10.11/5.12)
- Supply of strips of card with boxes on for Activity 10.14
- Mail-order catalogues (Activity 10.15)
- Imitation order forms for mail orders (Figure 10.2)
- Microcomputer, with program (Figure 10.3) for Activity 10.16
- Cards with layout for *Calculator sentences* (Activity 10.18)
- Work-sheets with graded exercises for each model of $+,-,\times,\div$, in the context of money (Activity 10.19)
- Supply of blank grids for Activity 10.20
- Money-notation work-sheets (Activity 10.21/5.13)
- Work-sheets with headings for *Say, press, check, write: money* (Activity 10.22)

ORGANISATION

Lesson structure: an activities circus

A simple structure for a typical seventy-minute mathematics lesson for our group of low-attaining 9–11-year-olds is shown in Figure 10.4. The model employed here is essentially that of an activities circus, sandwiched between some brief whole-class activities.

It is not envisaged that every lesson should follow this format, but simply that this might be a useful, basic model to follow much of the time. The time allocations in Figure 10.4 are, of course, very flexible.

The structure incorporates a short period of about ten minutes at the start of the lesson given over to a whole-class activity. Activity 10.1 (*Estimate cost*) is an example of the kind of activity which might be used here to focus the whole class's attention on the topic in question. Alternatively, this time might be given over to a class discussion or question-and-answer session about some key ideas, such as the correct way of writing a sum of money using pound notation, or the relationship between pence and pounds.

The bulk of the lesson is then given over to small-group activities and individual (or paired) work. This is referred to as an 'activities circus'. Setting up these activities will obviously require some time.

In the middle of the central part of the lesson structure, I have built in an 'interruption'. In my experience, many low-attaining pupils find 45 minutes working on the same kind of activity to be too long. In Chapter 3 it was suggested that some concessions may need to be made to these pupils' difficulties in concentrating on one task for any length of time. I find it helpful therefore to stop them after 20 minutes or so and do something else

10 mins	whole-class activity
5 mins	organisation
20 mins	activities-circus: small group and individual or paired work
5 mins	interruption
20 mins	activities-circus continued
10 mins	clearing-up and whole-class activity

Figure 10.4　A possible structure for a mathematics lesson

for a few minutes. For example, the teacher can deliberately look for a problem or something of interest which has turned up in some of the pupils' work or activities which can be usefully shared and discussed with the whole class. Sometimes this interruption could be used for a short class game, or to show some completed work, or for a mental arithmetic test, or even just for a chat about what the children did at the weekend.

The final ten minutes is allocated to clearing up and a further short period of whole-class activity. This could be used regularly to focus on basic number knowledge. The kind of activity to incorporate here is something like *Turning the tables* (Activity 10.5).

A framework for the activities circus

I will assume that our low-attaining set consists of 24 pupils, who will be referred to as A, B, C, . . . X, arranged roughly in order of mathematical ability, with the least able pupils at the beginning of the alphabet and the more able ones at the end. Some principles for grouping these children for various activities and for the selection of activities have been outlined above under *Principles of Procedure*. These principles can be worked out in practice within the framework shown in Figure 10.5. This diagram applies to the activities circus, i.e. the section of the lesson given over to the small-group and individual or paired activities, and provides a basic structure for a sequence of four lessons.

Groups

	A - F	G - L	M - R	S - X
Lesson 1	Moving forward	Small-group extension activities	Small-group extension activities	Individual or paired work: consolidating
Lesson 2	Individual or paired work: consolidating	Moving forward	Small-group extension activities	Small-group extension activities
Lesson 3	Small-group extension activities	Individual or paired work: consolidating	Moving forward	Small-group extension activities
Lesson 4	Small-group extension activities	Small-group extension activities	Individual or paired work: consolidating	Moving forward

Figure 10.5   Framework for activities circus for four lessons

The framework assumes that the teacher has first organised the pupils into four groups, A–F, G–L, M–R and S–X, roughly according to ability. This is a starting point for organisation and does not mean that the pupils will work only in these groupings.

Secondly, the framework assumes that there are three kinds of activity in which the groups will engage:

1. Assessment and moving forward: during this time the teacher will aim to sit with the group in order to assess and to teach them, checking the pupil's progress against some of the objectives, diagnosing difficulties, maybe introducing new material, clarifying ideas previously found difficult, explaining procedures.
2. Individual or paired consolidation work: during this time the pupils will be working individually, or in pairs, on work-sheets, puzzles, or computer activities, designed to consolidate their learning, based on the teacher's work with the group in stage 1.
3. Small-group extension activities: during this time pupils will engage in appropriate small-group activities, calling on and extending their mathematical knowledge and skills within the given topic.

As far as possible, the activities will be selected so that only the group scheduled for assessment and moving forward should make heavy demands upon the teacher. Since, in the framework of Figure 10.5, there are two groups engaged in small-group extension activities at any time, there is some possibility for flexibility in the groupings of children for these activities.

Overall plan

It should be stressed that Figure 10.5 is no more than a basic framework for planning a series of lessons. A considerable degree of flexibility from one lesson to the next will be required, as the teacher responds to the events of each lesson.

It is certainly not envisaged that all the lessons in the weeks devoted to this topic will be organised strictly along these lines. For example, a few lessons might be set aside for the whole class together to engage in Activity 10.3 (*Best-buy investigation*) or Activity 10.2 (*Shopping frieze*). Then, towards the end of the topic, perhaps a whole week would be given to the project described in Activity 10.4 (*Planning an event: refreshments stall*). During this project there will be further opportunity to vary the groupings of the pupils, so that some less-able pupils might get the benefit of working alongside more able friends.

So over a period of twenty days, the scheme might develop like this:

Days 1–4	Activities circus
Day 5	Whole-class activity (Activity 10.2) *Shopping frieze*
Days 6–9	Activities circus
Day 10–11	Whole-class activity (Activity 10.3) *Best-buy investigation*
Days 12–15	Activities circus
Days 16–20	Class project (Activity 10.4) *Planning an event: refreshments stall*

FIRST LESSON PLAN

The proposed plan for the first lesson in the scheme is shown in Figure 10.6. This uses the lesson structure outlined above in Figure 10.4.

Opening activity

Introduce the class to *Estimate cost* (Activity 10.1), explaining that this will be done at the start of each lesson for a number of days, to see how good they are at estimating the cost of various purchases. Use a child's sweatshirt, costing, say, £7.50: each pupil to write down their estimate for the price on a slip of paper. The teacher should provide some explanation of the pound notation for money and encourage pupils to write their estimates in this way.

Activities circus

The activities circus section of the lesson is based on the plan for Day 1 in Figure 10.5: pupils A–F will be the main focus of the teacher's attention, for

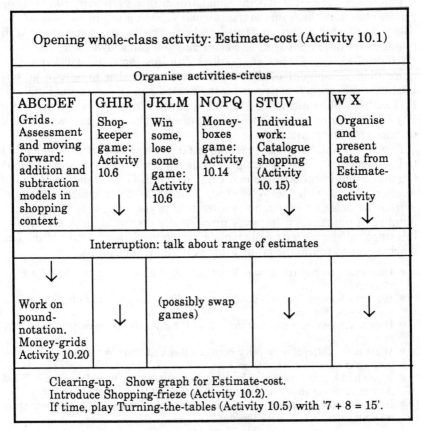

Figure 10.6   First lesson plan

assessment and moving forward; pupils G–L and M–R are to be organised for small-group activities; pupils S–X will spend this time on individual or paired work.

Pupils W and X will be given responsibility for organising and representing the class's estimates for the cost of the article. It is assumed that, since this activity is a regular feature of any work on measurement, these pupils have done this before with estimates of length, time, capacity or weight, so will not require very much instruction. If necessary, an example of the kind of graph to be produced might be provided by the teacher. The four other pupils in this group (S, T, U, V) will work individually on *Catalogue shopping* (Activity 10.15). This is a new activity for them, so it will be kept fairly simple to begin with: for example, choose 5 items, spend up to £20.

Pupils N, O, P, Q will play the game *Money boxes* (Activity 10.14). They are familiar with this game in the original version given in Activity 5.6, so will require only a little instruction about playing the same game with pound notation. Pupils J, K, L, M will play the game *Win some, lose some* (Activity 10.13/5.11). They are familiar with this game and will require no more than a reminder of the rules. It is possible that these two groups might swap over their activities for the second half of the lesson. Pupils G, H, I and R will be introduced to a new game, *Shopkeeper* (Activity 10.6). Pupil R is a fairly competent and responsible child and can act as bank manager for this game.

Pupils A–F will be given some simple *Grids* (see Chapter 5: Activity 5.9) to keep them purposefully occupied while the teacher gets the other groups organised and introduces the new game to pupils G, H, I and R. Then the teacher will sit with the A–F group and assess their understanding of various models of addition and subtraction in the context of shopping. A number of purchases with prices prominently displayed, in pence only at this stage, will be placed on the table. Each child will have a calculator. The teacher will go round the group asking questions such as:

- How much to buy these two? What do you enter on your calculator to work this out?
- How much more does this cost than that? What do you enter on your calculator to work this out?
- How much less does this cost than that? What do you enter on your calculator to work this out?
- What is the difference in price between this and that? What do you enter on your calculator to work this out?
- If you had 45p and wanted to buy this, how much more would you need? What do you enter on your calculator to work this out?
- If the shopkeeper reduced this by 25p what would it cost? What do you enter on your calculator to work this out?

The children's responses to these will be noted and used to determine which *Calculator sentences* or *Graded exercises* work-sheets (Activities 10.18 and 10.19) will be given to them in the next lesson to follow up this assessment.

The teacher will also spend some time with this group on pound notation, and then leave them with some *Money grids* (Activity 10.20), in order to check up on the progress of other groups of children. A supply of these *Money grids* should be available as fillers for any pupils who complete their activity before the end of allotted time.

Interruption

Half-way through the time allotted to the activities circus, the teacher will give the class a few minutes break from their activities. This will be used to talk about the range of estimates which pupils W and X have discovered as they have organised the data from the opening activity. The actual cost could be disclosed at this point, and estimates which are excessively low or high could be compared with this.

Closing activities

Assuming the graph of the class's estimates is completed, this will be displayed and discussed. The class will be challenged to try to get everyone much closer to the actual cost in future estimates. The idea for the *Shopping frieze* (Activity 10.2) will be introduced and the class invited to bring in labels and packages from home with various prices shown on them.

If there is time left, the teacher will write '7 + 8 = 15' on the board and play *Turning the tables* (Activity 10.5/8.5), with questions such as:

- What is 8 add 7?
- 15 take away 8?
- What is the difference between 7 and 15?
- How much altogether for a pen costing 7p and a pencil costing 8p?
- You have 15p and spend 8p. How much left?
- You have 7p and want to buy a ruler for 15p. How much more do you need?
- I have 15p and you have 8p. How much less do you have than me?

QUESTIONS FOR FURTHER DISCUSSION

1. If pupils are consolidating skills through work-sheets or puzzles, what are the advantages and disadvantages of their working individually or working in pairs?
2. What is your view of my suggestion for a planned interruption in the middle of a mathematics lesson for low attainers?
3. How would you plan the second lesson in this scheme?
4. What criteria would you use to evaluate the scheme outlined in this chapter?
5. Return to the questions at the end of Chapter 2 about the low-attaining pupils studied there. Answer them again in the light of what you have read in this book.

BIBLIOGRAPHY AND REFERENCES

Ainscow, M. and Tweddle, D.A. (1979) *Preventing Classroom Failure: an Objectives Approach*, John Wiley & Sons.

Bell, A., Burkhardt, H., McIntosh, A. and Moore, G. (1978) *A Calculator Experiment in a Primary School*, Shell Centre for Mathematical Education, University of Nottingham.

Biggs, E. (1985) *Teaching Mathematics 7–13: Slow-Learning and Able Pupils*, NFER-Nelson.

Biggs, J.B. (1967) *Mathematics and the Conditions of Learning*, National Foundation for Educational Research.

Blake, G. (1985) 'Using maths to make things happen: the mystery of the forgotten shower unit', in T. Booth *et al.* (eds) *Preventing Difficulties in Learning*, Basil Blackwell in association with the Open University.

Bloom, B.S. (ed.) (1956) *Taxonomy of Educational Objectives: the Classification of Educational Goals – Handbook 1: Cognitive Domain*, David McKay Co.

Bowers, J. (1981) 'Excursion to Boulogne', *Struggle: Mathematics for Low Attainers*, no. 4 (ILEA).

Brown, M. (1981) 'Number Operations', in K.M. Hart (ed.) *Children's Understanding of Mathematics, 11–16*, John Murray.

Carraher, T.C., Carraher, D. and Schliemann, A.D. (1985) 'Mathematics in the streets and in schools', *British Journal of Developmental Psychology*, Vol. 3, no. 1.

Carraher, T.C., Schliemann, A.D. and Carraher, D.W. (1988) 'Mathematical concepts in everyday life', in G.B. Saxe and M. Gearhard (eds.) *Children's Mathematics*, New Directions in Child Development Series no. 41, Jossey-Bass.

Clement, M.A. (1980) 'Analyzing children's errors on written mathematical tasks', *Educational Studies in Mathematics*, Vol. 11, no. 1.

Cockcroft, W.H. (chairman) (1982) *Mathematics Counts* (Report of the Committee of Inquiry into the Teaching of Mathematics in Schools), HMSO.

Denvir, B., Stolz, C. and Brown, M. (1982) *Low Attainers in Mathematics 5–16, Policies and Practices in Schools* (Schools Council Working Paper 72), Methuen.

Department of Education and Science and the Welsh Office (1989) *Mathematics in the National Curriculum*, HMSO.

Dickson, L., Brown, M. and Gibson, O. (1984) *Children Learning Mathematics: a Teacher's Guide to Recent Research*, Holt, Rinehart & Winston.

Dienes, Z. (1960) *Building Up Mathematics*, Hutchinson.
Donaldson, M. (1978) *Children's Minds*, Fontana.
Duncan, A. (1978) *Teaching Mathematics to Slow Learners*, Ward Lock Educational.
Easen, P. (1985) 'All at sixes and sevens: the difficulties of learning mathematics', in
    T. Booth *et al.* (eds) *Preventing Difficulties in Learning*, Basil Blackwell in asso-
    ciation with the Open University.
Girling, M. (1977) 'Towards a definition of basic numeracy', *Mathematics Teaching*,
    no. 81.
Glennon, V.J. (1981) *The Mathematical Education of Exceptional Children and
    Youth: an Interdisciplinary Approach*, National Council for Teachers of Mathe-
    matics (USA).
Hart, K.M. (ed.) (1981) *Children's Understanding of Mathematics, 11–16*, John
    Murray.
Haylock, D.W. (1986) 'Mathematical low attainers checklist', *British Journal of
    Educational Psychology*, no. 56.
Haylock, D.W. (1987) 'Towards numeracy', *Support for Learning*, Vol. 2, no. 2.
Haylock, D.W., Blake, G.F. and Platt, J. (1985) 'Using maths to make things hap-
    pen', *Mathematics in School*, Vol. 14, no. 2.
Haylock, D. and Cockburn, A. (1989) *Understanding Early Years Mathematics*, Paul
    Chapman Publishing.
Haylock, D. and Morgans, H. (1986) 'Maths to make things happen', *British Journal
    of Special Education*, Vol. 13, no. 1.
HMI (1978) *Aspects of Secondary Education in England*, HMSO.
HMI (1984) *Education Observed 2*, HMSO.
Hughes, M. (1986) *Children and Number: Difficulties in Learning Mathematics*,
    Basil Blackwell.
ILEA Learning Resources Branch (1985) *Count Me In*, Inner London Education
    Authority.
Jones, K. and Charlton, C. (eds) (in press) *Learning Difficulties in Primary Class-
    rooms – Delivering the Whole Curriculum*, Macmillan Education.
Jones, K. and Haylock, D. (1985) 'Developing children's understanding in mathe-
    matics', *Remedial Education*, Vol. 20, no. 1.
Krathwohl, D.R., Bloom, B.S. and Masia, B.B. (1964) *Taxonomy of Educational
    Objectives: the Classification of Educational Goals – Handbook 1: Affective Do-
    main*, David McKay Co.
Krutetskii, V.A. (1977) *The Psychology of Mathematical Ability in Schoolchildren*,
    (J. Kilpatrick and I. Wirzsup, eds; J. Teller, trans.) University of Chicago Press.
Low Attainers in Mathematics Project (1987) *Better Mathematics: a Curriculum
    Development Study*, HMSO.
Lumb, D. (1978) 'Mathematics for the less gifted: project report', *Mathematics in
    School*, Vol. 7, no. 2.
Moore, G. (1985) 'Calculators and remedial education in mathematics', *Remedial
    Education*, Vol. 20, no. 1.
Moore, B.M. (1988) 'Achievement on basic math skill for low-performing students:
    a study of teacher's affect and CAI', *Journal of Experimental Education*, Vol. 57,
    no. 1.
National Curriculum Council (1989) *Mathematics Non-Statutory Guidance*, NCC.
Nesher, P. and Teubal, E. (1975) 'Verbal cues as an interfering factor in verbal
    problem-solving', *Educational Studies in Mathematics*, Vol. 6.

Open University EM235 Course Team (1982) *Developing Mathematical Thinking*, Open University Press.
Open University PME233 Course Team (1980) *Mathematics Across the Curriculum*, Open University Press.
Poulter, J.G. and Haylock, D.W. (1988) 'Teaching Computational Estimation', *Mathematics in Schools*, Vol.17, no.2.
PrIME (Primary Initatives in Mathematics Education) (1991) *Calculators, Children and Mathematics*, Simon & Schuster.
Ross, D. (1964) 'A description of twenty arithmetic under-achievers', *Arithmetic Teacher*, no. 11.
Royal Society and Institute of Mathematics and its Applications (1986) *Girls and Mathematics*, The Royal Society.
Saxe, G.B. (1988) 'Candy selling and math learning', *Educational Researcher*, Vol. 17, no. 6 (American Educational Research Association).
Sewell, B. (1981) *Use of Mathematics by Adults in Daily Life*, Advisory Council for Adult and Continuing Education.
Underhill, B., Uprichard, E. and Heddens, J. (1980) *Diagnosing Mathematical Difficulties*, Charles E. Merrill Publishing Company.
Womack, D. (1988) *Developing Mathematical and Scientific Thinking in Young Children*, Special Needs in Ordinary Schools series, Cassell.

INDEX